PANICS AND PLEASURES
OF A PET SITTER

Wal Kiesman

PANICS AND PLEASURES
OF A PET SITTER

Vanguard Press

VANGUARD PAPERBACK

© Copyright 2023
Wal Kiesman

A CIP catalogue record for this title is
available from the British Library.

ISBN 978 1 80016 438 3

*Vanguard Press is an imprint of
Pegasus Elliot Mackenzie Publishers Ltd.*
www.pegasuspublishers.com

First Published in 2023

**Vanguard Press
Sheraton House Castle Park
Cambridge England**

Printed & Bound in Great Britain

This work is a recollection based on real events. Names have been changed for the privacy of individuals.

Introduction

How did it all begin? Where did the idea come from?

Well, we'd never realised, never thought seriously about it, but we'd already been doing it for years.

Both my partner and I had various pets as we were growing up, and as a couple had twin mongrels from Battersea Dogs Home (both born in the same sac rather than just from the same litter) that shared our lives, the ups and downs, never judgmental of our flaws, and always giving us their loyalty, their devotion, and their love. After their loss, it was too difficult to contemplate going through again, so for the next more than a few years we regularly looked after our good friend's dog, a Jack Russell cross, who just presumed it was normal for any self-respecting canine to have two homes. Since he was young, we had taken him out, he had stayed with us, sometimes for two weeks at a time while they were on holiday, and he treated our home like his own (occasionally not a good thing)!

It was another animal encounter however, that enabled fate to give us that extra little nudge, (doesn't it always)… and in no time we found ourselves 'working' in one of the most enjoyable jobs you could imagine (that is if you like animals, but I'm presuming you wouldn't be reading this if you didn't)!

We had been invited to have dinner with the ex-boss of my better-half, and during the evening, he and his partner kept commenting that their cat, who didn't usually waste time on strangers, had given us his seal of approval, allowing us to stroke him and even feed him cat treats, quite a unique occurrence it seemed. From the moment we arrived at their flat, Harley had been interested in making our acquaintance, as head held high, he strutted confidently along the hall towards us, allowing ample time to admire the way his sandy Burmese coat perfectly matched the carpet as if it had been chosen specially to complement him. He observed our human greetings with his owners, then as our hosts ran round getting drinks and making sure the food didn't burn, he dutifully kept us amused, obligingly chasing one of his many toys that we had found in a box conveniently placed next to the settee. It could have been a subtle feline way of keeping an eye on things, but it kept all three of us entertained until his owners returned.

The evening progressed, the wine flowed, and they half-jokingly commented again on how well he had taken to us.

"We're going to need someone to look after him while we're away at New Year if you're available," one of them casually threw in to the conversation.

"It wouldn't be far from the London fireworks display as we're right on the Thames!"

Not needing as much as a look of confirmation between the two of us, "We could do that," we agreed, adding the cheeky proviso of, "if my Mum could join us for the festivities."

Somehow the conversation digressed and nothing more was said on the subject, the four of us not quite sure who was joking, who was serious, and nobody admitting whether they meant it or not.

A few more drinks later and a farewell nightcap meant that by the following morning, both with fairly substantial headaches, any memory of the conversation was so blurred we definitely weren't sure if they meant it or not, in fact, no fit state to even be sure if we meant it or not.

After a day of recovery, the haze cleared a little, so we sent an email clearly explaining that we were available for the cat sitting if it was required, but still giving them an escape route if they had regretted their 'less than sober' invitation.

Chapter 1 — Harley

The escape route wasn't needed, and the day after Boxing Day, as agreed, we arrived at their flat.

Slowing all the traffic rushing down the embankment, I cautiously turned one hundred and eighty degrees in to the small car parking area, drove into the one available space, then not wanting to miss anything, hurriedly jumped out of the car to follow my better half who was somehow already halfway to the foyer to collect the keys from reception. It could have only taken a couple of seconds to reach the half a dozen steps up to the doors but by the time I did, my other half, now holding an envelope, had re-emerged and was heading back towards me, so I quickly turned round and went to start unloading. Trying our utmost to act quite nonchalant, we trudged up and down an excessively long corridor to the lift, carrying bag after bag... after bag... after bag. The concierge, who for much of the time kept his face hidden just below the level of the desk, would glance up to open the doors and somehow maintain a deadpan expression as most of the contents of our bedroom and kitchen passed before his eyes. I couldn't help thinking he must have wondered just how much food, just how many clothes, just exactly what could possibly be needed for a ten day stay in a flat merely fifteen minutes from our own home, but my better half was taking no risks.

Annoyingly, the glass windows along the corridor provided a perfect view of our car as we walked past on the inside of the building, the lift frustratingly only a few yards from our parking space, but there was no shortcut. Any hope of a fire exit being opened was promptly dealt with, something about being against one rule or another, so we had to walk practically the width of the building outside and in every luggage load. Several journeys later, we had accumulated enough bags for one trip up to the fourth floor, so the lift was called, and we began loading them as quickly as possible, both of us jumping in unison each time the doors tried to jolt shut, presuming we had been given ample time. Eventually, each taking a deep breath, we crushed ourselves in to what little space remained, as they finally got their wish and slammed shut.

A few seconds later, we half-stepped, half fell back out, and now knowing how impatient the lift was, I quickly tried using one bag as a door stop while we unloaded the others. Unfortunately, the chosen bag was much too light and soon dislodged by the restless doors, so I resorted to pushing one leg solidly against the doorstop bag, whilst attempting to hop round with the other. As you might expect, this also was not an effective technique, and in spite of my best efforts to stay put, it just resulted in both the bag and my leg being easily shoved aside on the slippery marble tiles. While I was absorbed in attempting to stay upright, it was down to my other half, who, with lightening reflexes sprung in to action, and took one almighty lunge at the doors, just managing to prevent our remaining bags going off on their own. After sharing a quick sigh of relief, the first load was placed by the door of the flat, before returning to the ground floor for even more of our belongings… this time feeling rather more self-conscious as we yet again walked past the doorman, knowing he could have just been watching the whole episode upstairs on CCTV.

Approaching the car, through the windscreen I could see the rather bored expression of my mum, who must have been wondering what was taking so long, but having moved the majority of our belongings, she could now emerge, no longer needed to guard our provisions. Noticing she walked with a stick, the helpful concierge immediately suggested we temporarily park in the underground garage where she could walk straight into the demon lift, allowing us at the same time to realise with absolute irritation that we could have saved ourselves all the lugging had she appeared earlier. At least for once it wasn't such a trek, and we could transport our remaining luggage with relative ease, even if various contortions were needed to actually pack and unpack the impatient elevator.

Having ascended to the dizzy heights of the fourth floor again, my mum was volunteered as the latest door stop, while we trudged the final bags over to the entrance of the flat, but predictably, those determined doors had other plans. Yet again they tried to jolt shut, completely putting her off balance, and in spite of another valiant last-minute attempt by my partner diving at the lift button to prevent it from leaving, we just had time to see an ever-narrowing view of her smile transformed in to eyebrow raising surprise before she disappeared off to some other level. I knew she wouldn't know which floor we were on, but no need to panic… by pressing the lift button belatedly, she would be back eventually, and we could do nothing more than wait.

At least it gave us opportunity to concentrate our attention on what was yet to be another nemesis, the unlockable door.

You would think that two, dare I say, 'sensible' adults, faced with two locks and two keys, could logically, by means of elimination somehow work out how to open a door… but no!

We both tried unlocking each lock with each key, tried them the other way round, went back to the original combination, stared at the keys, tried them again, tried them the other way round again, all the time snatching the keys from each other impatiently. Several minutes and a surplus of irritation later, we finally realised that only one of the keys was necessary, the second lock was already unlocked, and the door, (yet another troublesome door), just needed a bit of a shove. It had however, taken us so long to solve the problem, that my mother had actually found her way back to our floor after being down to the basement garage, up to the seventh floor and who knows where.

Feeling as if we had just undertaken a thorough workout, both physically and mentally, we finally pushed open the door to walk in… just as Harley, having heard all the commotion, was trying his best to get out. All arms flapping around in a panic, the three of us managed to create a mobile barrier and working like a team of farm dogs rounding up a stray, carefully steered him back indoors. Looking slightly ruffled by the experience, and far less impressed than on our first meeting he strutted down the hall not in the least interested in any greeting whatsoever, but by the time we had shoved our numerous bags through the door his composure was regained, and he teasingly rolled over on his back in front of a warm radiator. We took turns to say our hellos, stroking his tummy and scratching his ears, then I suggested that my already well travelled, jet-lagged mother should continue to pamper him and otherwise distract him, while my partner and I transported our belongings and hers into the appropriate rooms.

Harley, coolly stared at the countless bags gradually invading his space, barely interested but he was more than happy once everything was in place when he realised we were making a beeline for the cat treats. His aloof persona was quickly pushed aside so he could eagerly trot after us into the kitchen to munch his way through a few goodies, while cups of tea all round were in order for us. I filled the kettle and stood in the kitchen waiting for it to boil, staring through the patio doors at the icy looking Thames, doubting we would be opening them to step on to the balcony and take in the view at this time of year. At an exact right-angle to the kitchen, the lounge patio-doors were framing the figure of my mum who was also staring at the bleak landscape until tea arrived, and I suspected she might be thinking exactly the same.

We soon made ourselves at home, and that evening we were keeping Harley amused by working our way through the vast choice of toys from the box next to the settee, mice bouncing on elastic, birds on elastic, various other unknown objects also bouncing on the end of a stick, (it was irrelevant) and as long as we were willing to keep them animated, he would keep chasing them. Although being totally engrossed, doing the same as any other cat, he somehow maintained a poise and demeanour that could not disguise his true pedigree, and as warned he always liked to keep at a distance. The chance of him sitting on someone's lap was more than remote, but it wasn't going to stop us trying.

At the end of the game he just disappeared, maybe to get a drink, but suddenly he was gone, and we had no idea where his hiding place was.

I found out sure enough, as he suddenly jumped out at me from a chair tucked cosily underneath the dining table just as I was heading to the bathroom, and it caused much amusement for my mother and partner, as I nearly hit the ceiling with the shock. Returning a couple of minutes later, heart still rippling a little faster than it should, I stopped by the entrance to the living room, bent down and peered round the frame just in case the game was still on.

There was my mischievous pursuer patiently waiting, crouched and ready to pounce.

Intentions of revenge were already scuppered, my inexperience of cat tactics little competition for his finely tuned instincts, as without thinking I had carelessly blundered too far into the doorway and given my position away. Once he caught sight of me, he was poised, not moving, not blinking, just staring, more like glaring, daring me to make the next move as if I was some spooked-out mouse. Devoid of any clever strategy, I decided to see if he was interested in a simple game of hide and seek and retreated out of view before the icy stare had me frozen to the spot. I squashed myself behind a large trunk in the hallway, breathing as quietly as possible to wait for that renowned cat-curiosity to persuade him to come seeking. Crouched uncomfortably in my hiding place for what felt like an age, I eventually decided I was playing alone, and got up, feeling somewhat dejected and fairly stupid.

My feeling of disappointment didn't last long!

His patience had paid off, lying in wait just round the corner all this time, and Harley was completely successful in making me jump even more than the first time.

I could see it was going to take more thought to outwit this cat, but I wasn't one to give up easily... the only trouble was, neither was he!

The game continued each day, either one of us lying in wait, an ambush on the cards, or we would attempt to creep up on the other without being noticed, a task totally impossible for me. One reason was the massive advantage he had of being able to see my feet below the furniture and could follow my every move without me knowing. I attempted to keep the odds on an even playing field, by either hiding behind furniture that was solid to the floor, or sometimes lifting my feet out of sight but none of these methods worked for too long.

Another one of his favourite games, usually when everyone was quietly engrossed in television viewing, was to, out of the blue, spring on to the top of the settee in one leap, then in a gravity-defying manoeuvre hang sideways on the back and charge to the opposite end before he fell off. His sudden appearance about two inches from your ear was bad enough, but the sound of claws ripping a route just behind your back was a real shocker.

At the opposite extreme, he would sometimes prefer a solitary moment, peaceful and undisturbed, resulting in a total loss of logic by all three of us human beings more than once. Not having seen him for about three or four hours one day, we started to get concerned about our ward, and decided a search was in order before we could relax. It was a two-bedroom flat so there couldn't be that many places to hide I declared, but one cat-hunt later, calling his name repeatedly, he was still missing.

My calculations show that was the precise moment all sensible reason was lost, even when you definitely know something... definitely... absolutely... you still don't really know it a hundred percent.

For example, we knew we hadn't been out all day, yet my partner and I opened the front door, quickly closing it behind us again, and did a complete search of the landing just to check he wasn't there... But how could he be? We hadn't been out there until now!

I went through our movements since arriving in my head and deduced that there was never a time his paws could have touched the landing carpet, and besides we had seen him indoors after that, and no one had opened the door since.

There was no way he could possibly be outside the flat.

That was definite.

I was sure of it.

Once back indoors we then examined every window, then inspected the patio several times even though we hadn't been out there either. Minutes, hours passed by, one of us looking behind curtains, checking under beds, in beds, looking outside again, calling him but to no avail, until eventually, it was my mother that had to get our perspective back on course.

"Just sit down and wait," she ordered. "He'll come out when he's ready!"

We sat, begrudgingly at first, but it wore off and sure enough, a little while later, he just casually walked in and thankfully things could return to normal.

I must just mention at this point, that it was here I learnt just how easy it is to stroke an animal for a few seconds, then receive a shock of almost lightning bolt intensity when next touching anything metallic. The amazing thing about this fact is the number of times it can be forgotten, but the speed one remembers it again!

Another thing to note… this could also happen by the method of transference from some other cat stroking person, which was even worse!

Back to the story.

In spite of my pessimism, the weather turned fairly warm for December, and because the balcony was protected on two sides by the patio doors we found it to be quite a sun trap… hard to believe I know. Several times we were able to venture out with our morning coffee, sit around the table (wearing sunglasses I might add) and munch a few biscuits as we observed the river traffic below.

We had been told Harley was allowed to go out there as well, but to be on the safe side we had blocked every gap between the railings with plant pots or any and everything else we could muster to be sure he couldn't fall, then one of us, usually me, followed his every move ready to grab him. This wasn't too relaxing so it was better if he was snoozing somewhere else indoors, then we could really enjoy our surroundings.

Looking down we could see a whole alternative mode of city transport as boats, barges, tourist cruisers of all shapes and sizes constantly passed by below, separating us from the large buildings on the opposite side. At night the view was spectacular, the moon, all the lights reflected into a shimmering mirror image, and each time it was disturbed by a passing boat you could wait for it to settle again... this was the life!

Our New Year soon arrived, we had eaten a nice meal, had a few drinks and as midnight approached, we donned coats and gloves, made sure Harley was locked safely indoors, and took the lift to the ground floor. We waved to the now familiar doorman and walked round the corner to Vauxhall Bridge where we hoped to see the 'spectacular' fireworks, the perfect end to the day, and the year. It was already heaving with revellers, so we crushed our way through the crowd to find a good spot, one with a bit of space, then waited for the countdown. In the distance, we suddenly heard cheering followed by cracks and explosions, the sky behind Big Ben illuminated in a multitude of colours... and from our location?

Nothing!

Not a sign of a single firework!

We looked at each other for a second, then tried pushing our way through the rowdy mob to acquire a better view. Any kind of view would have done, but it was like walking in the opposite direction to a hoard of stampeding shoppers at the Harrods sale, and time was running out.

We had to give up… but I wasn't complaining!

Being jostled and knocked every which way by drunken party animals, whilst avoiding the alcohol they were spilling everywhere, was not going down well with either myself or my disappointed colleagues, so it was official… we were in total agreement… and as the noise of the fireworks came to an end, we beat a hasty retreat.

Not a word was spoken as we marched back in a line but entering the foyer we were unexpectedly greeted by the smiling doorman, who suddenly produced a bottle of champagne and handed it to my mother as a New Year gift.

She had obviously made a good impression!

The sombre mood changed in a flash as we all thanked him, wished him a healthy and 'Happy New Year', and all said we hoped that we might get to see him again in the future, as he would be changing shift after tonight.

Having said our goodbyes, we trailed our way down the corridor and returned to Harley, who looked as though he had slept through the whole thing, yawning and stretching his body to the longest, thinnest shape possible on his matching carpet as we all walked in.

Having un-donned coats and gloves I gave him a stroke as I passed, my mum did the same, and my partner followed suit. He joined the end of the line as we paraded towards the kitchen, three of us a little disgruntled but still going to crack open a bottle to celebrate the New Year. Perhaps it would help us forget the firework debacle!

It was a day or so later, I answered the phone to our friend's mother, who had forgotten they were away, not someone I had ever spoken to before, but during our friendly discussion discovered her to be a previous New Year cat sitter.

I was dreading the, "Did you enjoy the fireworks?" question, but when it came I felt so comfortable in our conversation that I could laugh it off, and admit the disaster… to which she commented, "I did exactly the same!"

I could hear the smile in her voice, as she explained that you only have to walk to the other side of the bridge to get the perfect view, and how I wished she had phoned a couple of days earlier, but too late now. When I eventually put the phone down, I didn't know whether to share the information or not, but in the end I decided I couldn't keep it to myself.

No one was that bothered!

It was only a brief moment during our stay.

Days passed quickly by and despite the few minor teething troubles we did enjoy our first sit immensely… so much in fact, that we decided to contact a pet sitting agency, and after an initial interview with the company it wasn't long before we were given our first official clients, so as my partner was working, I set off for my first preliminary meeting to see if we would get the job.

Chapter 2 — Duke and Duster

Excited at the prospect of our first booking but slightly apprehensive, I walked down the quiet road in North London, checking each number as I passed the smartly painted doors, glancing either side at well-tended gardens, but looking further ahead at a black door covered in cobwebs and dust, I just knew it was inevitably the house in which we could be spending a week on our first agency sit. I pushed open a heavy black metal gate, walked up several concrete steps to the massive black door, and rang an old-fashioned doorbell, anxiously waiting to see who lived on the other side.

After a pause, a voice shouted from the basement, "We're down here!"

With no handrail for support, I cautiously looked over the side of the steps, waved an amiable acknowledgment, then carefully descended to what must have previously been the tradesman's entrance, where, after a brief introduction, I was led through a dark hallway and ushered to a chair in the kitchen.

As I took my seat at the old-fashioned wooden table by the window, a slightly moth eaten looking black, curly coated retriever lolloped out of a much too small dog bed and put his face on my knee. Although he didn't smell too fresh, he was friendly enough, and his interest in me remained undiminished as I took out my agency interview sheet, and went through the first few questions to find out names of pets, feeding, sleeping, walks etcetera while his owner made coffee.

Having got to the question on commands, I, myself, was instructed to throw a ball for the dog now known as Duke, to demonstrate just how much he loved to play. The ball rolled across the kitchen floor and he promptly ran after it, promptly returned and promptly didn't give it back, seeming happier to teasingly rest his chin on my knee with the ball clamped tightly in his jaws, no amount of persuasion going to make an iota of difference to his decision. The game seemed to fizzle out, so trying to ignore his massive face on my leg, I took a sip of coffee and continued our questionnaire.

I didn't get very far before the owner deemed it necessary to go in search of another member of the family, so I politely sat with my avid companion, still with chin on knee, both of us listening to her footsteps on the wooden stairs as she repeatedly shouted to the absentee.

She reappeared with an extremely friendly cat, who, being placed on the middle of the table, found it to be a totally unsatisfactory position, and immediately strode across my notes and sat down on the middle of the page, staring at me with his nose about two inches from mine. As I stroked him, he purred loudly, looking happy enough with his assessment of my character, which I took to be a compliment of the highest order, but he still wasn't moving.

The appearance of Duster the cat, providing unwelcome feline competition for attention, ensured that Duke, not wishing to lose out, immediately unglued his massive face from my leg and now wanted to hand over his soggy spit-laden ball urgently. Fortunately, as I tried to avoid any contact with saliva, the owner had also been on the ball and quickly led him back to his inadequate looking bed. Inwardly breathing a sigh of relief, I again resumed our interview, watched intently by four scrutinising eyes, (not including the owners) and discussed all feline requirements. They were quite simple. He ate dried food on the top of a cupboard well out of reach of Duke and could go anywhere and everywhere indoors and out. The only stipulation was that he was in the house at night, so around nine o'clock in the evening the cat flap should be locked once he was home, and he then stayed in until the following morning.

Sounded simple enough!

Next, I was shown the remaining three members of the family, the first being a tortoise named Herman.

Jokingly I said, "Oh—after Herman Munster?"

Without even the slightest hint of a smile I was informed that it was the breed of the tortoise, so after that faux pas I wisely decided to keep quiet on the subject and stared through an algae covered glass tank looking for the other two prospective pet sit characters; one unnamed goldfish and another darkly camouflaged fish, also nameless. They just needed feeding once a day, and Herman the tortoise was to be put outside in the morning, brought in about five p.m. and fed salad and dandelions three times a day. I couldn't foresee any problems arising from such simple needs.

Just before I left, we were briefly joined by the lady's husband, who added a few extra words of advice that his wife had neglected to impart, such as how to mend the broken cat flap if ever Duke tried to poke his head through it, and explaining the reason for the padlock on the fridge being due to his ingenuity at getting pet sitter's chicken. I concluded there was more to this dog than I gave credit, and we should definitely not underestimate him if ever we got the job.

With a polite handshake I took my leave, eager to report back to my other half.

Regardless of my indisputable inexperience on the tortoise front, we did get the job, and a few weeks later pulled up outside the house, car looking as though we had grabbed all our worldly possessions to flee either an erupting volcano or some evil dictator. Although I had been told there was off-street parking there was no visible evidence of the fact, so I rushed to the lower entrance while my trusty partner vigilantly kept watch for any overenthusiastic traffic wardens patrolling the area. The owner of the menagerie came out gesturing towards to some overgrown bushes, and I realised hidden amongst them were two gates. I squirmed as he scraped them over the grooves already carved in the pavement, then retreated to the safety of the driving seat, as he revealed a drive just wider and just longer than our car, yet with an incline that would have been just as happy somewhere in the hills of San Francisco.

My partner got out of the car to avoid being imprisoned once cosily inserted in the driveway and watched as I nervously accelerated the car onto the pavement and turned into the gates. To my relief, the owner was returning to the house and didn't witness my expression, not altogether dissimilar to that of a child just having reached the top of a roller-coaster for the first time and now waiting for the sudden drop. The car tilted downwards, and I immediately braked to avoid a face-to-face confrontation with the garage doors, then having successfully negotiated the overgrown gap, I squeezed out, sidled back to the path, and wondered why I had ever made such a big deal about the occurrence. Perhaps it had been the unfamiliar situation we were blindly heading into, or perhaps it was the lack of vision through our evacuation-technique packed car, but so far, so good (little did I know it wouldn't be too long for things to change)!

Having arrived early, due to the fact they had phoned my mobile, (which was turned off while I was driving), to say come later when we were already 'en-route' we suggested unloading our luggage while the owners greeted several extra members of the family who were joining them on the expedition. Luckily, they took up our advice so could not see us dragging our belongings through their overgrown garden, wincing as we were stabbed in the leg on each journey by some sharp spiteful vegetation. I was either getting weaker or every bag was getting heavier on each journey up the concrete steps, through the upper black door, to a strange room leading finally into our bedroom, and I seriously wondered why, yet again, we had decided so many items from our own home were essential to survive in someone else's. Whatever the reason, we'd allowed for every possibility and our backs were going to pay for it.

After the compulsory recuperation period, my other half enthusiastically suggested we take Duke for a walk to look keen, but luckily, (as you will read later) having decided against the idea, we just sat quietly in the strange room upstairs and tried to concentrate on reading until their moment of departure. My eyes scanned round as I looked up from the page for the umpteenth time, and I realised it resembled and felt more like a doctor's waiting room than any identifiable room in a home, large plants filling every window, with several chairs, none of them matching, placed in two rows against opposite walls. Just as I was experiencing the nervous anxiety of waiting for my name to be called for my appointment, the inquisitive cat, Duster spotted us. Sauntering over, he rubbed against our legs in turn as if checking the static content of the material, immediately followed up by his familiar technique of close scrutiny... extremely close scrutiny, somehow getting himself up to a sufficient level where he could stare you right in the eye, straight through your eye to the inner workings of the brain and understand your every thought.

The mesmerising effect of the hypnotic feline was brought to an abrupt halt as his concentration was interrupted by a flurry of people running about downstairs. The three of us listened as bags were dragged through the doorway, someone was shouting a request for their coat not to be forgotten, then the owner dashed upstairs having remembered we needed some keys before a final shout goodbye, slam of the door, and they were gone.

As the sound of the taxi faded into the distance we went down to the kitchen, followed by Duster, and stared at our new companions, stared at each other, stared at them again, and although feeling a little apprehensive, decided now would be a good time to go on our first walk to the local community park with Duke.

Talk about in at the deep end!

As instructed, we clicked the red lead on to his collar, emerged from the basement kitchen door and headed up the steps to the creaky gate with the six stone, twenty-seven-inch-tall stranger. Duster the cat scooted between all of the legs and feet and leapt onto the nearest windowsill where he could smugly observe.

We set off, me hanging on to the red lead tightly, flanked by my partner who was overseeing proceedings. Nearing the pub at the corner of the road, the volume of conversation and laughter increased by several decibels as a crowd of people, taking advantage of the good weather sat at the outdoor tables savouring a Friday afternoon drink before heading home from 'work'. With perfect timing, ensuring a perfect view for the onlookers, Duke suddenly acted as if he had been possessed by some demon, and took an extreme dislike to his so-called favourite red lead. Trying not to look too embarrassed, I desperately tried to hang on as I was pulled along the pavement, shook in several directions and almost dragged into the middle of the road as he showed his disdain for the blood-red leash. Luckily my sensible other half had brought a backup lead, and as if trying to grab some writhing serpent, she eventually managed to attach it to his collar, then with both of us hanging on for grim death somehow got back home in one piece.

Being somewhat shaken by the episode I would have stayed there all week but acknowledging the proverbial advice of getting straight back on your bicycle, I knew we had to brave the situation again, and with the encouragement and determination of my partner, who would not be beaten by a dog of any size, off we went again with two leads… neither being the red one.

Duke seemed more relaxed this time (disappointingly for our avid audience at the pub), and trotted along quite calmly, even if it was at the speed of an Olympic walker. We knew if he took it into his head, we could have easily both been dragged anywhere, but luckily, he was intent on getting to the park, and only stopped once to investigate a banana skin, causing us both to nearly experience the feeling of a dislocated shoulder as he suddenly came to an abrupt halt. It was short-lived as he was assertively told to leave, immediately refocusing him on his prior objective, but now he had to make up for the lost time he had spent sniffing the banana skin, so off we set again at an even greater gold medal winning pace.

It was about this time as we breathlessly tried to keep up, immersed in our new unintentional workout programme, that I became aware of every other pedestrian on our route hurriedly crossing over as we approached. This came to be a regular occurrence on all of our walks, and it was quite amusing watching the different techniques of passers-by, some casually crossing over as if it had always been their intention, others just blatantly running across the road with a fearful glance to make sure we were not following. Nervous parents grabbed their children and scooped them out of our path, whilst people on bikes considered it to be safer riding on the wrong side of the road rather than pass within a metre of this gigantic force.

Having arrived at the park, neither of us felt confident enough to let Duke go free, even though it seemed as though any differences between us had been settled, so we thought it better for one of us to hang on to the extending lead while the other threw a ball.

I was the nominated thrower, and the second the first ball left my hand I felt my heart jump into my mouth as I realised it was going to go further than the length of the lead. A mere detail like that wasn't going to stop the overenthusiastic Duke, so I watched helplessly, not daring to let the slightest hint of a smile cross my face, as my partner, who only a second ago had been stationary, suddenly move with a velocity that should have impressed even Jeremy Clarkson.

Frozen to the spot I held my breath as she checked the condition of her already overstretched shoulder, then turned round revealing a somewhat aggravated face.

This was not the time for any type of conversation or comment whatsoever.

Oblivious, Duke happily dropped his ball by my feet, and in silence I dared to look over to see if it was safe to throw the ball again. Hopefully judging the situation correctly, I took another throw, this time with more care so Duke could reach it within the length of the lead, but to my horror, as he bounded along at top speed to catch the escaping sphere, I realised he would not be able to stop in the required time. Helplessly I watched the almost perfect replay, him running along for several more yards, my speedy other half not far behind and it was growing harder to contain my amusement... sensibly, I was just about managing...

That was until Duke decided to give the ball to my other half instead of me.

Quite flattered by the opportunity she threw the ball in my direction, not taking the lead into consideration whatsoever, and was only momentarily static before once again racing along. I just caught a brief glance at her shocked expression as she sped past me behind Duke, charging between the bushes to make sure his precious toy was not lost.

That did it!

That was the final straw, and I had to laugh out loud, no matter how risky... in fact, for the rest of the evening, at intervals, the image would creep into my mind and either a stupid grin would come over my face, or I would suddenly burst into peals of laughter like some madman, much to the un-amusement of my partner.

We returned home fairly quietly that day, still faster than most of the bicycles trying to avoid us by one method or another, but both felt relieved that the initial ordeal was over, and perhaps Duke was too!

Once safely indoors, my better half-filled Duke's gigantic bowl with fresh water, then we stood watching it flood all over the kitchen floor as he pushed most of his nose into it and drank noisily, more slopping even further as he lifted his head to turn and see if we were still behind him. At least he looked grateful for our efforts, and as we paddled through the water to find a mop, I was sure we could do better tomorrow with our new friend who was nothing like the wild animal we first thought.

By five o'clock the temperature outside had cooled, so we had to go and find Herman the tortoise, who had been outside for the day, as he always was in the summer. Having carefully opened the wire to his pen, I watched my every step as I led the way to his favourite spot lodged between two broken bricks in the surrounding wall. I wanted to be brave but just couldn't bring myself to prise the reptile from his cozy nest, so sheepishly called for backup, in the form of my speedy partner. She was a no-nonsense person, and sporting a plastic glove, she just gently pulled him away from the wall, and took him indoors to his vast tank as if she had done it every day of her life.

I was more than impressed!

Next on the agenda?

Defying all the rule books, we decided we could relax over our own meal much better if all animals had eaten first... which was not a reflection of pack hierarchy by any means. There was only one boss round here... and... it wasn't me!

Duke and Duster were first. Their dried food lasted all of thirty seconds, so moving on quickly, I gathered some nice crisp salad leaves and dandelions from the fridge and dropped them into Herman's tank, who was now warming up under the light in his tank. We were amazed at the volume of the crunching as he worked his way through the juicy snack, but not as amazed as we were at the amount of liquid that came out the other end as he relieved himself. We stared as it flowed all over the newspaper lining the bottom of his tank and were both quite aware that it couldn't stay that way. We weren't going to be eating until this soggy mess had been dealt with.

Pushing him to one edge, the paper at the opposite end was removed, the slates washed, and dried and newly ripped strips of paper placed over the tiles so that end looked pristine. Moving him to the newly refurbished half of the tank we then repeated the process until the whole tank looked brand new, a stark contrast to the fish tank directly above it.

Once I had dropped some food into the fish tank, they were still hidden within the murky depths of the green camouflage, all animals had been fed for the day, and once the lights to both were turned off, fish, reptile and warm-blooded pets could settle down. Finally, the human beings could get some well-needed food, then get down to watching television for the rest of the evening.

Eventually it was time to retire, so after letting Duke out for the final time and saying goodnight with his last treat of the day, we closed the gate at the bottom of the stairs and headed up to the bedroom, blissfully unaware that someone was right behind us. With trips to the bathroom undertaken, my other half got in the bed, the moment the silent stalker had been waiting for, and he made his move.

Duster the cat appeared from nowhere, jumped on to the bottom of the bed, and with his tail completely vertical like some slumber-detecting aerial, strutted the whole length to the pillows where he paused momentarily to weigh up the situation. Seeming almost oblivious to our presence, he then turned and slid under the cover next to my partner, rotated one hundred and eighty degrees and reappeared, placing his head on the pillow next to hers.

Seconds later, realising he wasn't moving I nervously pulled back the duvet my side, and got in next to him, hoping he wouldn't mind the intrusion, but he looked cosy enough and soon the three of us must have been asleep.

The following morning I started to wake, taking a little time to get my bearings in the unfamiliar bedroom, until the memory of our feline bed companion flashed into my mind. I quickly turned to look at his spot on the pillow, and sure enough, it wasn't a dream. He was still there, eyes tightly closed, looking extremely comfortable, and enviously still sound asleep.

Still harbouring a certain amount of jealousy, I got up, hurriedly dressed and went downstairs to see if Duke had been okay overnight. There was no reason why he shouldn't have been, but my anxiety at being put in charge of so many animals on our first sit made me extra cautious.

An exuberant welcome put my mind at ease and after letting Duke out to relieve the stress on his bladder, I renewed the water close to the top of the bowl allowing for plenty of spillage, threw more fresh leaves into Herman's tank (who was still quite slow without his light bulb), and made tea for the minority group in the house.

Everyone was soon up and when nine a.m. arrived it was time for Herman to go to his outdoor quarters, which took up almost half of the small garden. Following instructions to the letter, Duke was securely locked indoors, lodged in his undersized bed, and like some well-practised army manoeuvre, I opened each of the four ties, my partner put Herman carefully inside, then I secured the wire door again, each knot under the close scrutiny of my other half. With a final check on the ties, we returned to the back door, where a black furry shape was now squashed through the broken cat flap. On further inspection the black furry figure seemed to have a wet, shiny nose and two dark-brown eyes, but on hearing our approach it struggled and contorted itself back in to the kitchen until there was no evidence left.

We opened the door and Duke, surprisingly 'still' in his bed, but somehow now facing the opposite direction gave us an innocent doleful look, with suspiciously familiar looking brown eyes.

We played along, and he looked delighted that he had outwitted us, but we wanted to make sure he was in an agreeable mood, because soon he would be sat in the back seat of our car while we drove him to a much larger park where he could run to his heart's content. Having watched him yesterday trying to exercise in the tiny confines of the local park, and moreover not wanting any visits to the local A&E with dislocated joints, we had decided to risk the journey, and what's more, with the permission of the owners, we were going to consider if we thought it safe to let him run completely free off the lead.

Embarking on our mission, my partner waited on the pavement with Duke, while I slid in to the driver's seat and grabbed the handbrake, momentarily returning to my previous state of illogical fear as if passing my driving test had been a total fluke, but again my nervousness totally unfounded as I reversed out and waited for my co-pilot and passenger to board. Through the side window I watched my better half open the rear door, and without hesitation, Duke jumped straight into the back, and for a few seconds took on the persona of a wobbly jelly as he tried to balance his weight on the springy seat while he circled until he found a comfortable spot to land. Once convinced he was settled, my partner slammed the back door again, then fastened herself in the front and we were off. Watching his every move, his every expression in the rear-view mirror, Duke looked as though he was taking the journey in his stride, and only starting to look interested when he realised we were close to his favourite haunt.

By the time we pulled into the car park his excitement had reached fever-pitch, much like my temperature as I tried to park before things escalated any further. Duke was panting and bouncing from one side of the seat to the other, and fearing for the upholstery, we braced ourselves and opened the back door. He shot out, and the expression on the face of my other half wasn't exactly one of confidence as she clung on to the taut lead, so I rapidly snapped the extending lead on his collar as backup. One lead or two, it didn't matter… consenting or not we were all racing along again as if driving down the hills of Monte Carlo in a car with faulty brakes. This considerably sped up our decision of whether we should let him off the lead or not, it had already been decided because both of us could hold him not a moment longer.

We had unclipped both leads and released him back to the wild.

What an anti-climax! Once off the lead, he walked right beside us, eagerly looking, coaxing us to throw his beloved ball and as long as it was in our possession he wasn't going anywhere.

(Occasionally on our trips, we spotted other dogs coming along, and always held our breath in anticipation of trouble, but Duke took the widest curve round them, looking back nervously as they passed—I think he was just worried that his tennis ball might get stolen).

Once armed with a tennis racquet to give a good wallop, it became a bit of a competition to see who could make Duke run the furthest, so he certainly used up all of his energy, meaning we could return to the car at a much more natural speed, his tongue hanging out of his mouth waiting for liquid refreshment. Like two efficient boy scouts, we were prepared, and much to his delight, produced a bowl and a large bottle of water from the boot. As the first drop was poured, he immediately started drinking, causing half of it to spill all over his head, and unfortunately over the feet of my other half who was standing right next to him to top up the bowl. I was too late to pretend I was looking in the boot, and too late to prevent a grin seeping to the surface, but it didn't matter. Our invigorating walk had put us all in high spirits, and my partner laughed, I laughed, and Duke looked up happily from his bowl. After a cooling down period everyone was ready for a peaceful journey home.

Arriving back at the house, our first thought after rehydrating the panting Duke and mopping the spillage was to check on Herman. By now it was his lunch break, so we went through the ritual of the entrance opening and placed some lettuce, tomato, and fresh dandelions in his path. He took no enticing and started crunching loudly again, so we both stepped back quickly, just in case there was also a repeat of movements at the opposite end. He seemed quite content munching away, so we left him to it and returned through the gate security like some U.N. Officials or wardens at a high-risk prison and went to get our own lunch.

After our feast, the sun beckoned, so we sat at the outdoor table while it digested, and for the first time had more time to take in our surroundings. A stone wall sat opposite the table providing one edge of a fairly large pond complete with running waterfall build at waist level, and as the sunlight glistened through the splashing droplets, it looked so pretty. The end of the wall continued into a few rocks and pots, then three steep steps led up to a sparse lawn which was the route to Herman's office at the far end.

Further round the corner on ground level however, the view was spoilt by several soggy black bags piled up, some of them blocking the path to the grate, and as I tried moving one, (just as an experiment) thousands of jumping insects tried to hide or make their escape.

I hadn't a clue what they were, I just knew they shouldn't be there!

Best to leave them where they were and forget about them, I thought, turning to see if my other half was looking.

Why is it I'm always completely wrong? Why did I ever move that bag?

Our relaxing afternoon consisted of shifting all the unsavoury insect laden bags, moving plants, moving pots, moving tools, sweeping mud, swilling the whole place clean.

No wonder Duke and Duster were nowhere to be seen.

By the Thursday, we were feeling so pleased with ourselves, our first sit almost complete and a total success, bar the first walk. Yet again the sun was shining, we had already taken Duke for his usual outing, so we thought we could have lunch outside and maybe even have a glass of wine. With acute perception Duke and Duster sensed the exact moment food was being prepared, and tried to be the ones who could get closest to it, neither of them being averse to a little theft, so careful table arranging was of the utmost importance. Firstly, Duke was so tall his head could just reach on the table and grab anything left unprotected too near the edge, and secondly, Duster could just leap from any number of surrounding surfaces if there was a landing space big enough, so things had to be spaced extremely accurately. We now had it off to a fine art, but not after a few early mistakes.

Lunch safely prepared, and eaten, wine satisfactorily drunk, we all retreated out of the sun, but it wasn't long before Duke could stand the confines of his tiny bed no longer, and opted for searching out a shady spot outside instead. We opened the door and left him to his own devices, whilst Duster watched closely as we cleared up, hoping to spot any leftover bits of chicken or ham that we had overlooked, and like a magician, make them disappear without us noticing.

Just then, Duke made a sudden return and got straight into his bed.

I attributed it to his often-bad choice of outdoor sleeping locations, some being nowhere near any shade, and once having chosen his bed he was going to lie in it until he could stand it no more.

A while passed and he didn't move a muscle, not an inch, showing no interest in stealing leftovers, and when the kitchen tidying was complete, and we were heading back out again he didn't budge. 'Strange'!

How unusual for him not to try and scramble out of the kitchen door before us.

My other half went first, admiring all our work on the patio tidying and tile cleaning, but before she could utter any congratulatory comments, something moving on the lawn attracted her attention.

She let out a gasp that I understood to mean something serious, and hurriedly started to climb the small steps to the lawn, at the same time saying something about Herman that I couldn't hear.

I followed, simultaneously trying to put two cups down on the outdoor table whilst my feet kept moving to catch her up.

Reaching the lawn I could now see the reason for all the commotion, and why Duke had looked so sheepish when he came in. Rocking to and fro in a dip in the lawn, was an upside-down Herman, who had somehow dug his way under the fence like some escaping P.O.W but instead of freedom had come across Duke the guard.

My partner bravely (without her gloves) lifted him up, and we could see teeth marks forming an extra pattern down one side of his shell, no doubt matching perfectly the dental profile of one Duke, and even worse, on closer examination blood was visible, coming through the shell.

I don't know about Herman, but the two of us were panic-stricken... what should we do first, phone the owner... phone the agent... phone the vet... would he be all right?

We decided the owners would prefer if we ring and interrupt their holiday rather than anything happen to Herman, so mentally rehearsing my lines while I dialled the number, I prepared to tell them the news. After that big nerve-racking build up, all I got was voicemail, so I quickly left a short message and then tried their alternative mobile number to see if that got any response.

It didn't!

Waiting a few more minutes for a reply, my imagination was running completely wild, and my partner, who only the day before had been announcing how you could never get attached to a tortoise, was now just about holding back tears while she constantly stared down at the wounded Herman. Neither of us having much medical knowledge about tortoises, in other words none, we scanned the internet for advice, all the time knowing we would always end up at the vet, no matter what it said, no matter if we paid for it ourselves, no matter what! We weren't going to rest otherwise. After informing the agent of the predicament, and not feeling any more reassured by her insistence that we were doing exactly the right thing, I immediately phoned the vet and arranged an appointment for A.S.A.P. then quickly finding a suitable box to carry our injured reptile, all got in the car and left. Although I had asked the receptionist how to find the surgery, my distracted mind could not concentrate for long enough to remember the instructions from beginning to end, and with every traffic light turning to red as we approached, emotions and frustrations were running, let's say, high.

As the time of our appointment loomed closer, I allowed myself a tiny sigh of relief as we had somehow found the right road, but as I was commandeered out of the car to scout for the building, it was nowhere to be seen. I scanned for a knowledgeable looking passer-by, and tried to retain a calm exterior, whilst inwardly screaming for the directions to the vet's surgery (having already unsettled him by acting like some mugger chasing him up the street). He thought it was only half a mile down the road, so I dashed back to the car, called to say we were almost there, and looked for a suitable spot to turn the car round... but there was no point!

We were on a one-way street, the surgery behind us, and we needed to go round the block again to reach it. I should never have allowed that premature sigh of relief, but this was no time for deliberating.

I joined the traffic which was now building up for rush hour, and drove round the block, barely faster than Herman could have walked there I'm sure, so by the time we reached the veterinary college, had sat in the waiting room for what seemed an age, it was more us that needed treatment rather than Herman, who walked faster than I had ever seen before, almost strutting across the middle of the disinfected surgery floor looking spritelier than ever. We related the sorry tale, then stood sombre faced as he was given a thorough examination by the vet, who managed to calm our fears slightly, but not our guilt, which hadn't abated in the slightest, even though it was no fault of our own. After an injection of antibiotics, armed with medicine to bathe the injured tortoise, we left, Herman's every move being watched as he tried to escape the box from the back of the car, and I could see my partner getting more emotional every second. Relieved to arrive back at our temporary home, we carefully placed Herman back in his tank, still observing him like some mad scientists, then tried to concentrate on feeding Duster the cat and Duke, who my partner now referred to as 'Tortoise Eater'.

Throughout what was left of the evening we attempted to watch the television, but kept staring in the tank, and what would any other night look like a tortoise sleeping, tonight caused utmost alarm, looking like a tortoise that wasn't moving.

After an extremely restless night, not including Duster who slept like a baby between the two of us, still bleary-eyed I hurriedly went downstairs to look in the tank, and could see Herman still in much the same position we had left him, so I crossed everything, put on the sunlight bulb and tried to distract myself with the usual morning tasks. The minute my equally bleary-eyed partner arose, she also headed straight for the tank, and fortunately, I was able to let her know that I had seen movement since the light had warmed him up. She still insisted on a tank-side vigil until our walk with 'Tortoise Eater' which probably would not even have happened, except for some information imparted by the vet the previous day. We had learnt that one of the favourite foods of the tortoise was clover, so after seeing who could do the longest tennis shot for Duke the ball boy, we spent about an hour sitting in a shaded field picking individual stalks of fresh, tasty clover. We walked back to the car with our foraged food, and after cooling Duke down with his drink, drove back and immediately set about our tasks.

My partner took Duke indoors, while I navigated the drive then gave Duke his fresh water. In the meantime the clover had been washed, we both meticulously sorted out the best bits, then rushed to the tank to see if this tempting treat would get a reaction.

It did, and he loved it!

He munched through the stems, and looked quite enthusiastic, (as much as a tortoise can) looking round for seconds. Once he got the flavour, he started tucking into his favourite red crunchy lettuce, a few bits of red pepper and tomato, so we hoped the worst may be over. We still kept him indoors for the rest of the day, which meant going through the tank-cleaning ritual a couple of times, then watching as he lost no time in relieving himself on the fresh clean paper immediately afterwards. It meant more cleaning out, but we didn't mind as long as he was okay!

Over the next few days he was bathed in his antiseptic lotion by my partner, we collected clover and dandelions every time we were out with Duke, (now returned to his original name) and Herman showed no ill effects from his unfortunate episode.

The end of our stay soon arrived, and as we had accumulated quite a bit of washing, thought it was good idea to get it all done the day before leaving and return home with fresh smelling, clean laundry. By now the weather had changed and wasn't really clothes-drying friendly, so I decided it must be okay to hang garments over the chairs in the kitchen, as the owner had already done it on the chair in front of the window, leaving her underwear for all to see. This would have been fine except I hadn't counted on my other half being so unobservant.

Had she not noticed anything all week?

Returning later to get the dry washing, I stood motionless staring at the chair backs, that is the empty chair backs, the ones with nothing wet or dry on them. While I was off doing some other chore, my helpful other half had efficiently gathered up every bit of the underwear, and now the owner's items had disappeared along with ours, and were probably lying next to our case ready to be packed, that is if they weren't already.

It took me a while to persuade my better half that there was a mix up, and both feeling rather uncomfortable, then had to investigate the size and make of each pair of knickers to decide which should stay. Typically, they were all the same well-known brand, unluckily they were all the same colour, and bewilderingly, even after our inspection, nothing was obvious.

All other clearing up forgotten, we sat glued to the spot, staring at the underwear, and mentally going through the options, but unable to find an un-embarrassing solution, or a way to even start the conversation.

What should we do? Leave any three pairs? Leave none at all? Now I was starting to doubt that there were any there in the first place! But surely no one would want to admit they had left knickers on the kitchen chairs when they went on holiday... especially if pet-sitters would be there... but what if someone did? I know they did... and now they were missing! And did we really want to ask if any belonged to anyone?

We decided, not an immediate decision, more after a debate of marathon status, to leave three pairs of the afore mentioned on the back of the kitchen chairs, and hope for the best.

The following morning, the day of our departure, we did the usual feeding and walking routines, but also had to wash bedding, vacuum rooms, pack clothes, get everything from the fridge and freezer, and wipe them out. Our numerous tasks meant the day was soon gone, and by midnight, and with all of our belongings now squashed back into our car, we were just waiting for a call. My other half decided to put out the final rubbish bag, and from the kitchen I listened as the front door opened and the bag clanged into the metal bin outside. Instead of the expected sound of the door closing again, I heard my name being called in a panicky voice, so shut the door on Duke and walked out into the hall.

Just as I was about to see what was amiss, the phone in the sitting room rang, so with no other choice I calmly said, "Hello!" Hoping my partner would not call me again... which she didn't... but more to the point... why didn't she? And where was she? And why was the door still wide open?

On the phone, the returning owners were enquiring about our sit, and I said Herman was okay, and everything else had been absolutely fine, hoping it still was, as I attempted to stretch the cable to where I could see the front door, but to no avail. I tried to end the conversation quickly, hoping I didn't sound in too much of a hurry, so I could go and see what was going on, especially now I had been told our hosts would be back in half-an-hour. Wasting no time, I slammed the phone back on the cradle, and dashed out of the open front door (Duke still safely closed in the kitchen), and ran up the steps, looking round to see what the panic was about.

Across the road, I could see my other half staring through someone's garden fence, whispering desperate coaxing sounds to presumably Duster, who was pretending he couldn't understand her, and carried on walking between their plants, sometimes completely disappearing to add to the tension. Now with both of us trying to track his movements, he reappeared on the spongey lawn, and flopped over on his back, before enjoying every second of flexing his claws in the grass, all the time listening with deaf ears to our pleading, watching our frustration in the corner of his eye.

I decided sneaky tactics were necessary!

Not holding out too much hope against yet another smart feline, I looked round for a stick and pushed it through the railings, wiggling it teasingly, while my other half became a Covent Garden statue, not moving a muscle that may distract him. It was ignored for a while, but eventually his innate hunting instincts got the better of him, and he started to crouch and stalk in that way only a cat can, his bottom swaying from side to side as he flexed the muscles in each back leg alternately.

He made a dive for the stick!

My partner made a grab for him! But he was too quick.

He had now moved back again, so I stretched my arm further through the fence to keep his attention, and several times he managed to keep just out of reach as he charged the stick, the time ticking recklessly away. Thankfully, just as my partner was reaching the 'tearing your hair out stage' he ventured near enough for a desperate grab.

Timing was essential, so as Duster started tapping the stick with one paw, I stretched my free arm through the railings as far as possible, my other half creeping in to a back-up position. Fully concentrating on catching his prey, he let down his guard and followed the stick right up to the fence. I quickly dropped the stick and without the expected struggle, (and clawed fingers) managed to grab him tightly with both hands. My cautious partner stood to my side, ready to make a secondary grab if I could not contain the cat, but he had already surrendered… and lay quietly in my arms, purring all the way back to his house. We walked in, shut, locked, and bolted the front door as if it was Herman's pen, then I dared let go of Duster, who casually ran to the kitchen door waiting to get a drink.

My better half may be able to pick up tortoises, but I can catch cats… what a team!

Duke looked bemused as the kitchen door swung open and Duster strolled past, but concluded nothing was awry, everything was still going well in the tortoise tank (thank goodness), so we sat in the kitchen, not wanting to disturb the freshly plumped cushions on the settee in the lounge.

We had spent so long apprehending the runaway, that a taxi was soon heard pulling up outside, and suddenly the flurry of owners and companions were back. Duke and Duster greeted them excitedly, we on the other hand stood nervously, waiting our turn to explain the breach in tortoise security. Having been appraised of the situation, followed by an inspection through the spotless tank at Herman, the owners assured us he would be okay and not to worry, a similar incident had occurred previously.

That Herman must be one tough cookie!

Job now complete, we said our goodbyes to everyone, went up the steps, then with one reminiscent final panic I reversed out of the forty-five-degree drive, my partner jumped in the seat beside me and we were on our way home.

(I did phone a few days later to see how Herman had got on with his vet's appointment, and all was well!)

After that initiation we were ready for anything!

Chapter 3 — Martha and Lexi

The next sit we were offered would last for nearly one month, but as the venue was only fifteen minutes from home, we could pop back occasionally, check post and generally make sure squatters hadn't moved in during our absence, so we were happy to go ahead.

Our initial visit had taken place on a lazy Sunday afternoon a few weeks earlier, meeting the two dogs we would be looking after — Martha, a scatty French basset who jumped around excitedly, while Lexi, the smaller of the two, limped awkwardly towards us, her arthritis plainly obvious but not going to stop her meeting new people at any cost. Inquisitiveness satisfied, she was soon eager to return to her blanket, the exact opposite of Martha who charged around the furniture like a maniac until eventually, she had to be put outside before we could continue our meeting in peace.

Everything had soon been settled and we left the family to enjoy what was left of the weekend.

Now back for the sit, the sun was shining again as we pulled up at the large Georgian terraced house, so we were led straight out into the garden for coffee, while we went through all codes for alarms, broadband, anything else we needed to know before they left. One of the things on our instruction list would be a new experience for us and we were both looking forward to it immensely... a visit to a therapeutic swimming pool for dogs. Coffee over, cab having arrived, the owners gave their pets a final cuddle with instructions to be good while they were away, and quickly left.

Wanting to make the most of the beautiful weather my better half opened the brand-new kitchen windows while I pushed open the bi-folding patio doors to their widest, then did the same in the television room, the indoors and outdoors instantaneously blending in to one as the whole wall disappeared. Martha trailed behind us as we explored the ground floor of the house and garden for a while, but it was no good putting off the daunting task of lugging numerous bags upstairs to the bedroom and trying to find space for the massive amount of food we thought we would need.

Yes... yet again we had allowed for every eventuality!

Would this town in the middle of London be the only one not to have any supermarkets!

What if every single shop was closed every day!

Whatever happened we would be prepared and somehow survive.

By now, there was no unexplored corner to investigate. Muscles flexed, as we plodded back and forth laden down with our excessive supplies, I made a mental note to slimline all clothes and provisions on our next assignment, but how successful that would be was another matter.

After several journeys to our bedroom up on the second floor, we could now settle into our latest premises and started preparing a summery lunch to eat at the large table outside. The unusually hot temperature made it feel like we were the ones on holiday as we sat savouring both the food and the weather. A massive, heavy umbrella stood next to the table, but neither of us dare tackle it, even though my hair felt so hot I could hardly touch it as I baked over my salad, and I could see my partner having a constant struggle trying to stop her sunglasses sliding to the tip of her nose at every mouthful of food. Still, we might as well soak up the sun while there was chance… it didn't happen that often so we stayed basking a while to let lunch digest.

By the time we had dragged ourselves back indoors, now thoroughly exhausted from the heat, cleared everything up and found the right place to put it back, it was time for a walk to the nearby common with Martha. The leads jangled together noisily as I removed one of them from the hook in the hallway and both dogs appeared.

Because of her severe arthritis, Lexi was only allowed a short walk every other day so she wouldn't be able to come with us and looking down at the two big brown eyes staring pitifully back at us, my better half and I both felt terrible about it. Lexi realised what was happening, and headed slowly back to her bed, just pausing to turn and give one last hopeful glance before finally lying down resigned to being left behind. The feeling of guilt my other half and I was accumulating couldn't have got any worse, but the only consolation was that she could have her short walk up and down the road as soon as we got back.

We'd better get on with it!

I expected getting Martha to stand still long enough for a lead to be clicked on her collar to take a fair while, but she managed to contain her excitement and off we went. She was not a bad walker on the lead, but it only took a few steps to realise all items thrown or excreted on the pavement on our route, (of which there were many) had to be avoided, otherwise they would be promptly consumed. To prevent this, I spent the whole journey to the common staring down at the floor, shouting warnings to my other half who was steering Martha around any obstacles a few paces behind, but we did eventually discover that by walking much faster she didn't have time to grab anything, which gave me a much more pleasant view.

It became my routine to take her to the common every morning, and once all the necessaries were done, we could carry on to the tube station, pick up the free newspaper, get back home and deliver it to my other half who sometimes hadn't yet felt the urge to leave her warm, cosy bed. Every other day we would slowly walk up and down the steep road with Lexi, and although it looked painful for her, she enjoyed the little exercise, stopping to sniff every tree, every plant, almost every blade of grass as we went. Our sedate outings could take almost as long as walking Martha but there was no point trying to hurry her along, like all dogs she was stubbornly going at her own pace, and strong enough to stop any hasty walker in their tracks.

This could soon change however if treats were on the cards. Somehow, she could change gear, bustle past Martha who would be sat with her neck stretched to its limit and jump in front of her to get the pick of the goodies on offer. They needn't have worried; they were always shared equally.

Chewing as fast as possible, they would surreptitiously look over to confirm that in fact, and the second the goodies were finished they would sneakily change places and inspect the area as good as any forensic team, just in case anything had been missed.

Both dogs were extremely friendly but definitely had opposite personalities.

Martha could turn on and off as quick as a light switch, one minute racing round chasing a ball, the next she was almost asleep on the floor as if nothing had ever happened, whereas Lexi was more on an even keel most of the time and took life at the leisurely pace she could manage.

One thing they did have in common however was their long, tangled coats, so we thought over the next three weeks we would try to brush them regularly so they could impress their owners with a sleek silky sheen on their return... not as easy as we thought!

Lexi would only put up with a gentle brush for a while, all the time sporting an accusing pained expression to make even the hardest of men feel slightly conscience-stricken. She would then shuffle round to face the opposite direction and you knew that was enough.

Martha, on the other hand, wasn't going to sit still while somebody tried to brush those knots away. She would gradually sink lower and lower until her back legs were stretched out flat behind her, then slowly (so as not to be noticed) pull herself along the floor on her front elbows. Whichever one of us was brushing would crawl along with her, but she gradually worked up speed until it was a sudden race to try and brush any leg or tail that hadn't got quite out of reach yet. This usually set off a chain reaction of manic ball chasing followed by the sudden flop of disinterest, which then allowed another few seconds of brushing, and off we would go again.

One evening I decided to attempt communicating with our companions in their own language, so tried a howl to call in the pack. Taking everything in her stride as usual, Lexi glanced up momentarily appearing to humour the attempt politely, but there seemed to be a slight reaction from Martha who was still staring inquisitively, head tilting to one side.

Clearing my throat I tried again, giving it a little more gusto!

Martha suddenly tilted her head back, pursed her lips and gave us the benefit of her best wolf-howl, showing how it was really done, and once she got going, she couldn't see any viable reason to stop!

I couldn't help having another go myself now I had heard the real thing, and this really got a reaction, both from Martha, and from my better half, who after a brief half-hearted attempt herself, was trying to tell us to stop... but we could hardly hear her.

"The neighbours will be coming round to see what's wrong!" she said loudly... and very seriously, and after a brief contemplative pause, I knew she was right.

I nodded my agreement... just before I threw my head backwards and howled again to get Martha going... we were both enjoying it so much.

Saturday was the much-anticipated visit to the doggie swimming pool, and we eagerly loaded their two beds into the back seat of our car so both dogs would be comfortable on the journey. A visit to the common was next on the agenda (to hopefully prevent any accidents on the way), and it provided a welcome change of scenery for Lexi. Once lifted out of the car, she sat contentedly next to my other half, observing everything in view, breathing in every scent within a two-mile radius while I explored with Martha, being towed along as she haphazardly darted from one tree to another.

It did the trick, and once we were en route the dogs soon settled, until an hour later, following the hand-drawn map, I turned into a gateway and drove down the steep farm track where we could see a car park between the trees. Pulling up as close to the entrance as possible Lexi was carefully lifted out, while the excitable Martha shot out of the opposite door, impatient to find out where we were. As the four of us walked towards the reception all the staff seemed to know our little dog, shouting hello, making a fuss of her, and although acknowledging them with a polite wag of her tail, she kept turning round to look longingly at the car, wanting to get back in and leave. Lexi knew exactly where we were and what this scenario meant, even if Martha didn't!

Inside, our appointment was checked, then one of the therapists brought over a small, red life jacket, which she exchanged for her collar, then coaxed the tentative little dog to follow her down the ramp into the warm water.

The three of us watched intently.

This session would consist of several laps round the pool, resting every other one, and we were informed that it would be good to keep shouting praise and calling Lexi to keep up the momentum, as it would be tiring for her.

No problem! No persuasion needed!

We were calling, praising, shouting, whooping like some crazy cheerleaders as we walked round the perimeter just in front of her. Martha looked slightly bemused but was enjoying the rumpus, and her feathery tail was perfect as it continuously swished round like some built-in pompom. Down in the water, Lexi was doggy-paddling for all she was worth to catch up, her short tail just peeping out of the water at the back, and her eyes fixed on the source of all the racket at the front. Each time she rested, cradled by the therapist, we knelt by the water for a quick stroke, then it was back up, parading round the pool like a marching band as we coaxed and encouraged to the max.

Eventually, a weary little dog slowly walked back up the ramp, the life jacket dripping furiously to rid itself of the extra weight, and we all gathered round to congratulate her on the massive effort, all getting splattered in the bargain, as she shook from top to toe. Nobody could have cared less.

The soggy red jacket was unclipped, her collar replaced, so the only remaining chore was to shower the disinfected water from her coat, then we could grant her wish… to get out of here, and fast!

The doggie showers were near the far exit, doggie shampoo provided, so we ran the water and started washing Lexi's coat, but an opportunity like this was not to be overlooked. Making sure the staff were otherwise occupied, we steered the unsuspecting Martha under the other shower, quickly gave her a wash and rinse before she could escape, then I hastily shuffled her out of the door. Lexi, once rinsed, was not far behind and after a mutual sniff at each other, both immediately wanted to rid themselves of the fresh clean smell. We looked around, checking if anyone was watching as they both wriggled around in the grass to get dry, and my observant other half spotted a building which seemed to have the canine equivalent of hairdryers. While Lexi was partially dried, I kept Martha outside, fearing the hot air might launch one of her scatty episodes, and we didn't want to draw any more attention than necessary. Coiffure done, we hurriedly ushered them both back in to the car and drove away.

Curling up in the beds on the back seat, Lexi was soon asleep after her strenuous workout, and Martha also snoozed away for most of the journey, dog telepathy only stirring them as we pulled up near their house.

Back indoors they both deserved a treat after all the excitement, which was soon devoured with more snoozing to follow.

The rest of the days followed the same routine, two weeks later we were back at the doggie swimming pool, and before you know it, a month had passed and it was the end of our stay.

We washed, tidied, dusted, vacuumed, hauled our numerous bags back into the car, then sat waiting in the house that looked as though we'd never been there in the first place.

It no longer felt like our temporary home.

Now on the brink of leaving, we were merely visitors again.

Hearing the front door open, both dogs disappeared into the hall, then a second later Martha shot back, skidded round the coffee table, dashed back into the hall, then charged back to us again, by which time her family had managed to wade through the barrage of welcoming and could greet us. Lexi lay blissfully in her owner's arms, listening intently as we confirmed that the dogs had been very good in their absence, as requested. Martha was being pampered at floor level, hardly able to sit still for a second with all the excitement but who could blame her.

Job done, we gave the dogs a last stroke and said our goodbyes.

Chapter 4 — Honey and Cotton

We didn't have to wait long for our next assignment!

Our next sit would be taking us slightly further from home, into Kent if we got the job, but we had to have our meeting with owners and pets first.

We arrived on a Monday afternoon, after embarrassingly having to ring them to locate their house as it only possessed a name rather than a number and could have been anywhere on the long winding cul-de-sac craftily hidden from the rest of a quaint small village. As I ended my call, a door burst open not far behind us, and our client rushed to the end of the drive, arms waving frantically as if she was a marooned sailor alone on a desert island trying to get the attention of a distant boat, rather than us just a few yards down the road. I returned the enthusiastic wave then reversed up to the driveway where we introduced ourselves, then were shown into a large sitting room where we met two rather subdued canines. An attempt to stroke them failed completely, and they disappeared to follow their owners who had themselves disappeared to make coffee, leaving the two of us alone, quietly waiting for our hospitable clients to return. They soon did, armed with the coffees and a plate of biscuits for accompaniment, then we could begin.

Our conversation began worryingly with a warning that we should only decide if we wanted to do the sit after being told of the incidents we might have to face, and looking down at the angelic faces, one of them slightly askew, of the little white Bichon Frise dogs, I wondered what dreaded secrets were about to be divulged.

The first problem, it was revealed, was of a rather unsavoury nature, entailing plenty of clearing up, and also keeping a constant eye on toilet activities, so any little packages could be swiftly and efficiently removed before they were re consumed. The second one was more of a psychological nature, and in the absence of their owners, particularly overnight the dogs could suffer from separation anxiety, resulting in yet more toileting accidents, so one would have to have their wits about them when getting up and walking into the kitchen every morning.

As we worked our way through the questionnaire of doggy requirements, we were offered numerous apologies for the smell, due to both dogs suffering from some sort of bug. It made me wonder if my partner and I were suffering identical nasal problems, because we didn't really notice anything untoward (which was rather disconcerting).

In spite of their cautionary information, we agreed that we could handle whatever they may throw at us, in whatever form, in whatever direction, and from whatever end, so leaving our coffee and biscuits we were led on a tour of the house, firstly heading into the kitchen where we were given extensive instructions on their beds, their food, their treats, their walks, their pills, anything you could mention, then shown the garden where we would be on twenty-four hour look out.

We could have been there much longer I'm sure, but our tour was abruptly cut short as the husband appeared, worry etched across his face, announcing that in our absence, Cotton had taken the opportunity to eat an unguarded mini chocolate cake, along with its silver wrapper, and there was now a distinct possibility we might witness first-hand what the warnings had been about.

Not wishing to put them through any more embarrassed apologies, and as they seemed happy with our interview, arranged a time of arrival, then with a knowing look telepathically decided on a quick exit.

On the Saturday of their departure we arrived with plenty of time to spare, and not wishing to intrude, parked at the end of their drive, with nothing more to do but watch the minutes tick by. We weren't there for long, because the husband had spotted us as he walked out with two massive cases ready to pack into their car. Dropping them with a thud to free his hands, he beckoned us to approach, so emerging obediently I tried to quickly stretch a few muscles back into shape watching my partner surreptitiously checking her trousers for any furry reminders of our previous sit. Within that time his cases had been slung into the boot, and he was already heading back, so we hurried down the long path and followed him through the front door to greet our nervous charges. By now they had recovered from their bugs and were much livelier, looking quite happy to be stroked. The husband left to carry on with the packing, keen to keep to their departure schedule, but his wife seemed to be dragging in her preparations, and kept going over instruction after instruction, perhaps for her own peace of mind, but merely avoiding the final 'au revoir' as long as possible.

After lots of reassuring, and an agonisingly slow goodbye, finally, they were ready, and we watched their car disappear round the corner.

Not a minute later it reappeared and pulled back into the drive. The two dogs glanced up at the sound of the kitchen door opening, followed by the sound of the fridge door opening and closing, but they didn't go to investigate. Tummy tickling was taking priority, even when their mistress popped her head round the door for another grand farewell. Their false start was due to having forgotten lunch, whether intentional or not, but at least it provided an opportunity to dispel some fears, as she could see her babies contentedly flopped on the carpet, soaking up the attention to such an extent they couldn't even be bothered to move. The door slammed again, a little louder than before, and she returned to the car with lunch.

Their second attempt to leave was successful, although we sat listening for a few minutes, almost expecting the door to open again.

Because we'd been told how sensitive these little dogs were, we grabbed toys by the handful to take their mind off the 'painful' moment, we kept sympathising with their plight in stupidly high voices, and we stroked and pampered them as much as is humanly possible.

But just a minute—Let's try a different approach.

It occurred to us that maybe nothing was actually wrong. They looked content enough, and if anything they were more than likely bemused by our odd behaviour. We decided not to play to their insecurities, from now on we would treat them like any other dog, hoping that was exactly how they would feel... and it seemed to work perfectly.

As it was, they had no time to pine once we started loading our bags and boxes of food through the kitchen door... they were too busy being nosy, more interested in what they might find to eat, so nothing could be left unguarded. All attention then shifted to the front door, which was a more direct route to the bedroom, and as more bags appeared both dogs insisted on accompanying us on every trip upstairs, checking anything being unpacked thoroughly, like sniffer dogs combing an airport for drugs.

It was now definitely time for coffee, so we all headed downstairs again.

Tiny feet pitter-pattered on the wooden kitchen floor, following whoever moved, as we paced and scanned the kitchen for a microwave, an essential item needed for heating milk to froth for a cappuccino. I knew there was one somewhere, but it certainly was well camouflaged, so looking like we were both losing our marbles, my better half and I stupidly started searching the cupboards, until we realised it was down at knee height, level with the oven.

Coffee finally made, the two of us, followed closely by the two of them, moved into the lounge.

My other half placed her coffee on a small table, I copied, and we both flopped on the large sofa.

As soon as we landed on the soft cushions, two little white bodies jumped up, and landed, one on each lap... I could detect no sign of separation anxiety here, and as we sipped our coffee, their eyes started to close.

Later that day, the little dogs who seemed to have no trouble relaxing without their owners, jumped up and ran to the front door as we grabbed their two leads ready for our first walk. What a difference to the massive Duke and the scatty Martha I pondered, as we calmly set off towards the field.

They lived in a very pretty village, but one of two halves. On one side of the only road passing through were large old houses spaced well apart, on the other, a vicarage and church hidden between thick foliage, which then led into a modern but affluent looking cul-de-sac on the left (where we were staying). A little further along going in the opposite direction was a road with fairly new houses, which we had to pass to reach the field, quite a distance for eight tiny legs. Honey strutted along happily, but Cotton did look a little nervous, and having been informed that they only walked to the entrance of the field before wanting to go home, we didn't expect to be out for long.

No one else was around as we reached our turning point, and the dogs weren't exactly pulling us back home, not even the nervous Cotton, so after a brief discussion we were through the gate and striding our way round the perimeter. My partner and I were on high alert, constantly scanning from side to side, checking behind to make sure no massive dogs were about to pounce on the tiny twosome, so, when out of the blue, a cockerel squawked loudly from the other side of the hedge, we both jumped a mile. The booming bird seemed to belong to a small farm, and once he'd found his voice, boy… was he going to use it!

That was the end of our walk, because Cotton had been spooked by the loud outburst as well and was now attempting to drag my other half back to the gate. We didn't want her upset, and retraced our steps back up the hill, over the road, in to the cul-de-sac and down the long path, surrounded by the equally long lawn, to the front door.

Made it!

We were safely home.

As we had passed the triangular shaped shrubbery on the corner, I tried not to notice the weeds and nettles dominating the other plants, but it was blatantly obvious, and I knew what we'd be doing sometime over our stay.

After dinner, television viewing was the order of the day, but our early morning was soon taking its toll, and we were both struggling to stay awake. For once we would have an early night, but there were things to be done first. I walked through to the large newly decorated conservatory, slid open the massive patio door and both dogs jumped over the metal frame like tiny ponies at a gymkhana. We were right behind them, resembling two bumbling Private Eye's as we tried to observe from a distance without putting them off their stride. They scurried around the lawn, which started out nearly level, but halfway towards the hedge dropped steeply to almost a forty-five-degree angle, so as we kept watch, the little white bodies abruptly disappeared, causing a momentary panic, and mad stumbling in the dark to relocate them. It was short lived because they were just as eager as us to get back inside and charged straight back towards the door. Both did their miniature leap, then ran straight to their beds in the kitchen to wait for the final treat of the day. We scattered newspaper by the back door and the kitchen entrance, then put towels in front of the sink and their beds, gave them their goodies and said goodnight, closing the baby gate as we left them, hoping for the best.

The following morning, I left my better half wrapped in the duvet, and went downstairs, braced myself, took a deep breath, and walked towards the kitchen.

My arrival was no surprise, and I could see two balls of fluffy white fur pressed against the baby gate, waiting to get out. I clicked the lock on the gate, and Cotton rushed off to get one of their fluffy toys from the toy box, while Honey trailed behind my feet, wherever they went.

I didn't want to acknowledge them yet.

Instead I grabbed the door keys so I could get them outside quickly.

Outside, I stood in the middle of the lawn to get a good view in all directions, but soon realised I had made an error, as I felt the early morning dew gradually seeping through my shoes, while I waited for them to do any bathroom necessities. They weren't overkeen on the morning dew either, and both made a quick dash for the gap in the doors, so I followed, abandoning my soggy shoes on the conservatory floor, and went to inspect any overnight damage in the kitchen.

What a surprise!

Everything was exactly as we had left it the night before.

No accidents!

No sign of separation anxiety to be seen!

Still slightly suspicious, I inspected the kitchen floor again, picked up the towels, gathered the sheets of newspaper, fully expecting something to be slightly damp at least, but all was well, and I couldn't believe my luck. This news was too good to be true, and had to be shared immediately, so I went up the stairs, closely followed by my two shadows, and woke my better half... a risky move I admit, but luckily she was just as pleased to hear the success story, and congratulated them both.

Let's see how tomorrow goes!

Cotton was always ready to relax at any opportunity, preferably on someone's lap, and seemed to have a built-in radar system that could detect anyone approaching the settee, allowing her to be there within a couple of seconds. Honey was much livelier and liked nothing better than chasing one of the many toys that were heaped in their toy box, so I usually ended up doing the playing, while my partner provided a comfy pillow, and could peruse as many films on Sky as possible.

Instead of just throwing the squeaky bone, I decided to make the game a little more interesting.

Firstly, I pretended to throw the toy, and as Honey dashed off to retrieve it, I ran off in the opposite direction. Quickly realising she had been tricked I could hear her tiny feet charging after me, and I was soon caught red-handed with the stolen goods as I tried to hide behind a door. Her little pom-pom tail was swishing from side to side happily, so I did the same, this time dashing into the kitchen to try and hide, but she was too quick. There were three doors to the television room, so I opened them all wide, one to the conservatory, another to the games room, and the last to the hall which also provided an alternative route through the games room to the conservatory. I now had a perfect circuit to escape from my pursuer.

She had been following as I prepared the game, and now stood poised for my first throw, concentrating on every bit of my body language, already facing the way she would be running, with her head stretched backwards to watch my actions. I decided on a normal throw to begin and watched her feet skid across the conservatory floor as she tried to stop once she had grabbed the bone. Unprepared for a different direction, it took a while to retrieve my second throw which went into the games room.

This was it!

I pretended to throw, and as she went careering into the conservatory, I dashed through the door into the hall. I paused at the games room listening to those little paws galloping ten to the dozen trying to change direction, then as she scurried back through the television room through to the hall, I was already continuing through the games room and into the conservatory from the other direction. I felt like some escaping fugitive. My heart was pounding, I was on edge as I desperately looked for a hiding place, knowing time was running short. Panicking, I decided to crouch behind the armchair in the corner, but as I looked down, a tiny, extremely pleased, cute face was staring up at me.

Busted!

This dog was fast!

I could see this turning into a long running competition, much like the game with Harley, but I didn't mind one bit.

Over the week, the distance of our walks got gradually further, and both dogs looked quite at ease, and we all got used to passing the noisy farm, even Cotton. The only hiccup to cause a little dissatisfaction to the dogs occurred one afternoon, when we had to take refuge under a tree to shelter from an unexpected deluge. It was getting harder to avoid the drips seeping through the foliage, so we reviewed our options!

Should we wait for it to abate?

Or should we make a run for it?

It was a tricky choice.

If we stayed put, who knows how long we could be there, and our companions were already shivering under their bedraggled fur. On the other hand it could soon pass, and we would all have got totally drenched for nothing.

After getting dripped on for another couple of minutes we decided to scurry home.

My partner and I lifted up a dog each and tried our best to protect them from the downpour, even though neither of us had a coat. I was so glad they weren't any bigger... trying to run with a dog in your arms, especially uphill, is harder than one might think.

We convened by the front door, my partner and I breathless from the dash, and the dogs still shivering as they were returned to ground-level. I unlocked the door and we all bundled through, then while my other half and I battled to remove Wellies with cold wet hands, the trembling twosome were running their heads along the hall carpet to get dry. Presuming they needed a little assistance I went to grab their unused towels from the kitchen to soak up more water, but they squirmed and wriggled around so much it was useless. They embarked on more head wiping, first one side then the other and it looked much more fun.

The week turned out to be a complete success and although prepared for the worse, I was pleasantly surprised every morning to find nothing amiss.

Their owners could hardly believe it.

They may have been just a little upset that their babies had no symptoms of the much-anticipated separation anxiety.

Nevertheless, they knew they could call on us again, perhaps with less trepidation next time.

Chapter 5 — Molly and Biscuit

Arriving at the impressive looking farm for our pre-visit, I was just trying to decide where to park in the large white stone covered expanse, as two small dogs came charging out at the car, barking incessantly to sound the alarm to the rest of their pack. I quickly stopped, and as we both got out, they turned tail, job done, and raced back to their owner, who was by now, purposefully striding out to meet us.

After a business-like handshake, we followed him with an invitation to meet his wife.

Trailing past various outbuildings we walked down three concrete steps and turned towards a massive lawn opposite the house, obviously well cared for (as was the rest of the garden) and followed to an outdoor table where his other half was savouring a cold lager. We were offered a cold lager ourselves, which looked extremely tempting to me in the unusually hot weather, but as we were aware they hadn't had sitters before, a good impression was essential, and we declined.

A few minutes later, sat in the blaring sun sipping red hot coffee, I was subtly trying to mop an increasingly obvious band of sweat gradually forming across my brow as we went through our usual questions.

I tried not to stare at the lager, but I was definitely regretting my decision.

We finished our part of the interrogation, then the owner stood up to show us the surrounding land that belonged to the farm... then we all stood up as he pointed out the large field where we would be taking the two little dogs for walks.

Molly and Biscuit, a mother and daughter who looked nothing alike were on tenterhooks, just waiting for the signal that it was time to be taken on their regular outing, but this was just going to be a practice run for us, not the real thing. A collar which produced a slight electric charge if Molly got too near the fence was removed, then we all went through the gate, the dogs racing into the distance until they disappeared altogether.

"Don't worry!" We were told. "They do that and as you walk round the perimeter they reappear."

As this was just a demonstration we returned to the farm, both trying hard not to look back, and sure enough, after a while, two breathless dogs, looking extremely pleased with themselves, shot like bullets back through the gate, trying to barge each other out of the way in their rush to be first to get a well-needed drink.

Our tour continued indoors and it was immediately obvious that this was a true farmhouse, in actual fact it was two farmhouses joined together, but in the one kitchen, an old-fashioned Aga cooker took centre stage, accompanied by a good old-fashioned kettle to boil on top, none of those new-fangled electric kettles, and definitely no microwave to come to the rescue if we had forgotten to take our dinner from the freezer in time. Luckily, we usually cooked food from fresh ingredients so were not reliant on heating up supermarket-ready meals, otherwise the raw food diet would have been required for the duration of this sit.

Having seen the rest of the house and everything agreed, we left, saying we would see them in about a month's time. Both owners and dogs watched our departure, the stones crunching noisily under the tyres as I turned the car round, and we were soon on our way home.

One Month Later

Always thinking I can remember things much better than I actually can in real life, we drove down the M4 towards our destination, and I kept reassuring my much more realistic other half that we would recognise our surroundings en route and get to the farm again with complete ease.

Conscientiously I had made sure to pack all of the information needed for our sit, but somewhere amongst it were the instructions and map how to get there. By the time I realised my error, my bag was well and truly buried deep in our packing, and it would have taken much too long to find, especially with two eyes glaring down at me.

How is it that I can never find anything if my other half is watching?

Things seemed to be going according to plan however, and either one or the other of us would see familiar landmarks as we went, getting to the village flawlessly, but then with our promised time of arrival looming dangerously close, and knowing we must be within about half a mile of our destination, the end piece of the jigsaw seemed to be missing. We both remembered the place where we asked directions on our first visit, but neither of us could remember the most important bit, where we went after that. As it was barely dawn, there was no one to ask this time and even without red, hot coffee I could feel that band of sweat forming on my forehead again. Beginning to panic I turned the car round so we could go back to a few shops in the village and hopefully try to relive our route.

For some reason it wasn't working, and even worse, neither of us could see where we were going wrong. Losing all sensibility whatsoever I started to drive up a track we had not investigated, knowing it didn't look quite right but hoping that was also a trick of my 'not so good now' memory and willing it to transform into the road up to the farm. It didn't of course!

Feeling the rapidly increasing anxiety of my partner, and the clock ticking nearer to late o'clock, in desperation I started to drive back up the road, past the spot where we had previously decided we had gone wrong, and although it looked totally unfamiliar somehow miraculously ended up on the right road.

Like film heroes diffusing a dastardly bomb, we drove along the farm drive, past the few small cottages on the corner, past the massive barn and pulled up on the noisy pebbles with seconds to spare, trying to look calm as the owner, unaware, complimented us on our punctuality.

They were well organised, and it wasn't long before they were ready to leave, so employing our usual technique we tried distracting the dogs while the recognisable sound of their owner's car faded into the distance. As usual this was followed by the canine technique of not being distressed one little bit, not even bothering to look for their owners, so as they were quite settled it meant we could begin our unloading.

Being farm dogs we thought the duo would be eager to return outside the second the door was re-opened, enabling them to take over responsibility of patrolling the property in the absence of their pack leaders. In reality, however, the call of the Aga was altogether much more potent than that of the wild, and acting more like it was midwinter, they both snuggled up together as close to the oven door as possible, turning a blind eye and a deaf ear as we struggled past countless times.

Next on the agenda, a well-needed cup of tea.

Not being completely 'au fait' with the workings of an Aga, neither of us had realised we should have started to boil the kettle a quarter of an hour before we wanted tea, and could now easily comprehend where the saying, 'a watched kettle never boils' originated.

Half-an-hour later, now revived and rehydrated, and definitely not wanting to squander the good weather we explored the grounds, followed everywhere by the inseparable duo, the orchard on one side with bird feeders spaced between the branches (every tree laden with cooking apples), a vegetable patch leading to a greenhouse at the back, a flower bed on the other side, and at the front, the massive lawn that led to the fields. As we were already half way there, we decided to go on the first walk of the day, and it was amazing to see how quickly lethargic demeanour can be miraculously transformed.

Although a little anxious at the prospect, we followed our orders to the letter, firstly unfastening the electric collar, which instantly started a frenzy of excited barking, jumping, and barging as they impatiently waited for us to follow.

At least they were waiting for us!

The gate to the field was then opened and even before it was closed the dynamic duo had disappeared.

Feeling somewhat redundant we carried on with our walk around the perimeter, each of us glancing at the horizon in turn, time dragging slowly by, so when we reached the top corner of the field and were still alone, both of us were now getting nervous. A few steps later the sound of rustling undergrowth built to a crescendo, and two excited faces covered in bits of leaves and cobwebs shot out from the hedge beside us. With a final bound to vault the ditch they were back by our side and how happy they looked.

As we all continued, my observant partner and I realised that this field was absolutely crammed with blackberries, we had probably stared straight at them earlier, but had not seen them through the mild panic. Optimistically searching our pockets all we could find was one small plastic carrier bag, and it was soon filled with the succulent fruits.

It must have been perfect growing conditions because these were some of the biggest blackberries I had ever seen, putting every supermarket to shame, and what's more, they were free.

As soon as we were back indoors, we crammed our pockets with more bags, ready for a mammoth session of picking on our next expedition, and it didn't disappoint.

The little dogs were happy to do their own thing, and it meant they could stay out longer as we helped ourselves to as many blackberries as we could. We were laden down with them, and by that evening we had blackberries in dishes ready for breakfast, blackberries in dishes to sample immediately, blackberries made into a scrumptious looking pie for tomorrow, blackberries in the freezer for another day.

All that and we had only skimmed the surface... these dogs were in for some long walks.

Later in the week we set off as usual, but as we reached the fence, they both looked just like they were athletes on starting blocks, more so than usual, every muscle poised for action just waiting for the pistol to launch them into action.

Signal given and they were gone.

We could hear shuffling in the foliage close by, rather than their familiar disappearing act and this time it wasn't them that reappeared. A fox suddenly ran out, followed closely by the other two, and there was nothing we could do but watch as the three of them raced across the whole width of the field. Calling was pointless because their innate instincts had taken over and they now assumed the identity of two wolves, unusually small wolves perhaps, but definitely teeth bearing, flesh hunting wolves, chasing their prey. I made a feeble attempt at following (as if I would ever catch up), but what would I do anyway!

Fortunately, as the fox reached the opposite hedge, they slowed down, turned and nonchalantly trotted back to see what we were doing. They must have just been chasing him off their territory... what a relief!

Having had no more heart stopping moments we were on our last day, and as soon as we got up, washing the towels and bedding was a priority. We organised it into two loads and put on the first while we took the dogs for the first walk of the day.

Off came the zapper collar, the catalyst to start both dogs running around our feet impatiently and we donned Wellies and coats, as quick as is possible when two dogs are running between your feet and jumping up knocking you off balance and set off towards the field.

We followed behind as they charged and barged each other, looking like a cross between a race and a fight, but it was soon forgotten once there was investigating and checking the territory to be done on the other side of the gate.

While they disappeared to do the usual check on the hedgerows, we were going to make the most of our final opportunity to pick the massive blackberries that were still never-ending. We were getting choosy by now, and my other half reached over to reach a bunch of prize-winning fruits right at the top of an overhanging branch. The only trouble was that overnight there had been quite a downpour, and as she stretched over, nudging the lower branches, massive drips of freezing cold water splattered loudly on to her head and coat. She turned threateningly to see if I was amused, just at the moment I was trying to stifle a grin, which then turned in to a snigger at seeing the water sprayed across her face. My hilarity this time turned out to be contagious, my better half joining in the laughter, particularly as I got just as wet making another attempt to reach the best fruits by balancing on one leg, arm stretched way too far, and overbalancing into the bottom of the bushes, thus causing another shower of hefty drips. Nevertheless, cold water seeping through our jackets, water running down the back of our necks, soggy through to the skin trousers could not put us off our mission, and we continued regardless.

Half way down the first side I gave the dogs a whistle, and they raced back, saw nothing was happening and were gone again just as quick, probably wondering why we had bothered to disturb them in the first place, but it gave me a little assurance that they were in the vicinity.

We carried on picking, and it wasn't until we got round to the opposite corner that they decided to come running back again, but this time Molly was much slower, and seemed to be limping. She stared at us with the biggest brown eyes that would fit in this size dog, as if she was asking what was wrong, and could we make it better. Neither of us could see anything wrong, no thorns, no cuts, everything felt fine, and for some unknown reason we also checked the other three paws, as if that would make her limp on the first leg.

Inspection completed we stood back and watched as she tried out the supposed wounded leg, walking in front of us for a few steps. After a cautious start, she walked a bit faster, built up to a trot, tried running, and then charged off at full pelt shooting past Biscuit as if nothing was wrong. Who knows what that was all about, a touch of canine hypochondria perhaps?

By now, we had done our lap, and were totally soaked through, so the thought of the warm Aga was even more inviting than usual.

We all felt like charging in to get the best cosy position today, but us humans had to put our coats to dry and fill the slow-motion kettle for a tasty cappuccino (We would definitely have plenty of time to empty the first lot of washing and get the next load started before it boiled).

Once emptied, the washing was draped on the front of the Aga, on the chairs in front of the Aga, and as much as possible on top of the Aga (after the kettle had actually boiled), so it could dry quickly and be smartly ironed for their return. We were well ahead of schedule so we could savour our coffee and biscuits.

Refreshment break finished, we did our usual cleaning routine, leaving the Aga to do its drying extremely efficiently, so my partner decided to get out the ironing press while I packed our clothes, the remainder of our food… and mounds of blackberries.

Every time I walked past with a bag, the pile of sheets and towels that had been ironed was growing, so as the second load was now almost dry, we decided to hang the ironed items back over the chairs to air them and make more space. Manoeuvring the laundry, my other half suddenly noticed a brown line along the sheet she had been pressing and called me over to join in her panic. We looked at the sheet, and I bravely stared her in the eye accusingly, thinking it was a scorch mark.

After a rapid response of, "Don't look at me." I quickly turned my gaze back to the mark, trying to assess either if it was reparable, or working out how much would it cost us to replace. It didn't look quite like a singe, so what could have happened.

Closer inspection revealed all!

Where had we put the washing? Over the chairs… you remember… the wooden chairs with the wooden backs. The wood colour had seeped into the white sheets, the white pillow cases, the white towels.

The majority of our smartly-ironed washing sported a matching line.

The only possible solution would be to re-wash everything, and hope, everything crossed, that we were in time to remove the stains.

Forget the 'relaxing because we were ahead of schedule!'

Time was moving on a lot faster than we would have wished at the moment, but all we could do was wait for the machine to go through its cycle, so we had a rather worried lunch, and then as the washing machine beeped to let us know it had finished, both dashed over and counted down every second of the time-lock, waiting to see if the stains had been washed out.

What luck! It seemed to have worked so the second load had to be dealt with asap.

While I dealt with the next load of washing, the ironing press was soon in action again, and this time on totally white laundry with no stains.

We had been given permission to leave before the owners returned home, but due to our unforeseen circumstances were still loading the final bags into the boot as they drove up. Molly and Biscuit dashed to their side and escorted them back, where they thanked us then waved goodbye.

A few days later the agent rang, saying she had received a call singing our praises. Dogs had been well looked after, and property looked pristine.

Phew!

Chapter 6 — Saxon and Luca

On the way back from our farm experience we decided to call in for a meeting with our next prospective client as it was only a short diversion on the route home. We had been warned this house had quite large grounds but sat in our small car we were now staring at two massive metal gates, waiting for a response from the intercom.

None came, but the gates suddenly swung wide open, so cautiously I pressed the accelerator just in case it wasn't meant for us, and as we weren't suddenly surrounded by security men, continued up the long drive. This was the only house we had come across, that needed signposts within its own grounds to make sure you found it, and a quarter of a mile later we still weren't there… instead we arrived at another set of gates. I got out and pressed the intercom to announce our arrival once more, although I was sure it was no surprise.

Like vampires we were invited in, and as I parked in front of the house, the owner opened the door letting two massive German Shepherds charge out towards us. Convinced this was our first test, my partner and I stayed calm, and treated the dogs as two long-lost friends, they, in turn deciding we were worthy of entry through the impressive double doors to follow their owner. We walked into a large marble-tiled hall with an equally large staircase in the centre and were led to the kitchen at the far end, escorted all the way by the two guards.

I decided the owner must have been through the initial meeting procedure before, because all of our usual questions were redundant, all answered identically with, "It's all down on the instruction sheets, which you will see when you arrive for the sit."

Wondering why we were even there, I resorted to trivial chit-chat while we finished our coffee, the slightest movement still closely scrutinised, before heading back through the gates and off to our own home, which we hadn't seen for a while.

We must have looked respectable enough, and capable of handling the dogs, because we were soon heading up the drive again, this time for the real thing. The gates of the massive house were already open, and someone was standing by the door, ordering the two dogs to wait until I had parked. They obeyed temporarily but were too curious to see who had arrived and bounded over as soon as the car was stationary, ignoring any other commands, so not wishing to keep the person, who presumably was their other owner, waiting, we fought our way through the welcoming committee to introduce ourselves. He in turn shook both our hands in a sort of friendly but official way, then proceeded to lead us through the hall to the other room at the far end, opposite the kitchen. We passed someone busily cleaning the massive floor as we followed, and I felt guilty to leave a trail of footprints straight through the middle of her hard work, as the tiles were obviously being polished until you really could see your face in them.

We went through another set of double doors, and all you could see was cream (the off-white colour, not the dairy product). Every one of the windows had cream curtains and a cream blind for good measure, we walked across the cream carpet and sat down on the cream leather sofas positioned in a u-shape, so all were aiming at the giant television in one corner. We again had coffee, as we were finally allowed to read the 'famous' long-awaited sheets of instructions, but I spent most of the time concentrating on my mug... I didn't want to be the cause of any blemish in this perfect room.

Relieved at having finished my drink with no catastrophes, and all pages perused, we then had to trample all over the newly washed and polished floor again, to have a quick practice at setting the alarm. We both apologised, and inwardly I hoped our grovelling was sufficient to appease the meticulous cleaner, that had, we learnt, worked for the family for many years, and would doubtless be offering a much-valued opinion on our competence (What with her and the numerous CCTV camera's we had better not set a foot wrong).

This would be a different kind of sit, because these were guard dogs as well as pets, and a balance had to be maintained.

Our first task, before anything else, was to keep the dogs in the large hall while their owners threw the final luggage in to their Range Rover and disappeared through the gates. Saxon was just tall enough to watch them through the glass in the upper half of the doors, but Luca, unhappy at not being able to see what was happening, took things into her own hands, or rather 'paws', and cleverly pressed on the door handle, to let herself out. Shocked, but inwardly impressed at her ingenuity, I, and my equally jolted better half simultaneously shouted her name in panic, which fortunately made her turn to see what the fuss was about and divert her attention from the door before the catch was activated. That would have looked good! I mulled.

Were we not capable of keeping the dogs inside, even with all the doors shut?

We did find out at later time that it was quite a party piece of hers, on one occasion causing two workmen to flee from the two of them, one jumping on the roof of their van while the other scrambled up the climbing frame out of reach. What fun!

Back to the job in hand, and it would be safer to entice both to the kitchen with a promise of a treat I decided, trying a friendly smile at the cleaner as we wandered past, but not getting much in the way of a response. She was still engrossed in making everything sparkle.

The dogs were transfixed as I lifted the lid on the goodie container then reeled backwards as the 'aroma of pig's ear' slapped me in the face and wafted in to every molecule of air in the vicinity. Squirming I pulled out two similar sized greasy treats, narrowly avoided holding them up at either side of my partner's head to try them for size, then headed back towards the front door. This caused extreme excitement amongst our canine companions who nearly knocked me flying in their haste, and as my other half opened the door now that the owners had gone, it was an absolute scramble to get outside first. Saliva splattered on the marble tiles as we nervously held out a delicious goodie each, Luca snatching one from my better half, while Saxon snapped his teeth together about a centimetre from my fingers. We left them chewing frantically and quickly retreated back indoors to get as much info about rules and regulations from the cleaner as she would not be coming tomorrow. Our conversation felt awkward, even though she was being helpful, but I suppose we had only just met… and had spent the majority of the time ruining all of her hard work.

The afternoon brought more foreboding as it was time to venture out on our first walk, both of us wishing it didn't have to happen while she was still around, but it couldn't be avoided. As sure as night follows day, she would be observing on one of the numerous camera's outside. What a nightmare!

At the first chink of a lead, both dogs were leaping round like hyperactive springs, getting more impatient as we attempted, with fumbling fingers, to attach them, so temporarily draped them loosely over their heads instead, and hung on to the other end. Both dogs dashed down the steps, us right behind them, not looking in control whatsoever, and we were suddenly in the massive grounds. At least we should be out of view of the cleaner, (and the camera lens) I decided, and hopefully it would gradually calm the dogs down, so we could get a grip of the situation. That was the theory, but in practice there was no change, and decided it was just better to let them off again, so they could release some energy on their own.

As we walked further the smart lawn changed into a wooded area, which provided thick camouflage around the whole property, and the dogs raced off, chasing between trees, grabbing sticks to tease each other, barging, and growling playfully.

At least I hoped it was playfully!

I hurried to catch up but the bouncy layers of fern, covered with dead branches and sticks, interspersed with hidden rabbit holes was not making it easy. My better half couldn't reach them any quicker, having taken a different route that led straight through some ivy entwined, thorny undergrowth and was now preoccupied in gingerly getting out of it. My own progress was slowed even more as I began experiencing my first lesson on how to trip oneself up in two easy steps. Repeatedly I managed to stand on a long stick with one foot, raising it up at the opposite end by lever action, allowing my other foot to trip over it... and I was getting plenty of practice in the technique.

We had been engrossed for a while, and Saxon had got bored of the chasing game, now plodding along with a massive stick in his mouth. Luca, of course, wanted the exact same stick, no other would do, no other was as good... and she wanted it. She jumped at him and made a grab, but he swung his head round just enough to keep it out of reach, so she charged him again and bounced back barking constantly, basically getting on his nerves.

I could see his tolerance was wearing thin. Luca seemed oblivious to the numerous warning signals, the deep growls and Elvis' curling lip revealing a menacing set of snarling teeth were simply of no consequence to her. I didn't want his annoyance to escalate any further, so there was only one thing to do!

Get them back on the leads and attempt to walk them down to the road.

Well, you certainly can build up some good arm muscles in this job!

Straining from the effort, we held them back while I aimed the remote at the large gates (another zone that would be on view in the house), then as soon as the slightest gap appeared, they were pulling to get through. Both dogs were so strong that it took every ounce of energy to keep them at heel, especially as they both wanted to be pack leader out in front, but at least by now we were doing it out of sight. We struggled down the slope to the main gate, then walked up the muddy road opposite. Leaning backwards as much as I could, I hoped my body weight might relieve some of the pressure on my arms, but it was of little help. We then struggled even more, slipping and sliding in the mud on our way back down, but at least it had filled the time until the cleaner would be leaving. By the time we had made it back through the first gate, the dogs were actually much calmer, and when her car whizzed past us on the way to the gatehouse we just waved, looking totally in control.

Perfect timing!

The rest of the day was spent getting to know where everything was, getting to know the dogs a little better, and getting to know what films we could watch on the massive screen in the cream room, before retiring to our plush bedroom with snazzy en suite.

I could get used to this!

Waking before my other half the following morning, which was usually the case (although I sometimes wondered if this was just a ruse so I could check all was well, and then deliver tea in bed). I made sure I had the fob for the alarm and walked down the stairs. Both dogs looked up from their beds either side of the staircase as

I descended, but made no attempt to move, which I naively put down to their outstanding obedience training, but by the time I had reached the bottom, my focus on disarming the alarm correctly just held out, as I became more and more aware of an extremely unpleasant odour. Turning round to head to the kitchen, I now understood why both dogs had more of a sheepish air about them this morning, as scattered across most of the hall, from edge to edge, from one end to the other, was the result of the worst doggie diarrhoea I had ever seen. Obviously the one that had done it was worried about getting in trouble, and the one that hadn't done it was worried about being accused of it and getting in trouble.

I needed a plan of attack!

First, I swung the front door open wide, and both dogs shot out... who could blame them if they had been breathing in these fumes for too long. I quickly closed it again before they could change their mind. Next, vigilantly concentrating on every step to the kitchen, particularly taking extra care getting past the big splats with paw prints in them, as it was probably splashed around even further, I went to search the cupboards for disinfectant and anything else that might be useful.

Now ready for battle, taking a deep breath I stepped back in the hall to begin, until many paper towels, disinfected cloths, a mop, and bucket later, the floor was resembling something closer to normality, although minus the immaculate sheen of yesterday that only the cleaner could achieve.

I, on the other hand, felt and most likely looked a total mess.

Just then I heard the dogs run up the steps outside to wait by the door, as if they sensed it was all clear, so I let them back in, and watched as they both practically tiptoed back to their beds before staring across to see if they were in trouble. They weren't because it wasn't done on purpose, but I couldn't really give either of them breakfast yet... not after all that, so they probably thought they were being punished.

I decided to leave them, while I returned to the bedroom to freshen up, and my better half, who was conveniently just stirring, asked if everything was okay.

I just muttered a reply under my breath, before disappearing into the bathroom.

Later the same morning, we had returned from yet another not altogether successful walk, battling to keep the two lively dogs under control, and were in need of coffee to recuperate.

Suddenly, we could hear fierce barking and growling, and dashed out to the sight of them both jumping, practically throwing themselves at the gates to warn someone away.

Who could it be?

What did he want?

It was pointless trying to communicate with the unwanted visitor, because no one could hear over the threatening snarls, but he gave a friendly wave, walked over to the post box and pushed several envelopes through.

I realised it must be the gatekeeper delivering mail. The dogs certainly weren't keen on him, but he casually waved again as if nothing was happening, then pointed to the box before driving away. Calm was restored once more, but had we witnessed that kind of welcome when we first arrived at the house, I was sure we would not be here now.

By the following Tuesday, we were all getting into a routine and were taking our usual brisk outing down the drive, plodding through the grass rather than on the concrete path itself as it was slightly easier to anchor our feet. I was walking Luca a few steps behind my other half who had Saxon, blindly following their trail without really concentrating on the terrain. Surging along, my vision was totally obscured, so it was too late to avoid stepping on a half-hidden manhole cover, which promptly took on the persona of a magician's dodgy trapdoor and rotated ninety degrees as I put my full weight on it.

Suddenly, my left leg disappeared up to my thigh.

The abrupt shock, not to mention the pain annoyingly brought tears to the eyes as I floundered helplessly at ground level... doubly annoying as I noticed the amusement it had caused my other half who was unsuccessfully trying to suppress a smirk. She had managed to put the brakes on Saxon and turn him round, so was now on her way back to help pull me out, but seemed to be having enough trouble pulling herself together first.

I knelt on my free leg and pushed at the ground (looking as if I was on starting blocks for the one-legged race), and my other half, arm inserted under my armpit was making an attempt to assist, by stretching my right side twice as long as the left, hampered somewhat by having to hang on to two leads with the other. Saxon and Luca had actually stood quietly while all this was going on, and even when I was back on my feet and back on the move, our pace was much slower, as if they thought I couldn't handle it. At least it allowed me to do a bit more whinging, and I hoped it might eventually stop my partner sniggering, but from behind I could still see her shoulders shaking with laughter. I didn't find it so funny, and felt a period of sulking was in order, not that it was anyone's fault, but I just felt like it.

I trudged along gloomily all the way to the gatehouse, then we turned, and I did the same coming back up the hill, this time trying to leave a sensible enough distance to spot any obstacles, but Luca was having none of it, and pulled even harder to try and get to the front. At least we were going in the field within the grounds today rather than venturing out, and as I pushed open the wooden gate, I could sustain my sullen disposition no longer. The dogs looked so happy as they were let off their leads, and the feeling was contagious.

This was a much better idea.

They charged and barged each other for a few minutes, until other interesting outdoor scents took over... which was all very well, but we wanted them to get rid of some pent-up energy so they would sleep when we got back. In our wisdom, we decided that they would get more exercise if we went to opposite sides of the field and took it in turns to call them. Gradually we separated to make the gap between us wider, and they kept wandering between us a little half-heartedly, but that soon changed!

As they were nearest my partner, she called them over and asked them to sit.

From the opposite side I gave them two sharp whistles, and called them to heel.

Obediently they started running towards me, gradually picking up speed, and the view from my perspective, was one of two massive Germans shepherds charging at full pelt, and I was going to be the landing spot.

As they got nearer, I tensed, ready for impact, not daring to move, but at the very last second, they veered either side of me, so close I could feel their fur brush past both my hands.

I definitely needed my better half to experience this, so instructed the dogs to sit again. I signalled my better half to whistle them, and they immediately stormed off. I could see my partner frozen to the spot, enjoying the moment as they approached like two charging bulls, wondering if she was going to be the target. This was nearly as good from the rear view… watching them execute the last-minute swerve technique, only a cat's whisker away from a collision.

After seeing them greet the gatekeeper the other day, then watching them hurtle along, no burglar would want to come across these two!

By now the dogs were panting and needed a drink.

So did we after that… and made it a double!

Our final test came on the final day, as we were implementing the final packing, before the final clean up. Most of it was done, except for taking out the rubbish, getting changed into something more respectable, then squeezing the bag containing our scruffy dog-walking clothes in the car at the last minute. I heard the dogs barking outside and presumed it must be their best friend from the gatehouse somewhere in the vicinity, but when I looked up at the CCTV monitors, the gate was just closing behind the car of the owners, and they were pulling up outside the front door.

I looked at my watch. They were an hour early! Were they checking up on us?

I scuttled to the hall to warn my better half, but she had already found out.

Feeling slightly embarrassed at our attire, I gave a cheery greeting, asking if their break had been enjoyable, then went through any dog info, excluding my journey into the deepest workings of dog tummy disorders, while my partner made a hasty exit to sling the rubbish in the bin.

The husband also disappeared, I think to check the state of the house, because our predecessor had not been so heedful with their belongings but was still smiling as he returned. There was no point changing now that we had been seen at our worst, so I got the last bag and we said our goodbyes, receiving a nice tip as we left.

Two months later, we were on our way back, and on this particular day something unique and totally unexpected occurred on our journey... absolutely nothing... no traffic jams... no roadworks... no accidents... no arguments about routes, or should I say no differences of opinion.

We arrived at the first gates, I announced our arrival then drove up towards the next barrier, where the dogs had already heard a vehicle approaching.

As our car came to a standstill in front of the gate, we were faced with two pairs of unfriendly and extremely efficient looking teeth, lots of fierce growling and ferocious barking as they paced their boundary and jumped at the bars. Any previous thoughts I had of stepping out of the car to press the intercom had fizzled away in a flash.

I meekly poked my head out of the side window, and in a wimpish voice said, "hello."

The two guard dogs instantly transformed into two soppy animals, still jumping up at the gates but now it was to be the first to say hello to the two of us.

Before they had barely opened, both dogs were trying to squeeze through, which might have been more successful if they had tried one at a time, but eventually they made it, and proceeded to circle the car as I tried to drive in. It was the slowest entrance ever, so in the end my partner had to get out and entice them away, but even before I had parked, they were already rushing over. It was now a race to get out, before they jumped in to greet me, which I just about managed. Saxon bounded over, Luca bounded over, and then it was a free for all, both dogs trying to push the other out of the way, us just pushing to try and reach the house. Everyone was ready to leave, so again we all stayed indoors accompanied by our two guard dogs while the cars drove out of the gates, and as it was Saturday, no one else was in the house so at least we could unpack our clothes and food at leisure, not having to worry if we were in the way of the cleaner.

The dogs had other ideas!

They were well aware that it was nearing the time of their afternoon walk, and the dog clock is rarely at fault. As they both paced the hall like caged wild animals, it was obvious that we would get no peace until they had got their way.

They knew all the signals, watching us close doors, get coats, excitement building at each step, so by the time we picked up Wellies it was time for celebration. They both ran to and fro, knocking into us, knocking in to each other, treading on feet, tripping over shoes… it was better to let them outside quick. As I turned the handle, they pushed the door open themselves and rushed out, realised we hadn't followed, and rushed back in again to make sure we were still getting ready, saw that we were, rushed out again then rushed back in. It was havoc!

They always acted as one entity, rather than two separate dogs, both responding to whichever name was called, so it took us a few attempts to find the best way to put both leads on at the same time.

Previously I would ask Luca to 'sit', but before I had chance to attach her lead, she heard my partner telling Saxon to 'sit', and dashed over to sit next to him. I called her back, but Saxon then followed behind her and sat in front of me, looking extremely pleased with himself, much to the annoyance of my partner who hadn't quite managed to get his lead on in time. We could have carried on like that for hours, but now by standing as close together as possible, they could sit right next to each other for synchronised lead attaching. That tactic worked, so we headed out of the gates and down the drive to the field. I could hear an engine somewhere close and sure enough, one of the gardeners was cutting the grass in the opposite field, so it was going to be impossible to let them off today as we didn't want to be chasing after them, chasing after a mower. We circled the field a few times and would have clambered into the wood for a spot of exploration, but the ground was absolutely covered in bluebells as far as the eye could see, and I didn't want us to spoil the perfect scene by flattening a path through the middle of it.

We had to go back.

Back in the grounds both leads were unclipped, and Saxon dashed off to the water bowl standing on the porch, plunged his face straight in, and took a massive drink. After numerous gulps he lifted his head just above the water level, eyes fixed on Luca as she approached to get a drink, waited until she got near the bowl then dipped his head in again to do more slurping, enjoying making her wait. His head hovered over the bowl again, and she tried to push her nose in the gap but had no chance as he barged her out of the way to get more water. My better half had seen enough!

She grabbed his collar and steered him out of the way, then took the bowl to fill with fresh cold water and plonked it down in front of Luca, while she served as a barrier to stop any gate-crashers.

After a cooling down period, dog dinners were served, followed shortly by our own, and stomachs satisfied, we all relaxed until it was time to retire early.

I was, of course, up first the following morning (surprise, surprise), and as soon as I touched the handle of the bedroom door, I could hear the two dogs getting excited... happy that the day had begun.

They obediently waited in the hall below until I reached the bottom step, then could contain their enthusiasm not a moment longer. As usual, I opened the large front door to its widest, but neither were keen to go out, and instead accompanied me to the kitchen as if they were on a training exercise for the closest possible walk to heel. I made a cup of tea, then walked back to the front door, a dog seemingly glued to each trouser leg, to see if a trip outside was on the cards yet, and this time, Saxon was happy to go. After looking on from the hall for a minute or two, Luca managed to tear herself away, and they both disappeared onto the grounds. By the time they reappeared, Saxon had found a massive wooden post left behind by the builders and because it looked like a gigantic stake, I found much amusement in calling him Saxon Van Helsing, as he patrolled the surrounding land hunting down any vampires.

It was quite a while later when my sleepy partner stirred, but we were soon out on another trek.

Instead of walking along the driveway to the gate, we decided to clamber over the fence to make it quicker, so we unclipped the leads and directed the dogs between the wooden posts onto the field.

While they waited, I grabbed the top wooden bar, slung my left leg on the middle bar as if I was getting on a horse, and pulled myself up athletically. Imagine my surprise when my hands skidded round on the green, slippery wood, and before I could throw my right leg over the top I had spun backwards, and was now hanging upside down like a sloth, having to shout out to my partner for help before I fell off.

She ran over and grabbed my shoulders, but we were both giggling and had no strength. Eventually, with an extra surge, I was pushed up and managed to scramble through to the other side.

Our walk was shorter than usual, as most of our energy was already depleted, I definitely used the gate on the way back.

As soon as we got back, we set about preparing vegetables to go with a delicious Sunday roast, and by the time the chicken had nearly finished cooking, it was already late afternoon so it was the perfect time to take the dogs out for their second walk of the day, then we could relax. We went through our routine of lead chinking, stumbling through the doorway, and eventually we arrived back at the field, went straight to the gate, then the dogs could charge round the field to their hearts' content. Racing between the two of us a few times, combined with a circuit or two of the field and they were looking weary, which was good because I was feeling much the same, and the thought of dinner was becoming a priority. I strongly suggested we return to base, encountering no resistance to the idea, and as I unlocked the front door a mouth-watering odour of roast chicken crept out from the hall. I could see two dog noses twitching as the smell wafted past, and they both lifted their heads, sniffing the air to examine the flavour more closely. Everyone made a b-line for the kitchen, gradually picking up speed until it was practically a race to make sure no one was left out of any sample testing. My partner reached for the oven gloves, so the three of us queued by the counter, mouths watering as the foil was peeled back, and we all had a taste.

It was probably less than fifteen minutes later, and my partner and I were staring down at empty plates, well and truly satisfied, whereas the dogs, who had been creeping closer throughout the meal, seemed to have recognised the sound of cutlery scraping the last morsels from a plate, and were blatantly staring to remind us it was now their turn to get fed.

Their usual meal with a few pieces of the scrumptious chicken added disappeared even quicker than normal, then they wandered round the kitchen, hoping to come across any dropped morsels, but I didn't rate their chances.

I realised that the trouble with having a roast dinner plus all the trimmings, was the clearing up it caused afterwards. We'd already spent hours peeling and prepping veg, we were now going to be spending a fair amount of time tidying everything up again, and the actual enjoyment of eating it, was a brief fleeting moment somewhere between the two. My philosophising would have to wait, because I had noticed Saxon looking unusually suspicious as he left the utility room after a massive drink and acted rather shifty as Luca walked past to get a drink herself. I nudged the arm of my partner to watch, as with one final sly look out of the corner of his eye to make sure she was still occupied, he quietly disappeared round the corner. We couldn't resist following and tiptoed into the hall where we could see him at the far end by the door. He was too busy concentrating on something to notice and must have decided he was at a safe enough distance, because suddenly the silence was broken by an almighty crunching sound, the noise amplified by the hard floor tiles and high ceiling up to the second floor. Somewhere he must have found an overlooked dog biscuit on the floor, then had nonchalantly walked past Luca as if his mouth was empty, and taken it to the far end of the hall where he could eat it in secret.

Very clever!

That evening we sat watching television in the cream room, lights dimmed, both engrossed in some tense thriller. Luca was stretched out on the carpet, and Saxon had been lying by her side, but unbeknown to us had since got up and crept behind the sofa to watch the rabbits outside. Out of the blue, in one of the quietest parts of the film he let out a massive bark, diving at the window as some rabbit ventured too close, banging into the large table next to the window at the same time. Not only was my heart pounding at the sudden shock, I could also hear the giant vase on top of the table rattling from side to side, in danger of an impromptu impersonation of *Humpty Dumpty*.

I prayed another rabbit didn't stray too close before I could get to the vase.

Fortunately, it didn't, and all was well.

On our next visit to what was starting to feel like a second home, I had noticed, in fact, you couldn't miss a large bandage on Saxon's back foot, and the owner explained it had been quite a serious cut, so he could not be allowed off the lead until his stitches had been removed, which wouldn't be for another week or so.

He wouldn't be happy on a lead in the field, watching Luca racing round enjoying herself, I thought, as we waved the owners off.

Everything unpacked quickly, it was the perfect moment to test my theory as it was time for a walk.

By now we had got the dogs to sit and wait for the gates to open before trying to squash through them, so we set off quite relaxed and reaching the fence first, I handed over my lead. This time I cautiously clambered over without any mishaps, and as I jumped down, the dogs were quick to scramble through the lower bars. Once my better half had tackled the fence we were ready to start our walk and I unclipped Luca's lead. She charged off happily, half bouncing rather than running, then turned back and did a playful charge towards Saxon. He stared up at my better half, waiting for his lead to be removed so he could charge back, but that wasn't going to be happening for a few days yet. To distract Luca, I ran towards the woods and as usual she wasn't far behind. It was the loveliest sunny day, and we stayed a while to make the most of the shade, but it was also the perfect vantage point to keep an eye on my other half following Saxon as he did his exploring. He wasn't interested in Luca now, as the field was crammed with more varieties of wild flowers than I knew existed, and lots of bees were busily collecting nectar from every one of them. I could tell when any bee in that field moved from one flower to the next because Saxon jumped after them, bee after bee, and my partner, clenching his lead with both hands, would suddenly dash forward a few yards, her face surprised every time it happened. It only lasted a couple of seconds, but sometimes she had only just recovered her footing when another bee would fly away, and off she went again. It was all very amusing for me, watching as she lurched in one direction, then jolted in the other, and Saxon was having a great time, but as good as it was I couldn't stay here all day and stepped back out into the warmth again.

Before I knew it, she had closed the gap between us, the temperature plummeting to decidedly frosty as the lead was thrust in my hands with the words, "*Here! You* have him!"

Reluctantly, I took the lead, and it wasn't long before I was being dragged haphazardly from left to right. I was sure that was probably enough walking for one day, with his bad foot and all, so veering us towards the gate, I gently suggested we should go back... after all it was a hot day.

We usually took turns with each dog, because Saxon was quite strong and it took a lot more muscle power to control him, so it was bad timing, when a couple of days later, I needed to post a birthday card, and we decided to walk the dogs along the main road to the post box... it was probably just a quarter of a mile... what could possibly go wrong in that short a distance?

For a start, it was my turn to have Saxon, who is unstoppable when he wants to go somewhere, even if he doesn't know where he's going, so all the way to the bottom of the drive I was in a constant state of muscle tension, trying unsuccessfully to slow him down.

After a brief pause while the four of us waited for the gates to open, I was then dragged to the edge of the kerb, where I just about mustered enough strength to stop us heading into the traffic.

I didn't look back to see if the gateman caught a glimpse of our hasty exit, in comparison to that of my other half, who had been calmly walking along with Luca (who can be quite well behaved when she wants), both of them looking the model of perfection as they walked past his window.

We crossed over to head towards the post box, every muscle in my body still trying to create a force equal and opposite to that of Saxon (impossible as we were moving in the same direction), but I was just about managing. It didn't help that we weren't in top dog position at the front, however, after all, he was the alpha male of the pack… and kept trying to overtake to get there first, wherever it was.

To make matters even worse, I could see we were now approaching a parked truck only a few yards ahead, two workmen walking back and forth across the pavement as they unloaded the contents and with hardly any space to get by.

I paused, enviously watching Luca being lead between them, one of whom was now stopped right in the middle of the pavement for some reason, so using universal sign language, I tried to indicate for him to move aside while we passed. Unfortunately, he must have learnt a different universal sign language to mine, because he started coming towards us, which in turn, indicated to Saxon an imminent threat. Without warning we lunged forward, and I hardly dare look as his nose pushed into the flabby stomach of the shocked workman where it remained depressed for only a couple few seconds, but it felt like an age. Luckily, that was as far as it went, and the extra surge of adrenalin shooting through my body gave me the strength I needed to drag Saxon away and make a speedy exit. We weren't hanging around and walked off before anyone said anything, neither my partner nor I daring to look back until we thought it was a safe enough distance.

I don't know what I was expecting to see when we finally stopped to turn round for a look, but it seemed he was just carrying on with his job as if nothing had happened… what a relief!

I silently cursed myself for not having eaten more over the past ten years as my puny weight was no match for that of Saxon, especially with his unbridled enthusiasm thrown in, so, hoping she's not reading this sentence, I handed over control to my other half, who was more equipped to deal with the situation. Even with the lead wrapped around her waist, she struggled to keep him under control, and boy, were we glad to see that post box.

Only when we were out of sight did we acknowledge the event, and by the time we returned, strangely enough, the workmen were gone.

The weather on our next visit was really quite hot and extremely un-British like, so we spent plenty of time outside, patio doors in the kitchen swung wide open, and while Luca was sensibly lying in the shade, Saxon was again obsessed with searching out bees, and making sure they were chased from the property. He could focus on nothing else, and constantly had to be snapped out of his zombielike state, or he would have stayed in the heat all day.

On (not all together) Good Friday, we were in the kitchen, my other half preparing the lunch, as I worked on the laptop, when suddenly, the television clicked loudly... simultaneously with every other electrical item in the house. The CCTV disappeared from the monitors, the alarm started beeping, and not even a phone would work… anything powered by electricity was dead, the little 'on' lights were unquestionably off.

For a moment I had visions of a daring escapade to steal the contents of the house.

We were probably already surrounded by several masked figures dressed in black from head to foot, some watching through binoculars from a distance, others throwing ropes over the roof to scale the walls, and of course, the dogs lured away by two juicy steaks, leaving us, the innocent prey.

I was abruptly brought back to reality, as my partner asked, rather curtly I may add, if I had found the contact numbers yet, somehow making it sound as though I had been asked several times already.

I searched through all our previous instructions from sits, only to discover the one for here was the only one missing from the file. I must not have put it away since our last visit only a month ago, and I wouldn't want to be in my shoes when I imparted this knowledge to my better half.

To make matters worse, we had watched the owner delving into cupboards and drawers in the kitchen just before she left, and when she said she could not find her sheet of contact numbers, I just proclaimed that we had our copy with us, so no need to worry.

I could feel those beads of sweat forming on my forehead, my face turning a giveaway red as I nervously tried to look in the same cupboards without being noticed, leaving my confession as a last resort.

Unsurprisingly, my search was fruitless, and I finally had to send a text to the owners asking the whereabouts of the fuse box.

A considerable time later, with no response it seemed we were on our own.

I paced round the outside of the house with the dogs, mainly to keep out of the way of my other half, who was less than happy at the distinct lack of contact numbers, when my thoughts were suddenly interrupted by a loud engine noise which wasn't usually to be heard. I followed the sound, which took me to a rattling, vibrating, very uncomfortable sounding generator, even though it looked brand new. This wasn't going to make me feel any less uneasy... now I had to worry if it was in danger of overheating, even blow-up before my eyes.

This resulted in more searching for the phone number of their son, which fortunately was more successful now that I was more desperate, so I took my mobile outside to get signal (the house phone useless without power) and waited for an answer.

He wasn't at home... of course... and his wife said she would pass on the message and get him to phone back.

I poked my head inside the front door to see if any power had come back on.

No such luck! And as I continued my pacing, I suddenly realised that the noisy generator had now gone silent... so was that better? Was it worse? Who could tell?

As I was staring blankly at the machine, my phone rang, so with slight relief, I could tell their son what had happened, but any hope of a solution was short-lived, as he explained he was miles away, and could do nothing… but would come round after six p.m. and see if he could help.

That didn't offer much consolation at two p.m. when we were still half expecting the Police to burst in to see why the alarm had gone down… just as soon as the gates were open that is!

They were electrically powered too.

As it was, nothing happened, and another forty-five minutes later, we heard all of the appliances return to life… except for the alarm and CCTV.

That was a relief! We would just have to sit it out.

Much later than six o'clock, the dogs started barking, and outside the gate I could see two headlights, so went over, but the driver was absent. I called, just in case he was round the back of the vehicle but got no answer.

Just then I heard whistling, so walked towards the two padlocked gates half way down the drive, and in the dark, I could just make out the figure of the son, who had climbed over and was obviously being cautious with the two dogs. He could have looked like an intruder and wasn't taking any chances.

He went to the alarm, which still insisted on beeping every minute, but quickly realised the solution wasn't going to be that easy, so went back to the electronic gate problem, and came to a similar conclusion.

After a call to the gateman, the two of them, armed with various screwdrivers took the lock apart, and all that was needed was the power on the third fuse box to be restored and all would be well... So where was it?

In the garage of course... that required the power from the same third fuse box to open!

Not to worry, there was a key for the garage, so it could be opened manually...

So where was it?

After a fruitless unanswered call to his parents, he decided to try and break into the garage... another disaster as the door only opened a couple of inches, so all attention was on the alarm again, which would need the security company to come round to do a reset.

In the meantime, at least the gate was open... it was just a matter of getting it to close again, without it relocking... so we decided on my belt!

No one would be able to get through such high-level security!

As it was getting late, we were left to deal with the security man, who took about three minutes to decide he could do nothing... because guess where the alarm panel was?

Yes! In the garage, of course!

His van disappeared, and I fastened my belt round the gates again, checking a gap couldn't form, big enough for the dogs to escape. Giving an all-clear to my other half, I saw the front door open, and the dogs bounded out, sniffing everywhere to get the scent of intruders, as they had been confined to the kitchen all this time. After a brief search, they decided it was okay to return indoors, and as I walked behind them in the dark, my overactive imagination was at work again.

Who hasn't seen a film, where the view from the outside of a house is of unsuspecting persons, sitting in a brightly lit room, watching television, oblivious of several intruders, peering through infrared night goggles, gradually creeping up on them?

Well, I must have seen plenty of those films, but somehow, we lived to tell the tale.

By the following day everything had been put right, but we wouldn't forget this Easter in a hurry.

Chapter 7 — Bruno

We should have been more observant on our previsit, instead of focusing on the fact that we hadn't been offered any tea or coffee... even water. Our meeting with the owners of Bruno the bulldog seemed very business-like and passed by so quickly that practically all I could remember, apart from they were leaving at some unearthly hour before dawn, was that if he started chewing the glass coffee table to... "Err! What was that?"

I heard right!

If he started chewing the coffee table, to throw some water on him... just the sight of a glass sometimes worked fine. Looking at the coffee table, it not only displayed severe lack of coffee mugs, but I could also see that all four corners had deep grooves and had been ground down to varying degrees.

We were invited to arrive the night before their departure, but instead, opted for a five o'clock departure from home, in reality, leaving more like four-thirty as our alarm clock was always fast, and consequently found ourselves parked on a cold, empty High Street at five-twenty a.m. on a Friday morning. The time dragged by, neither of us capable of sensible conversation, so the best we could do was discuss the earliest we thought we could arrive at their house, then wait in icy silence, interspersed occasionally by my delicate partner brusquely asking how much longer.

After about the sixth time it was close enough.

I turned the car round, drove up to their house, parked, then we both emerged disguised as wide awake lively people that had just at that second, completed our journey.

Both owners came to the door to greet us but spoke very quietly, explaining that they didn't want to wake Bruno, which was acutely unsuccessful, as he suddenly made an intimidating thunderous charge from the living room. He sniffed each of us briefly only to disappear again just as quickly and must have only just had time to get back on his favourite chair when a loud snore started to vibrate throughout the whole house.

We all tiptoed our way into the kitchen, and this time did get a cup of coffee as we went through our instructions one more time, which did in fact seem more like the first time to me as our previous meeting had been so brief.

Scanning around as I sipped coffee, my bleary eyes were coming more into focus, as the husband swung open a cupboard door and generously proclaimed, "Just help yourself to anything you need."

I smiled at him politely, said thank you and turned to see if my better half had been looking, but she was engrossed in a different conversation with the other half of the couple, which sounded like our brave bulldog was frightened of the vacuum cleaner. I stared down at the floor, the rest of the conversation drifting somewhere in the distance, past my hopefully blank expression as I perused the remnants of food compressed in the spaces between the floor tiles.

The polite early morning dialogue struggled on, so we turned to the favoured topic of the British, the weather, the husband knowledgeably informing us that we were as high as Edinburgh and were bound to get the brunt of any snow in the area. Continuing, he added that the shovel could be found in the shed at the bottom of the garden if required, but from the expression on the face of my other half I could tell we were agreed, inwardly dismissing it as an unessential item… oh dear!

We were finally rescued from the awkward exchange by the sound of a taxi pulling up outside, and they were out of the door in a flash, the sound of snoring uninterrupted by the occurrence.

Abandoning the luggage for now, I started making space in one of the cupboards for some of our food, not wishing to get in the way of my other half, as I knew our early morning might have slightly agitated her.

"Afraid of the vacuum cleaner," I tutted, closing the cupboard door again. Strange for a dog that resembled a cross between a gorilla and a tank. I wondered if he would even hear it if he was able to sleep through his own raucous snoring, but just before I was tempted to try, a confused looking Bruno appeared from the darkened living room, wanting his first walk of the day.

The sun had reluctantly made an appearance, but the temperature was still in the negative zone, so we donned boots, coats, hats, scarves, and gloves... a chore in itself taking about five minutes, then it was Bruno's turn. Fastening the Velcro of his bright-red coat around his thick neck and ample stomach was a daunting task in itself, his head twisting left and right continuously, as if he was trying to spot a pantomime villain somewhere behind him, but it turned out to be a piece of cake compared to firstly working out which way round his harness fit, and secondly getting him to step in it, then keep all four feet in position while it was clicked shut. Another five minutes later, with the lead, our final piece of kit attached, we were finally ready.

Cautiously I opened the front door (remembering our first experience with a dog wearing red) and braced ourselves for the initial take-off. We had been advised that he didn't walk too far these days, but I didn't expect our maiden flight to consist of a three yard walk to the end of the drive, Bruno relieving himself, and a prompt return back through the front door, a walk altogether much briefer than the time it took to get dressed in preparation. Feeling somewhat cheated we took off the lead, the harness, the red coat, then reversed the five-minute operation and took off all of our own layers again. Might as well return to the kitchen for a well-earned tea and toast breakfast.

Three years previously Bruno had suffered a stroke, and it seemed difficult to communicate with him, although neither of us had any prior experience of bulldogs so couldn't tell if this was their general demeanour, but somehow, he seemed in a world of his own. Bearing this in mind and having been told he may not eat for a day or two (that separation anxiety again), we expected getting him to eat his breakfast to be a task of gargantuan proportion. Propped up against the settee, Bruno watched as I put the wooden log used to raise his bowl nearer head height next to the fireplace. Showing an extra nil interest as I placed his food in position, he at least sniffed the air to get the scent. It looked like time for the well tested and usually successful method of slightly warming up the food to get his juices flowing. It made the aroma much more tempting, and after carefully dropping a couple of bits of cooked fish in his jowly mouth to get the flavour, he actually decided to move and was soon tucking into breakfast enthusiastically.

Well... to a lady bulldog his table manners may have been totally acceptable, but the slurping, burping and sight of bits of food and slobber flying round the living room floor was slightly disturbing to say the least. As he finished, I threw the larger bits of the splattered residue back in his bowl before removing it, replaced the piece of log under his water so he didn't have to bend too far to quench his thirst, then wiped the remaining grease and spit off the floor. A mammoth burp vibrated throughout the room behind me, so I presumed that he enjoyed it.

We seemed to have already crammed so many things into just one morning, so that was enough of doing chores for one day, and a session of television viewing was in order, perhaps a little nap thrown in to make up for lost sleep wouldn't go amiss until our next exciting walk.

I stared at all the teeth marks on the television control briefly before going through a few channels, but I was too tired to think straight, and soon even the sound of the loud snoring couldn't stop either of us from taking forty winks as we were so weary.

I must have drifted in and out of sleep for a while, checking on my companions each time I came to, but no one was stirring, until eventually I managed to keep my eyes open, and got out of the chair. I could see my partner looking as bleary as I felt, as she stretched both arms above her head, and it wasn't until late afternoon that either of us began to feel almost normal again after the disturbed catnap.

A blow of fresh air would do the trick, so we all went through the same time-consuming prep for our walk, and opened the front door to set off. Bruno must have noticed the drop in temperature and teetered on the edge of the step, inhaling the atmosphere. My partner stepped round him and from outside tried a slight pull on his harness but it didn't encourage him to move. A stronger tug on the lead didn't make any difference and trying to pull him outside was useless… he was like a solid block of concrete, and a stubborn one at that. We both tried coaxing him as nothing else was working, until it looked as though he was going to take a step.

He did…

Straight back into the hall and we were going nowhere. Time to remove our unnecessary layers yet again.

The weather was getting even colder, but a while later Bruno could hang on not a moment longer, so we opted for a visit into the back garden this time. Once he had ventured out, I slammed the patio door behind him, to stop too much heat escaping, and watched as he lumbered down the three steps to the lawn, then crouched privately round the corner nearly out of sight. It only lasted a few seconds, and he immediately thundered back up the steps towards the glass doors.

Did he think they were still open?

He wasn't slowing down!

I fumbled for the handle in a panic to avoid dog concussion, and just managed to produce a gap big enough for him to bounce through as he raced back to his favourite chair. I looked at him in disbelief. Who would have thought him capable of such speed?

He was soon back to his favourite occupation, professional resting, and it looked as though his timing was perfect. Through the slatted blinds behind him I could see it had started to snow, and from the look of it, it meant business.

You could say that!

By the following morning the whole landscape had been transformed into one expanse of solid white, a thick layer of snow on top of the garden table, providing visual evidence as to the depth.

Bruno was still snoring (which obviously wasn't disturbing my slumbering partner), but I optimistically grabbed his coat, his lead and his harness, then calling his name, rattled all three to indicate it was time to venture out.

I presumed our outing wasn't going to take too long, but better to get it over with.

He barely opened one eye, and proceeded to thoroughly ignore the invitation, so standing a little closer, shouting a little louder, I repeated the action. This time he didn't even bother to look at all, although I knew he was listening because I saw his left ear twitch slightly, so I decided to start getting him ready. While his eyes were closed, I wrapped the red coat round him, squashed it between his back and the chair and fastened it round his neck.

I placed the harness on the floor ready for him to stand in, stood back and called his name again… no reaction!

I moved closer again and shouted his name again… still no reaction!

As I stared at Bruno getting his beauty sleep, leaning on the chair arm at an angle, his red coat resembling a red cape as it hung loose near his rump, he looked just like a 'not so action-packed superhero' either suffering from exhaustion or a hangover. I smiled as I imagined any world disasters having to be put on hold for the moment and decided I might as well leave him for a while as nothing was looking urgent.

Once I'd removed his superhero outfit again and made tea, I couldn't wait to tell my other half about the weather, and displaying only minimum resistance to my powers of persuasion, she was soon up to share the wintery scene. Immediately, I was volunteered to go outside to measure the depth of the snow still increasing on the table… it would stop further speculation. Ordinary boots were not going to be sufficient for this mission, so I went to check the Wellies we had already spotted in the garage and grabbed two pairs that seemed close enough in size to each of us (My partner would be needing the other pair if we ever got Bruno to walk out of the front door). Taking my ruler in one hand, I unlocked the kitchen door with the other and swung it open, immediately feeling the icy, cold air sweep straight through every layer of clothing to my bare skin underneath. I waded across to the table, hearing the door behind me rapidly slam shut, and sunk the ruler through the snow until it clunked on the wood in the depths below. After confirming the measurement twice, I briskly returned with the news.

"It's ten inches deep," I proclaimed, shutting the chilly climate out once and for all.

Living in London we hadn't seen this much snow for years, and as was usual on such rare occasions, we were lapping up the spectacle, staring out in wonderment, not really considering the practicalities of the situation.

All the commotion must have aroused some curiosity in Bruno, who wandered in, so my partner quickly put on the extra footwear, snapped Bruno's red coat in place, and positioned his harness on the floor in front of him. Helpfully, for once, he stood in the leg spaces so it could then be pulled around his back, also snapped shut, then his lead was attached, and we opened the front door waiting to see what would happen in this bleak weather.

Amazingly, he jumped straight outside, and my other half had been dragged almost to the end of the drive before I had time to relock the door. As I optimistically followed in their footsteps through the snow, he turned right and walked a little further, but in the few seconds it took me to catch up, he had already cocked a leg to do the necessary, and they were now both returning to base, mission accomplished. I turned tail, there was no point trying to change either his mind, or his direction.

Three breakfasts later, the morning schedule was looking fairly empty, so fearing the weather might worsen, we decided on a walk to High Street for bread and milk and thought we could do a good deed and knock next door to see if the elderly neighbours were okay for provisions. Expecting a similar shopping list to our own, we were taken completely by surprise hearing the words 'cat litter please', and that was the only thing they needed, thank you. I concentrated on maintaining my neighbourly smile while we gave a friendly wave, already considering just how heavy an average bag might be, but we had offered now. Once out of view, we could exchange surprised expressions, accompanied by a disbelieving smirk, but couldn't dwell on the subject. We wanted to be back home in the warmth as soon as possible.

Most of the sluggish journey was spent staring at the floor, hanging onto trees, fences, or hanging onto each other at any slope that could induce a slippery fall, rather than enjoying the scenery. Not a single vehicle had been down our road, and it was not until we reached the main route that we discovered other footprints, indicating others had braved an expedition. Mostly, we were on unchartered territory, being the first to make an imprint in the white expanse.

As we slid across High Street, our first port of call was just ahead, that well known store renowned for underwear, but today it was going to be providing us with food items... at least that's what we hoped.

Wrong! Everyone who had braved the weather had already emptied the shelves of any stock.

It was bedlam inside, the melted snow brought in by the crazed consumers had caused a treacherous film of water on the shop floor, feet were skidding everywhere, shoppers were hanging on to trolleys for safety, the staff were trying to mop the water. I was glad to get out in one piece, and the icy pavement seemed relatively safe in comparison.

A little further down the road we could see the local pet store, but as we reached the entrance, a test of the door and lack of lighting promptly confirmed no one was inside.

Our search for cat litter had not started well.

Quickening our pace very slightly, both now displaying early signs of shopping hysteria, we strode onward, to the far end of High Street where two more well-known supermarkets resided on the opposite side of the road. I was sure we would be successful in our quest at one or the other.

Arriving at the first, we separated at the entrance like two hungry velociraptors ambushing a film actor, and starting from the furthest aisles, methodically scouring each one, until a few minutes later we both ended up at the same spot.

An empty shelf where once cat litter had stood.

What was happening to all the cats round here?

I realised that it wasn't a sudden epidemic of feline dysentery, but an effective replacement for salt to melt snow, and everyone was looking for it.

We rushed to the next store now displaying full-blown symptoms, and while my partner interrogated an assistant, I was already heading in the direction he was pointing.

We were desperate! After going to the trouble of asking the neighbours if they needed anything, we didn't want to return empty-handed... failures!

As luck would have it, sitting alone on the bottom shelf was a slightly battered massive bag of cat litter, so I made a grab for it before anyone else could, expending enough force with which I expected to lift it in to both arms to carry to the checkout. All I could manage was to momentarily raise it to knee height, then had to let it thump down on the floor next to my foot (At least it was next to my foot, not on it). Taking a deep breath and flexing my arm muscles for an extra boost I tried again, and by some clumsy balancing and manoeuvring had just managed to cradle it in both arms when my other half turned up. She looked relieved, but I could detect a slight hint of shock at the size of the bag in her expression, so I was immediately sent on my way to the till, while she walked off to get our almost forgotten bread and milk.

I walked gingerly towards the checkout, the floor getting more hazardous each step nearer the exit, then dropped the bag down on to the conveyor belt, vibrating the till and almost the cashier with the force. My partner had already caught up and added her items, so we paid up, both wrestled the gigantic bag out of the shop, then paused outside while we worked out the best way to get us and our shopping home.

We gripped the one plastic handle at opposite ends and stumbled a few yards as the bag thumped alternately into the nearest leg. That wasn't going to work. We needed to keep in step to stop the bag rocking so much.

We tried again, and I was beginning to sense that familiar agitation exuding from the other side of the bag. By the third attempt, we managed to advance down High Street, and this time we weren't stopping. I was being steered along by the exasperated pace of my other half, and if we crossed paths with any shoppers, her route was totally uncompromising... we weren't veering from our course for anyone. I scurried between them trying to maintain the pace, keep in step, keep the bag level, catch up again without slipping, anything I could to prevent my by now, more than seriously ruffled other half from merely abandoning the cat litter on the spot.

Having done as much weaving and swerving as a fairground dodgem with a grudge, I was more than relieved to set foot on our road, and now out of the bustle we could pause to swap sides and save our hands from complete disintegration by the handle boring through the flesh to the naked bone underneath. By now it was difficult to even bend my arm due to the weight pulling on it, and my partner was not uttering a single word, she was blankly staring downwards at her feet like a weary zombie. We continued our struggle home, our stops to change sides more and more frequent, our pace getting slower and slower, and at one point I started to harbour suspicions that I could still be asleep, experiencing one of those perpetual nightmares where the horizon gets more distant, the more you try to reach it.

Against the elements... we made it!

I unlocked the door, and with a joint effort draining any remnant of energy we had remaining, the bag was hoisted up the step and into the hall. I looked across at my exhausted, still totally silent better half, and noticed her face visibly mutating into a bright, and I mean really bright red, as it heated up in the sudden return to warmth. It was wise not to comment at this moment, so I opted to check on our trusty companion instead. It's not as if it was difficult to track him down.

Sure enough, sunk deep in the cushion of his favourite chair, leant casually against the arm, he just stared across, fully aware that we were back, not the slightest bit interested. I left him to it, as I could hear the welcome sound of a kettle being filled in the kitchen... and one reviving cup of tea later we had built up enough strength to carry the dreaded cat litter round to our neighbours.

Trying not to trip over it, or each other, it took nifty footwork almost as complex as the Argentinian tango, as we manoeuvred through their awkward gate, then turned and twisted down the narrow path, causing a threatening exchange of scowls more than once, the final glare still etched across both of our faces as I rang the doorbell. We quickly adjusted our expression to a friendly smile as the door opened, and we could see our temporary neighbours looked extremely grateful, although slightly startled as we thudded the bag down on their hall carpet. As a token of gratitude, they presented us with a bottle of wine and although we hadn't done our good deed for a reward, I decided it might help numb the pain of our aching muscles later.

Still with little sign of a thaw over the next few days and having succeeded in making a considerable dent in our more than abundant supplies, we needed to do a more substantial shop. This meant taking the car, which also meant we would have to dig our way out of the drive first, which then meant we would have to get shovels from the garden shed before that.

Donning the house Wellies, we waded through the snow on the patio, then I lead the way to where I thought the path must be, checking each foothold as I went, because there were steps under there somewhere. My trusty partner followed in my footsteps, literally, to avoid finding any hazards that I had missed, then we huddled close by the door as I fumbled the small key into the lock. Shivering wasn't making it any easier, nor could I see much through the mist of hot air, formed by our breath in the icy temperature, but the lock clicked, and we quickly grabbed a shovel and spade, relocked the shed, then swiftly retraced our route back.

Was I wearing enough layers I pondered, as we were blasted by another icy chill opening the front door at the opposite end of the house.

I had no time to consider other alternatives.

My other half had determinedly marched up the drive, intent on rapid completion of our task and would not appreciate my absence at this crucial time. Head down, she was already digging around the car tyres, so I set about clearing the pavement at the end of the drive.

Loading the shovel with a hefty heap of snow, I swung round to throw it aside, only to find it had compressed in to a frozen lump and was hanging on like dried cement. Irritated at the immoveable ice, I walked to the side of the curb, then banged it down several times to remove the contents. The same thing happened for every shovelful, so it wasn't long before I realised my clothing was more than adequate for keeping warm at this job. After a minute I dragged the scarf from my neck before my head overheated completely, another few minutes and I was tearing off my coat to prevent it getting soaked in sweat, a few minutes more and my jumper was not far behind. The porch was soon littered with discarded garments from both of us and there was still plenty to do.

Needing a little respite we opted for an attempt at getting Bruno out for some 'exercise'.

Talk about a dirty look! He was less than impressed as my better half appeared with his harness and coat, and my powers of persuasion were of little effect trying to coax him from his chair. Emulating a red beacon once more, with the surplus amount of heat emitting from her face, and with the unfinished task weighing heavily on

141

the mind of my better half, she just walked round the back of the chair and tilted it forwards. Bruno could not escape the gravitational pull and had to concede.

While he was still taken aback at his unexpected landing I took the opportunity to fasten the coat around his neck and girth, his feet were placed in the harness, and before he knew it, he was ready for action.

The one occasion we would have appreciated the usual swiftness of the Bruno walk was the one time he decided to be adventurous, leading us frustratedly at less than a snail's pace to a small green island dividing the road about fifty yards away. We had already paused at every other house en route, Bruno scanning all angles of the neighbourhood, our body temperature dropping rapidly as we waited patiently for things to happen naturally, so as soon as they had, he was off home with my other half, while I did a clear-up, then chased not far behind.

Bruno was eager to get back indoors and barged through the doors as soon as they were slightly open, and now with my less than normal body temperature, I was happy to get straight back to the task at hand. Meanwhile, my other half had used our standing around time to mull over other plans to assist our snow removal.

I followed to the garage in a search for buckets or similar vessels, because she had recalled spotting a large bin of salt just round the corner... well, a fair old walk but only round one corner. We would fill our buckets, empty the salt on the drive and watch the snow melt away.

. Well, that was the theory!

In actual fact, there was a complete absence of buckets, so we ended up with one recycling box to tussle between us as we both tried to walk sideways on the dicey terrain. Just round the corner felt a whole lot further when carrying even the empty box, and we had both used up practically every irritated expression in our repertoire, so who knows how we would get on getting back. Throwing open the lid of the bin as if having just discovered buried treasure, it became all too clear that we were about two days too late, and the riches had already been plundered. I leant over the side, scraping the meagre crumbs in desperation, and threw a few pathetic bits in our massive box. My partner did the same. We even picked up any bits recklessly spilt around the outside of the bin by our careless predecessors, but they were lost in our optimistic sized receptacle. Deflated by the fruitless search, we grabbed a handle each side of the container to return home, and downcast, trudged back.

Our plan was thwarted, and it was back to the digging! Silent once again we recommenced the back-breaking assignment and over an hour later, both sporting the luminous beacon look, we had finally succeeded. Bruno was hotfooted out of the back door for any last-minute bladder action before we set off on our expedition, and once he returned, we were quickly out the front door.

I panicked briefly, wondering if I should have tried starting the car before undertaking our strenuous labours but it was too late now, so I jumped into the driving seat and turned the key. Thankfully, the car revved into action and after tentatively reversing up the drive and off the edge of the kerb, my other half got in beside me and we were soon on our way. The weather had been so bad that the main roads were still not clear, and as I pulled into the supermarket car park, it seemed to be a less than half speed version of its normal self.

Neither, however, were as perilous as yet another supermarket floor. One wrong move, one lack of concentration on the hazardous ice rink of an entrance could only end in one of two ways.

1) On the floor.

2) Performing frenzied gestures whilst trying to grab hold of the nearest secure object, brought on by feet sliding in opposite directions, resulting in total embarrassment.

Not finding either option too desirable, I doddered along slowly, doing what I presumed to be a pretty accurate impersonation of myself in forty years' time, unlike my better half who had sensibly grabbed a sturdy shopping trolley for support, and was gliding from shelf to shelf, freezer to freezer, getting item after item from our shopping list. My busy other half only paused to shout instructions for me to go in search of some isolated requirement from a distant aisle, and had disappeared by the time I returned, so I headed gingerly towards the tills presuming she wasn't hanging around.

I located the blonde hair turning round every few seconds to see if I was anywhere near, and could see it was framing a frustrated expression, as my better half was having to let people behind her in the queue go first while she awaited my arrival. Once I was spotted, she beckoned frantically, glaring as if I was dawdling for no good reason, and my item was abruptly snatched away and placed on the conveyor belt, while I got ready to pay for the goods. I have to say my better half is one of the most proficient and rapid 'shop and packers' I have ever come across, and as usual had everything back in the trolley, divided into several categories which were packed into separate bags by the time I was juggling the change back into my pocket.

Brilliant for unpacking with ease at the other end!

Pretending I was helping steer the trolley from the front, our exit from the supermarket felt considerably safer to me, and we were soon on our way back, after only a brief moment of dicey foot sliding whilst putting our bags in the boot.

I stopped on the road outside the house while my partner got out, then accelerated back up the kerb and into the drive. The shopping was piled on the porch, then I unlocked the front door, and we pushed each bag into the hall, then my other half slammed both doors shut before too much heat could escape. Bruno actually appeared from the sitting room to greet us, wagging his thin curly pig-looking tail. He got a stroke from both of us, then after a quick investigation of the bags he was gone. I rushed after him to open the patio doors before he could get comfortable on his chair again, and he went outside quite happily for once, cocked a leg against the stone wall and returned.

I joined my partner in the kitchen, and we both satisfyingly unpacked our fresh supplies into the pristine cupboards, then made tea and went into the sitting room to keep Bruno company, after all, he hadn't seen too much of us today with the snow moving episode. I slumped into one of the other chairs and grabbed the gnawed television control, while my better half sat on the settee and took a sip of her tea. She immediately slammed the mug down on the coffee table and shot up again.

The tea isn't that bad, I thought to myself, inquiring what was wrong.

Hearing some sort of 'yeuk' noise to accompany her screwed up face, which was now trying to twist one hundred and eighty degrees to examine the back view of her clothes, I decided I had better go over to see what all the squirming was about. The back of her trousers were warm and damp, and a quick investigation of the settee revealed that one of the cushions, unfortunately the one she had sat on, was suffering the same symptoms, totally saturated from a moment of either Bruno's incontinence or impatience. My horrified partner hastily left the room and marched upstairs, every hefty footstep a clear indication of her annoyance, every movement easily traceable through the ceiling as she stomped between the bedroom and bathroom to disrobe, and wash. She had already stomped back downstairs to throw her contaminated clothes in the washing machine by the time I had checked all other cushions, including the one Bruno was firmly planted in, so seeing me grappling with the tightly fitting cover gave more opportunity to release some pent-up anger. I hung onto the cover tightly as the inside cushion was wrenched out in one movement. Worries concerning the possibility of shrinking seat covers were hastily discussed, but pushed aside as something needed to be done, the quicker the better.

It was obvious that the washing machine was much too small to deal with this emergency, so we draped as much of it as would fit into a bowl, and my partner rushed it upstairs, while I followed, hanging onto the surplus like a bridesmaid holding a bride's train, all the way hoping it wouldn't have time to drip. Cold water seemed the best bet, so we added a slight amount of washing powder, and an even smaller amount of disinfectant to the running water and dropped it in the bath. All shades of grey and yellow were streaking across the surface like oil slicks, and I was keeping everything crossed that it wasn't the brown colour of the cushion cover. My other half let out the water again, we grabbed an end each to twist as much of the dirty water out as possible then repeated the whole process. Leaning almost upside down over the side of the bath, pinching the grime away, then wringing out the cover was causing nearly as much extra heat as snow moving, I contemplated, as we finished the third cycle, but at least the shades of water leaving the bath were now growing paler. Doing another impersonation of a mangle, we gave a final twist and shook the cover back into shape, giving it a gentle stretch before draping it on a clothes airer over the bath.

We returned to our lukewarm tea, and my better half checked the lonesome remaining cushion on the settee before deciding it was safe to use. She glared at Bruno, the same glare I had received earlier, as she sunk into the seat, then we got back to watching television, as nothing more could be done for now.

A couple of hours passed, and we decided to check on our hard work, but I could hear the gigantic drips still thudding on the bottom of the bath as I reached the bottom of the stairs, so there was no chance of judging any sort of collateral damage yet, and therefore no decision as to whether to go ahead with the rest of the covers or not. Neither of us could relax. We were agitated, impatient, we wanted to get it over and done with… if it was happening… and before the whole day was gone. Before you know it, the decision was made.

Almost immediately, I began to regret our reckless choice, as I tried to wrestle one of the back covers already stretched taught over a plump cushion like some ill-fitting garment two sizes too small, but I couldn't give up now. My other half was having the same trouble but there was no way she would let it beat her, although she had to consent to a little assistance in the end, begrudgingly no doubt. By then I was getting so annoyed at the amount of time it was taking, my anger was easily vented on another tussle with a back cushion, pummelling and dragging it away while my partner clung onto the cover.

I grabbed everything and slogged back up the stairs. For once it was me that had had enough, and my other half knew it. I had no conversation left as she ran the cold water, then I just slung the pile in the bottom of the bath and stared as the same grey and yellow colours leaked across the surface. Either the settee was going to end up a lot paler than the accompanying chairs, or the other covers had suffered similar consequences which had gone unnoticed by the owners. I feared it could have been the latter, and the evidence had dried away by the time they were home from work... I didn't want to dwell on the subject!

By the time we had squeezed as much water as is humanly possible from the rest of the covers, we were well and truly kna... exhausted. I was too weary to stomp back down the stairs, so I hung weakly onto the banister, slowly descending, trailed limply by my partner.

Yet again we were displaying matching red faces that could outshine the rear end of any orangutan, and the only possible cure this time was going to be a cold drink, if either of us had the strength to get it. My partner took a cold lager from the fridge and started to pour it in a tumbler, while I measured out a medicinal gin and tonic with ice and lime, then we exchanged glasses. If anybody deserved a drink it was the two of us, and they hardly touched the side.

The days progressed and we thought we were getting more used to the quirks of Bruno, so were surprised one evening as he took his evening wander out on the patio, and the usual return in thirty seconds was delayed. He was still staring towards the end of the garden five minutes later.

Curiosity aroused, we both stared out at the same spot.

Shock! A pair of eyes were staring straight back.

A dark shape was crouched underneath the bench sheltered by the trees, the outline only visible against the white of the snow. Nobody moved for another couple of minutes, but by now Bruno was getting bored of the situation. He relaxed his rigid gorilla pose, and turned, taking a few steps towards the patio doors. As soon as he did, the eyes in the distance started to creep closer. He must have sensed it, because he suddenly turned back and did a bull-like charge towards the lawn, culminating in the gorilla position again. The eyes quickly retreated and waited until they in turn sensed he had given up. Once again, they started to skulk nearer as Bruno did a U-turn.

It could have gone on forever, no one wanted to give in, and Bruno wasn't going to lose face, so it was a good excuse when he was ordered back indoors. He wasn't going to be disobedient this time.

Another few days and we needed another expedition to buy a top-up of milk, but little did we expect to yet again spend the rest of the afternoon wringing out chair covers. He had ventured out just before we left, we were back within forty-five minutes, but Bruno still managed to have an accident, this time on the other armchair adjacent to his favourite.

I was now getting suspicious of his motives.

It's funny how it was never on the one he spent ninety percent of his time!

Was he being instructed by his owners, who wanted a complete spring clean, including the furniture before returning?

Red faced once more, my partner and I slumped wearily on either side of the settee. I don't know what came over Bruno, but he plodded over and stared, until I understood it to mean he was joining us. Moving towards the arm, both cushions sunk downwards at the middle of the settee as his thick body landed between us. The three of us rocked to and fro as he circled on the spot, headbutting each of us alternately as he tried to get comfortable, but there was inadequate space, and he wasn't satisfied.

Bruno may have had a stroke, but he was clever enough to see a solution to the problem.

He forced his massive head behind my back, then gradually edged the rest of his body on my seat so I had to lean forward. I was much too weary to offer any sort of resistance, so when he began shuffling and shoving the cushions out of the way rather aggressively, I decided it was better to stand up. Normally I would never give in, but today I just couldn't be bothered.

On the last day, we went through the usual routine of cleaning up after we had packed our belongings, and the whole house looked spic-and-span, and I almost wished we could still be there when the owners arrived back, but they were not due until eleven p.m. so we were to leave at eight o'clock, and push the spare key through a friend's door, just in case they were delayed.

Wandering out of the front door for the last time with Bruno, a neighbour accompanied by his buddy, a golden retriever, were just setting off on their evening constitutional, so they came over to say goodbye, knowing we would soon be on our way. We had met often during our stay, usually on the last outing of the day, and practically every time we had been stationary, quite often shivering as we waited for Bruno to make a move, so a quick friendly chat helped pass the time, as well as take one's mind off freezing cold fingers and toes.

We waved as they set off again, and Bruno perused the road in both directions, then stood silently staring into space for a while. He wasn't a bad old lad, I decided, looking into the night sky myself, and wondering if we would be back to see him again. After a few more minutes he had done what he was there to do, so we all went back indoors, and my partner and I watched Bruno return to his chair. I turned the lights down low, and we crept outside as if he might be disconcerted by our disappearance, although I was sure pigs would be flying over hell as it was freezing over before that might happen. Nevertheless, I quietly pulled the doors shut so as not to disturb him, and quickly ran across the road to post the key.

With a final glance at the door we left, and another chapter of our pet-sitting was over.

A day later I received a text expressing an extremely grateful thank you from the owners, and I guessed we would be seeing Bruno again after all.

Chapter 8 — Timmy, Candy, Guiseppe and Carlo

As we rang the doorbell after another traumatic journey to reach our destination on time (meaning I had mislaid the directions), we heard a voice ordering an overly loud barking dog to get in the garage, and another dog to sit and wait.

Only when the commotion had abated did she open the door, so we politely said hello and entered the hall as if we heard nothing, but the serene mood was fairly short-lived.

A skinny, hyperactive Border collie charged at us from the opposite end of the hall, swerved round her owner and bounced between the two of us until her collar was eventually grabbed and she was made to sit. I could see her tail gradually picking up momentum even though she sat on it, her inner excitement only just contained, and ready to blow. Trying to calm her only lasted a few seconds at a time, so in for a penny, in for a pound, the owner decided to introduce us to the garage dog as well, giving him an unforgettable introduction!

Is it me, or does it put you on edge if someone says, "Don't stare at him or he might go for you!"

Having had a dog gnash his teeth at me, every one of those big shiny teeth, in my school years, it obviously left a weak spot that I hadn't realised was still there, so for most of our initial interview that phrase constantly echoed round and round my head.

We were also going to be looking after two cats, Guiseppe and Carlo, but they didn't bother to make an appearance, although they were fairly laid-back characters by all accounts and should be no trouble.

I kept hoping I looked as relaxed as my better half, as we went through our usual questionnaire, and it must have worked, because we got a call from our agent the following morning to say how professional and competent we had been, and how impressed the client was.

It felt good to receive a little praise, so as I drove back the following Friday, we were both full of self-confidence.

In my case, that was soon to be greatly diminished!

We had arrived much too early so the owner suggested we go through the walking ritual before she left, generally shown the ropes. Pondering why it was a ritual in the first place, I took one lead, as she handed the other to my partner, but it only needed the time it took to get to the end of the drive for me to realise that I had the young uncontrollable troublemaker, who immediately insisted on making me look totally incompetent, scrambling from my left to right, panting and coughing, practically strangling herself in the process, while my partner shined as the professional pet sitter, walking alongside the owner who was questioning if she had ever done dog training. Trailing behind, veering from one side of the pavement to the other, I eventually caught up with everyone as they waited at a pelican crossing.

Just the sight of it instantly triggered some weird metamorphosis in my dog, and I now had a shrieking writhing banshee on the end of a lead, crazily leaping and pulling like an unbroken horse at the rodeo.

She didn't warn me about this did she!

As the lights changed and the crossing beeped, things went from bad to worse, and while my companions strolled across calmly, I was now being dragged across the road by the schizophrenic hound as if a starting pistol had just gone off. I was already struggling to hang on to the extending lead, but once we had shot across the road, we were immediately on the common. My boots had no grip in the wet mud, and with no other way of holding Candy back as I skidded along, my only choice to bring us to a halt was to make a grab for the arm of the owner, who incidentally was about a foot taller than my vertically challenged self (as well as having suitable footwear).

Now safely anchored, but quite embarrassed, I tried to regain control, but it was too late to save face, and feeling rather dejected I handed over the lead to my other half, who had suggested we exchange dogs for a while.

All that excitement meanwhile had drained a little energy from Candy, who looked a little more behaved, so while my other half took up her position alongside the owner, I trailed even further behind with Timmy, who had to cock his leg at every possible opportunity, posing me with the quandary of either looking like I was trying to strangle him as I dragged him along to keep up, or look like a weakling, entirely void of authority as I did his bidding.

Still concentrating on some sort of compromise, we reached the end of the wood, and the owner, feeling confident that at least one of us was capable, said she was going to make a quick exit and head back to the house so she could leave for her flight. With only a fleeting glance from the dogs as she disappeared, we were flying solo.

It was only a few minutes later that my mobile rang. She hadn't been able to get in the house because the catch on the front door was down (as in locked), and she had given us the only keys to the back door.

I have a sneaking suspicion that I was the culprit.

I definitely was the culprit.

After we had got our bags inside, I had wanted to make sure all doors were safe before going out (particularly as we were used to being extra vigilant in London), but after everything else that had just happened, I didn't want to own up to that as well.

We needed to get back to the house, and with nothing else to do, the owner walked back to meet us but thankfully nothing was said on the subject and when we arrived back at the house, she just had enough time to load her bags into the car and leave, this time in full view of all pets, cats included, but none seemed to mind.

After unpacking less than usual, as this was only for a weekend, we had dinner, fed the dogs, then it was time for television viewing, and Candy immediately wanted to join us on the reclining sofa. Instructions said she had to be invited rather than leaping up, so we made a space between us and tapped the seat.

No second invitations were needed.

She was making herself comfortable, circling round a few times to get the perfect position before lying down, while we shuffled nearer to the sides to accommodate her. From a distinctly thin-looking dog bed opposite, I could see Timmy staring across enviously, and as he walked over, I felt sorry that he was left out of the pack bundle. I decided to risk extending the invitation, turning my head away immediately afterwards so he didn't think I was peering at him. He put his front paws on the edge of the settee next to me, so I pushed Candy nearer to my other half, my other half crushed closer to the side, I then shuffled up to Candy, who by now was in a much tighter ball and Timmy squashed in the small space left between myself and the other arm. It was impossible to move as we were all wedged in so tight, but we were at least forming a closer bond with our companions.

One of the cats ambled through to join us, but with all arms trapped and no possibility of a stroke he jumped on the larger settee, adjacent to ours for a catnap. Stretched to capacity along the back with all four legs hanging over the edge, he could practically defy gravity.

On the occasions he was able to procure a spot on the outstretched legs of my other half, he assumed a similar posture, one that looked as though his bones had the constitution of jelly.

This cat could really relax!

In some ways I was quite relieved when Monday afternoon came around. Every walk had been much the same as the first, nothing we tried had improved the fiasco at the crossing, not even walking across the road further along. I always returned from our expeditions feeling drained.

We were perched on the two settees in the living room, each accompanied by a dog when their owner returned, and they darted out to greet her, wriggling round on the floor as she spoke to them in a high baby voice, tickling their tummies and kissing their noses, then the cats got their turn.

She seemed somewhat relieved that everyone had come out of the ordeal unscathed, but I couldn't vouch for myself entirely and was more than ready to leave.

The only trouble was that we already had our next booking here, and we would be back very soon.

2ⁿᵈ Sit

Refreshed after a few days at home, off we went again, this time more prepared, and having reached our destination far too early on our first visit, tried to be more sensible about our time of departure.

As you might expect… by leaving a 'sensible' amount of time for our journey, we were then met by any and every obstacle you might expect to encounter, starting with a painfully slow traffic jam on Edgware Road. Although Police and Ambulance presence was needed, we could see nothing except numerous cars slowing down to see what had happened, and this had accumulated in a tailback of impatient yet more curious drivers, probably all complaining about the traffic jam, but all helping cause it. There was no sneaky back route, so all we could do was move an inch at a time, watching the minutes pass by at an alarming rate, the unspoken panic in our minds increasing as we mentally worked out how far we had to go, and what time we should arrive.

Eventually passing the scene of what we presumed must have been an accident, things started to move slightly quicker, but then it seemed every car in front of us suffered a chronic attack of politeness, inviting any vehicle at every junction to go first. I doubted whether there would be any hair on either of our heads left to tear out by the time we arrived, but believe it or not, we pulled up at the house only a few minutes after our ETA. The unconcerned look of our client (even though she was putting her case in the boot of her car ready to leave), dissolved the stress of the journey away in a second, and making our well-rehearsed excuses superfluous. She was more confident in our punctuality than we had been a few minutes ago, but all was well, and as we had been here only two weeks previously and we knew the routine, so this pet owner could leave quite happily.

This time well equipped with wellies we set out on our first walk, and again I struggled to stay sure-footed as the rain had turned the common into a quagmire of slippery mud. It was bad enough trying to balance as it was, but with 'Miss Scatty-Chase-Cars Dog' and 'Mr Protect-my-Territory Dog' every step was cautiously taken. Any sighting of vehicle or canine would mean one or the other of them would be pulling at the lead, resulting in a sudden change to the centre of gravity, and with no solid ground to get a footing, this could only result in a rapid landing with one big splat in the mud.

Fortunately, we made it to the field without an incident, and once on the grass could set a much better pace, but every time a car was heard in the distance, Candy got that glazed expression as if she was staring at the snake in *'The Jungle Book'* singing, 'Trust In Me' and it was nigh on impossible to distract her. It would have been nice to make her walks a more pleasurable experience, but it would take plenty of time and patience to put right whatever had happened to her before she found this home, so we just wanted to make the best of our second weekend together.

After a lap of the field we started the return journey, safely tackled the skid zone again, did the usual struggle at the crossing and headed back to the house.

There was always a sense of relief when we knew we were in for the night, so we ate, watched television, and soon it was time to let the dogs out for the last time, get the two bowls of cat food ready, and say goodnight to our pack.

The following day was almost like spring... the sun was out, the birds were happily chirping and our walk was really quite pleasant. Both of us still kept a watchful eye out for any cause of distress to either dog, but in no time, we were back at the house enjoying cappuccinos and chocolate biscuits.

The afternoon walk was much the same, so on our return we started to prepare the evening meal early as we had seen a good film would be on Sky at eight p.m. and wanted to have eaten, cleared up and ready for uninterrupted viewing.

Our schedule was going as planned, and as eight o'clock approached, we each took our unfinished glass of wine, plus bottle for a top up, into the living room and flopped on the sofa, ready to enjoy the film. It wasn't long before one of the cats came in to join us on the sofa, and purred his satisfaction at being stroked and brushed as he rubbed up against each of us in turn to get as much attention as possible... which was fine as it wasn't interfering with our film viewing, in fact it was quite relaxing for all of us.

That was until my wine glass caught his eye.

It was red wine so I quickly moved it out of reach, then decided it would be much safer to take the bottle back to the kitchen to prevent any accidents, so tipped what was left into the glass and dashed off. It's not as if cats were interested in red wine, but better safe than sorry.

My feet had barely touched the kitchen floor when I heard a high-pitched scream of, "No!"

Startled, I turned back to see my other half hurtling out of the living room, and I could tell by her face exactly what had happened.

We both grabbed cloths and kitchen roll and rushed back, where my worst fears were well and truly realised, my usual overactive imagination totally accurate for once.

This inquisitive cat had still been fascinated by the red wine, and thanks to his curiosity, the contents of the replenished glass were now dripping down the cream wall and seeping onto and into the cream carpet, not a drop left to drink.

Several irritations reared their ugly head, the fact that there was nothing left in the glass to savour, the fact that we were now going to miss half of the film whilst trying to clean up this mess, but mostly, the fact that the culprit and cause of this disaster was now curled up in a cozy ball in my seat, blissfully unaware of the situation.

I dashed back to the kitchen, hot on the heels of my better half and we both frantically searched each cupboard for any solution, deciding that salt was probably the best bet to soak up the offending liquid… but should we just leave it to dry… what if that wasn't the right thing and we were just giving it time to soak in even more, drying well and truly stained.

I tried wiping the wall down for a while so the salt could hopefully do its work, but I just had to have a peek, and scraped it away at one side. We agreed that it looked better… but not good enough, so I poured more on to the uncovered spot, and we sat down, barely aware of the film now. Neither of us were in a patient mood, and were soon brushing away the salt again, but bit by bit, gradually managed to get the carpet to a stage were we felt happy enough to leave it overnight and take another look the following morning.

Red faced (very similar to the wine colour), from all the bending, rubbing and wiping, we eventually tried to enjoy the remaining part of the film but couldn't really concentrate, one or the other of us would stand up and be there staring down at the carpet every few minutes.

With no wine, I decided on a cold lager to quench my thirst, so returning from the kitchen yet again, carefully sat down on the settee, glass held firmly in hand. The offender, now awake again, made another approach, but because the problem had been more or less sorted, I was in a forgiving mood, even imagining that he must be feeling guilty for all the mayhem he had caused, so allowed him to jump up. He rubbed his head, apologetically I presumed, against my hand.

Yes!

Just as I was taking a well needed gulp of my drink, and it promptly poured all over my face, down my neck and all over my jumper.

I started to laugh, causing my intrigued yet unobservant partner to ask the reason, but the more I tried to answer, the more I laughed. The best thing was to turn my head so she could get a good look, which then caused so much hilarity, neither one of us were able to regain any sense of composure for several minutes. It could have been hysteria, it could have been relief, or maybe it's just the kind of sense of humour you need for this job.

Having utilised any remaining energy on laughing, there was nothing to do but go to bed and get some rest, just in case there was further cleaning to do tomorrow.

Getting up the next morning I immediately went to the television room and cautiously looked down at the carpet… it didn't seem too bad. I was quite confident that another session of elbow grease would have it back to normal in no time.

Worries dissipated, I opened each of the doors where the dogs slept, and they both eagerly dashed to see what was left in the cat food bowls. Once any leftovers were finished, they said a friendly, "hello" to me, and then it was out in the garden to bark any sleeping neighbours awake.

As I closed the door behind them, something was still causing an uneasy feeling in my mind.

I had no explanation for it, but it could only be one thing.

I went back and looked down at the carpet to re-evaluate my previous judgement.

It looked okay… more or less… it seemed my fears were unfounded.

Yes, it was going to be fine after all…

Yet something didn't look right…

…What was it?

My eyes glanced a little higher, and immediately every hair on the back of my neck stood on end.

Last night we had been concentrating on getting the carpet clean, thinking that the marks on the wall just needed to dry out, but this morning they looked exactly the same.

In the clear light of day, it was apparent that the red wine had stained the wall thoroughly, and leaving it overnight was ample time for it to dry in a permanent dark reminder of the occasion.

I didn't want to look a second longer and went to wake my partner with the good news.

After a joint inspection, we optimistically decided that it could soon be rectified with more wiping, so after a quick breakfast went on the morning walk. It was so brisk that Candy hardly had time to go through her scatty episodes, and as it was Sunday didn't need to press the button at the crossing, so we were in the woods before she had time to screech. We went home the same way, and yet again crossed the road in silence. Was this some kind of progress?

On our return the dogs were given their breakfast, then we grabbed all cleaning implements and determinedly set about the wall cleaning.

I grabbed a wet cloth and started to wipe the stain with gusto.

It was going to need a little more persuasion, so I wiped harder.

After rubbing for a few more seconds the red hue seemed to be disappearing but leaning back to examine my efforts it wasn't cream I was looking at. What I was looking at must have been the previous colour, some shade of blue, starting to peek through. I felt yet another hot rush of panic sweep through the whole of my body, as I realised the more I had tried to rub the stain away, the more I was wiping the paint off.

I got my other half, who had been focusing on the carpet all this time, to view the wall, and from her alarmed expression I could see we were not going to get away with it!

"We'll have to see if she has any paint left over," I heard myself say before my brain had chance to edit the thought.

Still stunned at myself for even verbalising the ludicrous suggestion, I was even more stunned when she agreed that this was our only solution. My big mouth had already done the damage, and before I could backtrack, we were both strutting to the garage, where we had seen tins of paint and other decorating gear each time we had put Timmy in there.

Our mission... find a matching colour asap.

Many tins of slightly varying shades of magnolia later, we eventually found a tin that gave a glimmer of hope... something calico... and I hurriedly grabbed a small paintbrush to test the shade.

Brushing a little on to a piece of paper I was dismayed to find it looked nothing like the wall colour, but with the persuasive encouragement of my wiser other half, strongly urging me to, "Just try it," I pessimistically dabbed the paintbrush on the wall.

It blended perfectly... combined with the blue underneath it was a perfect match, even though it was a totally different colour on the piece of paper. I quickly continued painting, as if any lethargy in the task might change the shade slightly, and within a couple of minutes the stain was gone... the old and new paint had blended flawlessly... what a relief... job done!

Or so I thought!

Unbeknown to myself, while I had been engrossed in exploring the many paint tins, my observant other half had spotted a carpet cleaner, and decided it would definitely rid the carpet of any incriminating evidence once and for all, so we were soon hauling it out from behind crates, bicycles, and various other decorating implements that were all crushed at the back of the garage. Just acquiring it was hard enough, and I was already dreading having to get it back in the exact same spot, never mind everything else. My better half wheeled it onto the carpet, and with lack of instructions we both perused the machine from all angles to examine its workings. Pacing round it one last time, satisfied we had it mastered, I was handed the plug to find the nearest socket while my partner went to get water.

Once the tank was filled, I clicked on the power, then with one final glance at each other, simultaneously hoping we were doing the right thing, it was revved in to action.

My other half stepped backwards and forwards, rolling it over the now invisible stain, and it was quite clear that the carpet was looking as good as new, the only trouble being that the rest of it was still looking old, much duller than the one patch by the wall. I was resigned to my fate and had already started pushing the rest of the furniture out of the way, removing anything else on the floor as I went, while she swayed to and fro. All pets were keeping well out of the way and as soon as it was done we would have to as well, until it was dry.

I needn't have worried.

By the time the weighty appliance was cleaned, back in its place, surrounded by all the other items, hopefully in the same place they had started, it could have dried more than once.

With that problem out of the way the world seemed a better place, and with much relief we went on our afternoon walk with the two dogs... just what I needed... a little exercise.

3rd Sit

A month or two later and we were off again.

Remembering our last journey to this place, stuck in traffic jams, road works on nearly every road in London, the slowest ever queue past a minor accident, and every learner driver out on the same day, I suggested leaving two hours before our ETA. This may have seemed excessive, even an hour and three quarters was ample but we decided to play it safe.

Safe maybe, but why think a more than sensible amount of time would be sufficient for this journey!

As clear as the roads were up to the M1, as clear as the M1 was, as clear as the route was from the motorway to our destination, about three or four miles away from the house our progress was rather abruptly halted by an almost stationary traffic jam. Yet again our stress levels were sent soaring as we barely moved for the next fifteen to twenty minutes and was usually the case, once you get behind schedule, things can only get worse.

Getting dangerously close to the 'tearing hair out' stage again, having endured crawling at two miles an hour for the past three miles, the view now facing us through High Street was one of complete chaos.

It was market day!

Not only was the town centre a heaving mass of cars, stalls, cars, shoppers, cars, buses, cars, cars more and more cars, all of the shoppers were also persistently pressing every pedestrian crossing button in the distance, which seemed to be spaced at twenty-yard intervals as far as the eye could see. Another fifteen minutes and a hundred grey hairs later we should have been there, and were probably less than a mile away, but had only moved a couple of yards, and were again motionless, trapped amidst the mayhem, so could do nothing more than sit tight and try to be extremely patient.

We arrived at the house to see the owner loading bags in to the back of her car yet again, and she must have seen our red perspiring faces as we jumped out of the car apologising but she didn't look too worried. Instead, she led us indoors, calmly explained that everything was the same as usual, except Candy was now allowed off the lead once in a safe area, and she also had a new lead to prevent pulling.

We were given a quick demonstration as neither of us had seen one before, both concentrating on memorising the procedure, but I could guarantee that neither of us would be able to do it when the time came. No one was admitting it though!

With that, she said goodbye to the two dogs, goodbye to us and left.

We unpacked our usual survival provisions and clothes enough for eight people as quickly as is possible for us, then decided to take the dogs for their afternoon walk so we would be able to then settle in and relax for the rest of the day. Before setting off, donning dog walking clothes was particularly essential for the impending hazardous terrain, and both plodded upstairs to the bedroom where we could see Guiseppe the cat in his usual favourite napping place on the bed. As soon as he opened his eyes he demanded attention, so I obligingly stroked his head, before continuing to change. That wasn't enough pampering to satisfy this cat, so just as I was balancing on one leg to take off my jeans, he rubbed his head solidly against the other, pushing me completely off balance. I tried to take a step to compensate for the shift in weight distribution, but my legs were firmly shackled by my jeans around my ankles, and after a valiant attempt at hopping alongside the bed, I eventually fell on to it. My other half paused to grin as I scrambled to the edge of the bed, but there was no time to waste. Downstairs two impatient dogs had recognised the drill and already knew what was afoot.

My other half opened the door and we all scuffled to be first to get in to the utility room.

It was easy enough to clip on Timmy's collar, then I stared at the new collar for Candy, which had seemed so easy simple when we just stood watching someone else do it. I made a fumbled attempt as my partner watched but couldn't work out the part that had to go around her snout to stop her pulling. I could feel my other half edging closer, chomping at the bit, wanting to show me how it was done, but when it came down to it, she was just as perplexed.

Between us, we spent a few minutes pushing each other's hands out of the way, still thinking it was easier to do it from an observer's point of view, but finding it fiddlier in practise, but eventually, after having to search out the instructions we were ready to go.

Candy, in the hands of my better half, obviously wasn't impressed with her new collar, and every few yards would stop and mount a frenzied attack, scratching at it frantically with her front paws, but after several attempts realised it wasn't going to get her anywhere, so just walked along, head held so low it was nearly scraping the pavement, looking totally miserable. It was a relief for everyone else, as her unexpected stops had been causing a lot of fancy footwork to avoid ending up in a pile. However, the new collar seemed quite successful in preventing her usual frantic pulling, so it was worth persevering. The calmer she became, the more comfortable it was for everyone, so we were all feeling quite relaxed as we neared the common. We nevertheless had to keep a lookout for other dogs though, as Timmy was still an intensely territorial kind of guy, and was always ready to assert his dominance to any potential rivals if they came too close.

Just as we were approaching the wooded area we spotted a fellow dog owner, fortunately holding his dog on a lead, so confidently, I gave him a friendly wave and carried on walking, happy that nothing could occur. That was about one second before I heard my partner shouting my name, which was approximately one more second before Candy charged past, collar dangling loosely round her nose, no lead to be seen.

It felt like a sudden shot of adrenalin directly in my heart, which was now thumping all the way through my chest wall, as I envisaged her hearing the cars racing along the main road not that far away and bolting after them. It didn't bare thinking about!

As luck would have it, Candy must have been disorientated with the shock of being suddenly untethered, so when I called her name, she just came over automatically, and I was able to grab her and the collar. Checking it over, the first thing I noticed was that part of it was missing.

It was still useable, so I clipped it back together and we all retraced our steps to where the incident had occurred. From that moment we transformed into a forensic police line, painstakingly searching for the slightest piece of evidence. No stone was going to be unturned, so back and forth we patrolled, eyes down, methodically scanning every part of the area, until at last, I saw something glistening in the grass.

It was the missing clip! Bent out of shape, but at least we had found it.

My partner held up the piece and said we could mend it, and although I was adamant that there was still another part unaccounted for, we had had enough searching for one day.

Our next few walks always included the forensic search every time we arrived at the incident location, but as it turned out there was nothing missing, and as soon as I managed to persuade myself, irritating as it was that I was wrong yet again, I was able to bend it back into shape, and all was well once more.

Although we didn't feel exactly comfortable at the prospect of letting Candy off the lead, it would be good for her to expend as much energy as possible, because she had so much of it locked up in her body. Taking a last look around to see if anyone was nearby, we decided all was clear, undid the lead, then watched as she ran up to the top of the hill and disappeared into the woods.

I almost stopped breathing, time suddenly slowed down to half-speed, and it felt like minutes, lots of minutes while we waited for her to reappear.

Everything went quiet, we all waited, and even Timmy was frozen on the spot, eyes scanning the gaps in the trees, waiting to see where she was going to emerge, if she was going to emerge...

It couldn't have been that long, and suddenly the calm was shattered.

A figure shot out from the green, ran back towards us, whizzed straight past and hurtled back into the woods in the opposite direction. We all stood motionless again, waiting for the explosion of energy to reappear again, which it did as she circled round to find a new zone to explore. Fortunately for us, Candy never wanted to be too far from Timmy, she was too nosey so eventually needed to come back to make sure she wasn't missing anything, or who knows how long we could have been waiting.

Having exhausted herself, and every possible route in and out of the woods, she succumbed to ambling to the top of the hill at a pace the rest of us could manage, and we were just going to head into the shade of another wooded area when all ears pricked up at the sound of a distant engine gradually getting louder as it came closer. My partner grappled with the fiddly lead in preparation as I called to Candy, trying to get close enough to grab her collar again, but this time she was having none of it. I turned towards the dust track that led to the farm, but I could see nothing approaching, which would give us more time, but why hadn't the vehicle appeared yet? Turning back quickly to make another attempt at grabbing her collar, I could see Candy looking up, and in the distance a helicopter had just reached the opposite end of the field.

So that was the sound of the engine, not a car as we originally thought, and surely she would never chase a helicopter.

I didn't even have time to breathe a sigh of relief as she set off across the field, hardly watching where she was going as she stared towards the sky, determined to get to the noise overhead. The helicopter in the meantime was speeding in our direction, so even before Candy reached the far boundary, oblivious to our shouts and whistles, it suddenly zoomed straight over her head. Any other dog by now might have given up this reckless task as a bad job, but not Candy. Within a second, she had turned tail, resumed the chase and firstly hurtled past me, who had made a puny attempt at keeping up with her, then past my panicky partner and a confused Timmy. Not for one moment did she take her eyes off this tricky customer.

Surely, she would soon be exhausted... but it just goes to show what determination can do.

For a moment I had visions of her following the helicopter trail, the three of us following her trail, wherever it may lead, whether it be one mile away or fifty, but mercifully there was a dog-proof barrier at the other end of the field, in the shape of an extremely solid stone wall, too high for our friend to scale.

The cats would be seeing us tonight after all!

I wondered whether she might give it a try, having watched a few canines doing Houdini-style escapes on the television, but she must have realised how tired she was, and just looked like a panting pink tongue, with a very weary dog attached.

Boy, was that fiddly lead clipped back on as quickly as possible!

It was not until we were heading back out of the common that I spotted two boisterous Labradors on our path, so I thought avoidance would be much easier than facing an encounter from the macho man dog himself.

To do this we had to go up a bank to the pavement rather than the normal gate, so with the help of a sure-footed canine leading the way, I dug my boots into the muddy slope and reached the top in a couple of steps. My partner followed along and held out a hand for an extra pull up the grass bank. I looked for a solid place to dig in a heel and leant forward to test my footing, but before I could say I wasn't ready, she had lunged at the bank. Instead of grabbing my hand she had only managed to grasp the end of my glove… Too Late!

The finger of my glove looked like it belonged to E.T. phoning home as it stretched to its limit, and as it stretched further, her foot slid backwards until one shoulder could resist gravity no more and splattered in the mud. It all happened so fast and as I watched, she skidded back to the bottom of the bank, the whole of her right side now smothered with a lovely orange, brown sludge.

As was usual on such occasions, I knew this was not the moment to see the funny side of things and I cautiously enquired on how she was. The question was disregarded completely, as she pulled herself up with one hand, still hanging onto the lead with the other.

We were still in a hurry to get out of the way of the other dogs, and I could see a determined expression ready to make another attempt, having decided I was of no help.

Aiming a foot half way up the bank she launched herself from the bottom, but there was only ever going to be one outcome!

As she put her weight on it, her foot slid backwards again and in slow motion she glided to the bottom.

This time it was the left side that got it!

I dare not say anything!

I dare not move for a second!

Underneath my concerned look, I could feel a smirk developing, and in danger of revealing itself any second, I tensed my face muscles to try and stop it and turned the opposite way. As she shuffled to her feet again, Candy by her side completely confused by the change in direction once more, I turned back and very quietly asked if she was okay...

Again there was no reply. It seemed meeting the two dogs was definitely the preferable alternative by now, and she was already making her way to the proper exit, so I walked along the road, grinning stupidly until we met up by the gate.

I think I can safely say that I have never seen such copious and colourful amounts of mud on clothes before, especially clothes actually being worn, but thought I'd better keep it to myself for now.

I tiptoed behind silently all the way home, then it was action stations as soon as we got through the door, my better half washing all the mud from her coat as I put the rest of her clothes in the washing machine.

We could laugh about the day's events later, but I had extra entertainment the following day, when, as we walked the dogs in the great British weather the whole coat started to froth up where it had been washed, but not thoroughly rinsed.

With each spot of rain, I watched more and more bubbles gradually form into a white frothy layer, so by the time we returned to the house, it was totally covered in soapsuds.

Just another story in the life of a pet sitter.

Chapter 9 — Ellie, JJ, Puck, and Lottie

Out of the blue we got a call asking if we could possibly take over a sit looking after four cats, as their owners were going to be away longer than anticipated, and the present sitter was unable to stay longer than her original leave date due to a hospital appointment. We had nothing to stop us, and after the energetic dogs we had looked after recently, the prospect of just four feline companions seemed a breeze. This was going to be the venue for one of our future sits, so we already knew it also included feeding foxes and wild birds, but that seemed fine as we did the same at home, also including the local squirrels.

Only having to cater for a four day stay, an attempt at more sensible packing was finally made, working out exactly what we would eat for each meal and packing a minimum amount of clothing, Wellies not included as we wouldn't be going out on muddy walks. This was getting easier by the minute.

To ensure a smooth changeover I had to phone the present sitter to arrange our time of arrival and see if she could let us know the 'Rules of the House' in advance, but there was no need… in an amused tone she said, "I have some sheets for you to read because there's quite a bit to do."

She then continued, "Have you done a sit before?"

Momentarily feeling a little uneasy at the need for this inquiry, I replied with an assertive, "Yes!" simultaneously attempting to stop my overactive imagination going into overdrive.

Continuing like some village soothsayer, she warned that this house was unlike any she had ever visited, the couple it seems had done plenty of travelling and always brought back weird and wonderful mementos from every destination, which now filled the house. I could feel my eyes widening to saucer like capacity as I listened to the grand finale, the icing on the cake... as relishing every creepy second, she imparted the information that one lone sitter was so scared she just left and went to stay at a nearby hotel rather than remain there.

That was it! Every horror film containing weird houses suddenly shot in to my mind, my thoughts changing to cinematic black and white as I pictured poor innocent characters laughing and joking as they arrived at some massive gates barely visible in thick swirling mist. They happily took their luggage into the house, suspecting not a thing, but a few days later they were either dead, missing, or totally mad sporting extremely grey hair.

Stop! What was I thinking!

I jolted myself back to the present... and back in to colour... and assured the sitter everything would be fine. We would be arriving by three p.m. on the Sunday.

She asked if we could buy two wholemeal loaves en route for the foxes, because as everyone knows, no fox should ever be deprived of a honey sandwich, and with that I said goodbye, then immediately dashed to relay our conversation to my other half, hoping I could instil a similar creepy image of our destination in her mind.

How disappointing!

She casually said it must be an interesting place, so feeling rather deflated I began to get our clothes and food together.

On the Sunday, we got up at a leisurely pace, dawdled over a fried breakfast and nonchalantly went through our list of requirements. Stress-free, we packed the car, left with plenty of time to get the bread, and after only one brief moment of map chaos, arrived with relative ease.

As I parked next to the gate, it was the house next door that looked creepier, the last bit of paint barely hanging on to the door and window frames, and in comparison, our latest abode looked quite respectable. (I hadn't noticed the gargoyles staring down from the roof and the garage at this point)!

We both enthusiastically walked down the stone path, and I knocked on the heavy oak door, waiting only a few moments before it opened.

A 'grey' haired lady (still looking quite sane) appeared, introduced herself, then lead us past various statues and sculptures in the hall to the sitting room, where we could read our instructions and let her know when we had finished. For a second, I had a flashback of sitting an exam at school, only allowed to move once it was complete, but *better do what she said,* I thought. Obediently we sat down, while she disappeared to gather her belongings, and almost immediately a black cat came in to join us, giving us a complete inspection culminating in the comfortable lap test. I wouldn't have minded, except too much comfort seemed to make him slobber, and trying to make sure it didn't splatter my clean clothes wasn't easy, so prompt removal was the only possible option.

It didn't impress our new friend in the slightest.

He left the room again, not before turning to impart a look of total disgust, so I continued reading, although not really giving it my full attention, skimming over several pages, as my better half concentrated enough for the both of us, taking so long I thought she must be going through it all twice (So well informed, she would obviously do much better than me in this test).

The allotted examination time was up, and our fellow sitter returned, car keys poised in hand, and it looked as though she couldn't wait to leave (not surprisingly after being here on her own for three weeks). We were taken on a whistle-stop tour of the house, then after writing down her phone number in case we needed to ask anything, she grabbed her one bag (I was envious of her minimal packing), and waved goodbye as she headed down the path.

Before searching out the other cats, we got our remarkably few bags from the car, and carried them through the doorway to different rooms. I had more time to study the numerous souvenirs from their expeditions. Every wall in every room was covered in photos, hanging ornaments, pictures, clocks, masks... every shelf was full of plates, photos, more ornaments... and then various large pieces stood on the carpets. My mind briefly returned to the black and white screen, as I imagined some evil spirit still lurking in one of these foreign relics, just waiting to possess an unsuspecting passer-by, but glancing over at my untroubled other half getting on with the job in hand, I quickly and sensibly pushed the idea aside. Once food for the freezer had been dealt with, nothing was too urgent, so we greeted another two of our new companions, who purred in anticipation as they invited us to stroke them.

The other male cat was a solid tough-looking character, totally black except for one white toe, which no one was going to dare make fun of, and the female was a very pretty black and white cat with two beautiful green eyes, framed with long eyelashes staring out from long silky fur. She looked even more glamorous with a silver charm attached to her collar like some jewel, and although the others also had them, they couldn't carry it off with such style. Puck, a feral cat at the time had been totally bewitched by her beauty, and followed her home one day never wanting to leave again. He just moved in.

During our stay they were usually in the same room, sometimes their tails intertwined as they sat together, and they looked the perfect cat couple.

There was still someone missing from the pride, but according to instruction, we knew she could be found in the upstairs bathroom. Like a feline Howard Hughes, Ellie preferred a reclusive existence, so after an adequate period of adoration laden on the other three, we ventured up to meet her. Entering her domain, a large bathroom decorated with various pictures, all including cats, it would have been easy to overlook the little figure curled up on a towel by the shower. She was on medication and looked extremely delicate, so we tiptoed over so not to startle her, and my other half whispered her name. We waited for some reaction from this tiny cat, and after what seemed minutes, she lifted her head weakly, totally disinterested in two strangers that stared, then curled up in to a little ball again. We thought it better to leave her and look in on her again in a while, although we were concerned.

Having manoeuvred the final two bags up the winding staircase and into the bedroom, we returned to the bathroom once again, and cautiously stared down at the sleepy little feline. Sensing our presence, a little character resembling a kitten rather than a sixteen-year-old cat stretched a back leg before emerging from the side of the shower, but the closer she came, circles of grey fur surrounding her eyes, her fur flecked with distinguished grey gave away her age.

True to species, regardless of her years, it was her catlike duty to submit a thorough inspection of new persons now residing at her house, and also test their stroking ability to the limit. She was so cute, even though she was thin and fragile in appearance, but in days to come we would learn that if crossed by one of the other cats, she could give an extremely effective triple slap before you could blink an eye.

By now it was dark, so I collected the three bowls of honey sandwiches and dog biscuits sitting on the wooden table in the middle of the kitchen, already pre-prepared by our predecessor to demonstrate the correct amounts. It had been raining for a while, and they all nearly went flying as I skidded down the two steps from the back door, so with extra caution, I worked my way along the narrow path to the lawn, gingerly taking the smallest of steps as I tried to keep my balance on the slimy green stones. Once safely on the lawn, the three bowls were spaced well apart, so everyone, whatever size, would be able to get some of the goodies. I picked up the empty plate used for bird feeding so it could be refilled in the morning, then quickly retreated back indoors to the warmth.

My partner, in the meantime, had been preparing the downstairs cat dinners, and was surrounded by a hungry trio, all making their impatience known in various pitches of meows. They turned briefly as I made my hurried entrance, but realising I was of little importance to the speed of service round here, got back to heckling immediately. Their meals were also spaced well apart so Puck, the largest of the three couldn't eat his way through all of the bowls by himself, and as they tucked in, we stood watching like two burly bouncers patrolling a nightclub, ready to step in if any trouble started.

A few minutes later, eating had been replaced with lip-licking, and contented paw washing, so we now prepped up the fourth meal. Ellie only ate small amounts, so I opened up a tasty looking terrine of salmon, while my other half poured out some cat milk into a very colourful dish. We headed to the bathroom with our servings and placed them in front of her, looking like panic-stricken contestants on MasterChef, waiting for her to taste our efforts and pass judgement.

Big disappointment!

We didn't get through to the next round, because the reaction after one sniff was to lay down again!

As Ellie had something wrong with her thyroid, she needed to eat regularly, so I suggested opening a tin of tuna, and with immediate agreement from my partner ran downstairs to search our supplies.

What a time to get sensible with packing... we hadn't allowed for cooking a tuna pasta, making a healthy tuna salad, not even a stupid tuna sandwich. End result... *No stupid tins of stupid tuna!*

On the verge of going out shopping, forgetting it was after six p.m. on a Sunday so nowhere would have been open, we decided on a freezer search, and thank goodness... there on the top shelf, were some frozen cooked fish portions. We could explain to the owners later I decided, thawing some out, then warming it slightly to get the smells circulating.

We returned with our second dish.

That did the trick. She ate only a small amount, but it was sufficient for us to be comfortable enough to leave her, and finally get our own food.

After all the usual preparation, eating and clearing up, we sat watching television until quite late, eventually retiring to bed in the satisfying knowledge that we didn't have to get up early to walk any dogs in the morning.

Drifting to sleep with those thoughts still echoing through my brain, my slumber was interrupted barely a few hours later, when half asleep, half-awake I could hear meows coming from somewhere in the dark. Unable to get my bearings in the strange bedroom, I had to ask my other half, who was fortunately awake from the disturbance, to put on the light so we could see what was wrong at this time of night. The emergency in hand was of course something that could never be considered trivial.

Cat hunger… with a capital C, a capital A, and a capital everything else!

Downstairs, Puck now knew we were awake and started meowing almost constantly, so Ellie, who had been the alarm clock in the first place, made sure she was not forgotten by intermittently meowing at such a loud volume it thumped your heart straight up into your mouth, then sent it thudding back into your chest where it bounced round the walls for a while. Still in mild shock, I hung onto the banister for safety as I stumbled downstairs, my other half hanging onto me, and as we descended in to view, the glamorous Lottie joined in with the meowing. Were they exaggerating their hunger, or was this just a test of our devotion to cat comfort?

My path to the kitchen resembled that of a drunkard, focused on some destination point in the distance, but legs veering off in several directions, as I tried not to step on one of the cats running around my feet. At least preparing the first three breakfasts would be quick as it only consisted of cat biscuits. My bleary partner got fresh water for all, then next on the agenda was to make sure Ellie had her pill, crushing it in a small amount of food, then once it was gone, she could have as much as she wanted. Having struggled with her dinner last night, the easiest solution at this unearthly hour was just to put the crushed pill in a small amount of the leftover fish, so optimistically took it back upstairs with us, with extra to follow if all went well. We were both hoping it would be a simple operation, which it should be if she was as hungry as her volume had suggested, then we could soon be back in a warm bed, but even after a relatively short time of pet-sitting, our experience was that things like that didn't usually happen.

We put the water and fish next to her on the floor and braced ourselves.

Prolonging the agony, the little cat inspected both bowls deciding she needed a drink first. It must have been the slowest drink ever, or time stopped completely, but it gave ample opportunity to appreciate the full effect of the chilly night (or rather, chilly morning), which was already making both of us shiver quite visibly in spite of the under-floor heating.

We couldn't believe it… one more sip and then she started on the fish.

Yes? Would she be suspicious of the taste? No! We dared to exchange a smile as she continued to tuck in, and with another couple of mouthfuls it was gone.

A little face looked up and let out another alarmingly impressive meow to indicate a second helping was required, which was served immediately. We were so relieved the task was completed successfully and pleased that she was now so much more responsive than last night. We had been genuinely concerned for her well-being on our first meeting, but true to that star of 'Gone With The Wind' tomorrow really was another day.

All cats now satisfied, the house was silent once more, and we managed to get a few more hours sleep before the next feeding frenzy would begin.

From the warmth of the bed I again heard stirring sounds, but now it was light, so I tried to make my eyes focus on my watch, moving my arm back and forth until I found the perfect distance to see the time. After a few seconds I could see it was about eight a.m. which meant birds needed to be fed, and doors opened wide so all cats could go out.

I tiptoed into the bathroom and walked over to the shower where Ellie was now engrossed in her beauty sleep, and realised that I hadn't really paid much attention to the actual shower itself.

Looking round for the door, I noticed the tiny cat was lying right next to a large gap in the glass, so with only three and a quarter sides, surely she would be drenched if I turned on the water.

I gently slid her and her bed along the warm floor so she would be out of the line of fire once I got in, causing only a momentary shuffle, then positioned a bath mat in its place and stood at the side to stretch across to the tap. I gave the tap a twist, and immediately a surge of freezing cold water shot out of the nozzle straight down my outstretched arm, all the way down my body to my leg and onto the mat. The shock was bad enough already, but not wanting more water to spill on the floor I panicked and just got in.

Boy, was I wide awake now!

Fortunately, the hot water started to come through not long after I took my foolhardy step, otherwise my partner could have walked into a familiar shaped ice sculpture. I let the hot water soak through my traumatised body for as long as I dare, then quickly put on some clothes and dashed downstairs, fully expecting a queue to be forming by the cat flap... but nobody looked that awake. Nevertheless, I was doing things by the book, firstly opening both cat flaps, then opening the back door to allow the three cats to go out. They all gave me an irritated look in unison, as an icy draught pierced the warmth of the kitchen... but they were the lucky ones, I was the one that had to go out to feed the birds. Taking the plate of leftover cat food I hurriedly placed it on the lawn, my footing much safer now that I could see where I was going, then put a scoop of ground food in the container on the lawn, topped up the hanging feeders with ordinary bird seed, and finally collect the fox bowls from the previous night. It hadn't taken that long, but by now I was losing the feeling in my fingers, and I dashed back in through the door, already knowing it was too late to avoid an attack of hot aches any minute. Wishing there had been an ally present to offer sympathy, I danced around the kitchen squeezing my hands together for a while, and then as the pain wore off, I couldn't help a little inward smile... not one cat had moved, no one had even bothered to open an eye as I battled the elements, it was far too cold to do anything but sleep.

Why didn't they know that at five o'clock this morning?

As the morning warmed up slightly, I was joined by other members of the household, my partner included, and soon, feeling that she was missing out, the recluse from the bathroom ventured to the top of the stairs and meowed again. If this was to happen, it stated in the rule book, all other cats should be closed into one room, and the front door opened so she could go out, have a little wander, then have a clear path to return to safety without any encounters. We bustled the downstairs cats into the front room, noticing about four varieties of keep-fit machine taking centre stage in the middle of the floor, surrounded by antique looking furniture along every wall, every surface laden with old-fashioned photographs. By the time they were securely closed in the contradictory chamber, she had reached the bottom of the stairs and was quickly out of the front door. As pleased as we were that she was showing an interest in exploring more than the bathroom for a while, it now meant she was out in the big wide world, adding further concerns as to how easy it would be to get her back indoors. Not content with the front garden, she disappeared out of view round the side of the house, causing us to race from the front door to the back, staring out, hoping that she would soon reappear.

She did, thank goodness, but we were on edge the whole time, watching as she explored the furthest nooks and crannies. We didn't want to alarm her by barging out, and for some reason we seemed to have completely forgotten that this was her house, her garden, and she probably knew every inch of it perfectly. Nervously I pushed open the door and stepped back out of view. She looked interested in coming back in and a few seconds later, obviously having read the instruction sheet herself, ran back to her private quarters upstairs, blissfully unaware of our brief panic.

The door was rapidly shut behind her.

The other cats acted as though they had been under lock and key for years, longing for a taste of freedom, as one by one they squeezed themselves through the opening gap of the door to investigate, but there was no evidence of the short adventure.

With all the time we had spent loitering in the kitchen, my other half had noticed cat brushes just waiting to be used, so it looked like a grooming session was imminent.

The female cat, Lottie, looking every inch a pedigree with her long silky fur and demure appropriately named catwalk, was born to be brushed, and lavished the attention, front paws continuously kneading some invisible dough.

Puck, once a feral cat, had completely forgotten his previous life and was now equally happy being pampered, after being bewitched by the beauty, following her home one day, and never leaving, and finally, JJ was the easy-going guy, patiently waiting his turn and oblivious of his cool good looks.

I say finally, but of course, would we be able to brush Ellie, the Greta Garbo of the cat world upstairs?

Usually she did have some company when her owners were at home, because they had an office next to her bathroom, so we thought we should spend some time with her, and surely a brush would make her feel better. After a tentative start, she loved it, and kept leaning her thin body into the brush to get as much pressure as possible. I sat watching from the other side of the bathroom, and after a few brushes, she would run over so I could stroke her, then she would look back at my partner and dash back, so as not to miss the next few brushes. This would continue with her running between the two of us, soaking up as much attention as possible from both sources, until finally, somebody was tired.

On the Monday afternoon we received a call from our agent asking if we could prolong our visit for an extra few days and we didn't mind one bit. We would need to buy some extra food, so after giving the cats their lunch (this time ordinary cat food), we disappeared to explore the town and were soon struggling back, each with two bags that got heavier each step. We kept stopping every few yards to change the bags round, comparing the white ridges in our hands where the thin plastic handles were cutting through, but at least it was only a few minutes' walk away. The noise of the key in the door alerted the residents and as we entered with our goods, first JJ came to greet us, soon joined by Puck and Lottie. Who would have expected such a welcome, especially after only a short time, but these cats it seems, didn't always follow normal cat criteria. We went to say hello to Ellie upstairs, but she was still asleep, so we unpacked the shopping and then enjoyed a homemade cappuccino and chocolate biscuits.

Later, as the daylight started to fade, my other half decided to prep up the honey sandwiches, and placed four slices of bread on a board. The thick gooey honey, boasting practically identical properties to industrial strength contact adhesive, and should come with similar instructions was then applied to all surfaces, and once two slices were placed in position on top of the other two, there was only a small window to make any adjustments before they were well and truly stuck solidly together. She cut them into bite size pieces, shared them between three bowls, then topped them up with dog biscuits, so I opened the back door to tempt any cats to go out for the last time today. Once the fox food went out, they were locked in for the night, except

Puck who knew how to handle himself, but no one could be bothered to move, and they knew they had the safety net of indoor litter trays anyway. Bracing myself yet again for the icy weather, I stacked the bowls, walked down to the lawn, spaced them well apart, grabbed the bird plate and hurried back indoors. In the meantime the cat flaps had been closed, and once the cats had been fed, we could all settle in for the evening. Although we were watching television, we made sure we went to visit Ellie every now and then, although she would soon and loudly let us know if she wanted anything. Lottie, now renamed Miss Slinky Puss, had sunk into the duvet keeping my other half warm, and purred contentedly, eyes closed as the rhythmic strokes of the brush gradually hypnotised her. I was joined alternately by JJ and Puck on the settee directly opposite. Although not bosom buddies, they seemed mutually respectful, and gave each other a polite amount of space rather than a forced confrontation.

Because of our early morning call and disrupted sleep we were both weary and kept taking it in turns to somehow watch the television with both eyes closed, so it wasn't long before we decided it could be time to retire for the night. The lights were turned off downstairs and after a final brush for Ellie, we went to bed, hoping to get more of a lie-in tomorrow.

It seemed like I had only just got to sleep, when suddenly, I could feel cat paws treading over my legs, striding up the middle of the bed, and stopping somewhere near my face, to allow loud purring easy access to my ear. It was no good thinking I could ignore it, but stupidly I gave it a go, causing JJ to reassess his position, ultimately deciding it was probably better to sit atop my shoulder, leaning straight down to my unprotected ear.

I shuffled him off with a slight struggle, then wished I hadn't, as I could tell he was now going to try the same trick on my partner... too late!

She stirred, and once he knew it, he was going to relentlessly keep up the onslaught, so I jumped out of bed, grabbed a dressing gown, and lured the purring feline out of the bedroom with the promise of cat biscuits. JJ looked pleased that his plan was successful, and would have gone downstairs quite the returning hero if the other two had known it was him that got their breakfast served punctually this morning. After getting the fresh water, I dared to take a look at my watch, and of course, it was five-fifteen a.m. just about the right time for an early morning snack, so I went through the routine of crushing the pill, small amount of food, stand shivering, wait till gone, bit more food, little stroke (whilst shivering), back into bed.

Was this going to be the routine every morning? Would we forever be getting up in the dark at five o'clock?

Of course not! Sometimes it would be four-thirty instead!

The next couple of days ran smoothly, and by now our stay was going to be even longer, as the owners of this mini pride could still not return until their work had been completed, but as we were enjoying every minute (not so much the five o'clock wake-up call), it was no problem.

On the Thursday, we had leftover chicken from the previous night, so thought we would try and tempt Ellie downstairs and outside again. She had been indoors since returning from her little walk on Monday, although the pouring rain every day hadn't been too inviting, but this looked like a proper spring day and the perfect opportunity to get some fresh air.

Getting the smallest piece of chicken, I knelt on the bathroom floor, held it briefly under her tiny nose, and immediately got a reaction. It's a good job the other cats had already been closed in the kitchen, because she was after that food, and as I backed away to lure her down the stairs, she was right behind me and gaining fast. We reached the bottom step, and she only now seemed aware of the noise outside, looking as though she might turn and run back, so I held out the small piece of chicken, and followed it immediately with a big yelp.

My other half, who was on standby with more chicken jumped, then laughed as I said, "She bit my thumb!"

Ellie was already reaching out for more chicken, small but dangerous claws ready to snare some for herself, if it wasn't forthcoming, but now perilously empty-handed I promptly stepped out of the way, and watched my partner deliver the next helping, this time in the front garden...

"Ow!" (This time I jumped), "She bit me too!"

Neither bite had been too serious, it was more the shock, but it had caused some amusement, and it was also good to see her so enthusiastic about food, so we each gave her another small piece, then waited to see if she wanted to remain outside now that she was here. Once aware that food deliveries had finished for the time being, she just turned and walked back up the stairs, so not wishing to show any favouritism we opened the doors and gave the same to each of the other cats.

We usually had the fox-feeding routine down to a fine art, served approximately at the same time every day, but one evening our schedule had gone awry, and somehow we had been distracted and forgotten our duties. The foxes had been visiting this garden for so long, they were very tame, and apparently had excellent body clocks, but also didn't like to be kept waiting.

This wasn't good enough!

Complaints needed to be made!

A chilling cry emitted from the garden, causing us both to stop in our tracks, eyes widening as we listened. That was the sort of reminder that got things done, and no time was wasted making sure their dinner was ready urgently, if not before. My other half started buttering bread, while I gathered the other recipe items so they could be added immediately, but by now, another fox was now making us aware of his displeasure. I hoped it wouldn't take long, or we may be fending off unhappy neighbours as well as hungry foxes.

On this occasion, it was the turn of my partner to serve the dissatisfied customers, and for a moment all went quiet as I opened the door. She carried the bowls to the lawn, as I peered through the glass, ready to let her back in when the job had been done. No foxes could be seen, but just as the final bowl was being put in position, the creepiest, blood-curdling fox scream resonated from somewhere way too close, and even in the dark I could see the shock on her face. The three cats in the kitchen were totally silent for once, and completely still as the harrowing sound bellowed forth again, initiating a rather hasty return by my rather pale looking better half.

You can be sure that it was the last time fox dinner was served late!

Overall, our stay there seemed to be a definite improvement in Ellie both physically and mentally.

She was always pleased to see the cat brush, pills were easier to administer with tempting treats, and she was now playing with various toys that found their way to the bathroom. One morning, I awoke in the early hours to the sound of a ping-pong ball being thwacked for all it was worth, followed by the scamper of tiny feet. The bathroom had the perfect surface to keep the toy rebounding from wall to wall as she chased after it, but the amplified sound as it hit the hard tiles made the noise echo through the whole house. Wide awake yet again, I couldn't resist peeping through the door, and could just make her out in the dark, having a wonderful playtime and enjoying every minute. It was worth getting up for!

By the last morning, we were used to being woken by one cat or another, one method or another, and it was obvious that this was no exception, as I awakened to feel a small character using all claws to pull herself up the duvet and onto the bed. Without opening my eyes, I put out a hand out to stroke the little cat, hoping to put off breakfast for a while, but as any cat owner could verify, a hungry cat wasn't going to be palmed off with some 'tired' story. Half asleep, I kept holding out my hand to the persistent kitty, allowing a kind of do-it-yourself stroke as she walked underneath, but it was totally unsatisfactory. Drifting off again, I was soon reminded that falling back to sleep was not an option and was briskly reawakened by a method never experienced before, faster and more effective than any other I had ever come across.

Yes, I woke up with a furry cat paw tapping around in my open mouth, and what's more, I could distinctly feel too many claws next to my tongue, almost on the verge of grabbing it if it dared to move. Fearing for the safety of my taste buds, I rapidly made a grab for the little paw, removing it before any damage could be done, but it had the desired effect, and I was absolutely wide awake.

Still quite stunned by this creative rude awakening, I sat bolt upright in the bed, hardly noticing that my 'so tired' story must have worked a little, because my partner had already disappeared downstairs, deciding that the sooner she dealt with breakfast, the sooner we could get back to sleep. I could hear her coming back up the stairs, as could Ellie, who was now letting out one of her ear-splitting meows, before jumping off the bed to see what was on the menu.

Unfortunately, my partner had served up an unusually large breakfast containing the pill, and it wasn't eaten all in one go, so still had to be guarded from theft by one of the other cats until finished.

On first watch, my other half sat on the bathroom floor, quietly reading to pass the time. Puck, who wasn't the most light-footed of cats tried creeping up the stairs, and presuming we were both on the second sleep shift, casually sauntered in to the bathroom. He was too focused on the food dish by the opposite wall to notice he had been rumbled, but soon realised as he was swiftly pointed back from whence he came. A few minutes later, my partner was reliving the episode, like reshooting a film scene, as he yet again tried sneaking in, got caught red-handed and got sent packing. Obviously disgruntled by the determination of my other half, and extremely disgruntled at not getting any leftovers, he was going to put every ounce of energy into a third attempt. Putting all of his weight behind it, he catapulted himself from the bottom step, and at full pelt, charged up the stairs like a rhino. Having reached optimum velocity, he then skidded round the corner, through the bathroom door, and made a determined dash at the elusive dish. He hadn't counted on the lightening reactions of my partner, who stopped him in his tracks like some American footballer, minus the padding, and this time he had to endure the embarrassment of returning to the others empty-handed, or rather empty-bellied. I blissfully slept through all of these goings on, unaware that my better half had vigilantly sat on the bathroom floor, at intervals picking Ellie's dish up, and then putting it back down as if it was a new breakfast, hoping a little psychology might go a long way in speeding up the process.

A not-so-speedy three hours later, having finished reading her book from cover to cover, she had discovered psychology had not been the answer, but at least it had now all been eaten.

It must have been at this perfectly timed moment that I woke up again.

Chapter 10 — Emma and Lady

Well, there we were at six a.m. on a Friday, knowing perfectly well we weren't going to be getting back to sleep again, but still determined to try, eyes closed as if it might miraculously happen. We'd already spent most of the night awake, one or the other of us fidgeting or checking the clock, knowing the alarm would be going off at six-thirty and, as if it was a rare occurrence, didn't want to miss the spectacle. Giving up on the shut-eye, I shivered my way to the bathroom, waiting for my brain to catch up with my body that was somehow getting dressed on automatic pilot, then I went downstairs to put the kettle on.

Conscientious as ever, we had to make sure we were on time for this sit over a long weekend, because not only was it a new venue, it was also a last-minute booking so we couldn't do our usual pre visit, meaning this would be our very first meeting.

I hadn't been in the kitchen for long when my partner appeared, managing to conjure up a look that combined one of 'pure discomfort from cold' with that of 'extreme displeasure at being up at this unearthly time of day'! I was rather impressed, but we didn't have time for compliments.

Having experienced London traffic for many years, we both knew a trip of one hour could just as easily take two or more in a traffic jam, three or more in a traffic jam with a minor accident thrown in, who knows how long with the previous two combined with roadworks. Basically, that meant as we were heading to the opposite side of London and beyond, we were leaving at seven-thirty a.m. to arrive for nine-thirty, hoping we wouldn't come across too many delays, but at the same time not arriving so early that we had to sit a hundred yards down the road freezing until it was a suitable time to arrive.

By accidentally leaving ten minutes later than we meant, we arrived only half an hour early, and could just check up on a few details before pulling up at their abode, a very impressive large house nestled amidst several equally imposing properties. I got out of the car and pressed the intercom to announce our arrival, jumped back in as the large metal gates started to open, then pulled in to the gravel drive behind three other vehicles. The door didn't open as expected, so once out of the car, I now rang the doorbell and strangely enough had to announce our arrival yet again, because this time it was the wife rather than the husband that answered. As everyone was now more than fully aware of our arrival, the door did open, and the man of the house shook both of our hands then led us straight into the kitchen to meet our latest companions.

Two Labradors circled us until we were nearly dizzy! Stroking either one of them was an impossibility as neither could stand still long enough, their tails wagging so fiercely that their hind legs and bottoms joined in as well. We gave up for the time being to allow them to calm down and give us opportunity to start going through yet another book of rules, info and instructions produced by the owner. Under his close supervision, we were working our way through sheet after sheet, checking the numerous keys that were required for all doors in the large house when his wife returned from an extremely quick visit to work. She immediately checked to see if her husband had told us everything, asked us everything, recapping every one of his instructions almost word for word so we reassured her that he had been very thorough.

Just then our meeting was interrupted by the arrival of the cleaner, who only paused for a quick introduction before disappearing to get on with the job at hand, so our initiation continued with a tour of the downstairs rooms, out to the garden, tennis court and swimming pool, concluding with our choice of rooms upstairs. Everything was covered, and it was time for the departure, as reluctant as it was, but eventually the couple opened the front door, and as was quite often the case, asked if they could ring later to check if all was going okay (understandable even more so as we hadn't met before this day), then with a final farewell glance, left.

Only a few minutes later we thought we would take the dogs out, especially as we had been told that Emma, the eldest at eleven years, usually looked very miserable at not being allowed along on a trip with them. We donned our usual outfits (Wellies and coats), took the dog leads and strode towards the gate at the bottom of the garden which led onto the path next to the golf course.

Half way there, we sheepishly turned back, dogs looking perplexed as though amnesia had just erased all memory of a walk, because my other half had just remembered that we'd forgotten the key. We then proceeded to look totally inefficient as it took us, the cleaner and both gardeners to eventually work out which one it was.

Having actually made it all the way to the gate the second time, we unlocked it and pulled it open. With permission to be off the lead (unless water was in view), both dogs ran through, and eagerly watched while it was relocked, ready to lead the way, so we were extremely impressed as they waited for us to follow, but we had been told that they were very well behaved.

With that, they both immediately went through a well-trodden gap in the wire fence, where not far away we could see two golfers ready to tee off, both eyeing up the distance and one of them judging his shot, hips doing that golf sway from side to side as he prepared to give the ball a good wallop. Worrying that the dogs might go and steal a golf ball, or just give them the enthusiastic greeting we received earlier, knocking any and every ball flying, a flurry of panic erupted in my better half, and she started calling loudly and whistling them back. I hurried to catch up to her, attempting to shout a warning in a whispery voice, both arms flaying around as I tried to indicate that the noise might very well put them off. It was more than likely going to be us spoiling his best shot rather than the dogs!

The dogs, in the meantime, had now walked further out of reach on the other side of the fence, although they weren't so interested in the concentrating golfers, they were busy munching on the luscious grass, so once satisfied (which felt like twenty minutes later), they 'obediently' came out of yet another well-trodden gap.

Further along the path, the golf course disappeared behind a row of trees, so it was forgotten by all, but as the dogs ran out of sight, without thinking, I gave them one of my best loud RTB whistles, taught to me many years ago by my uncle.

Almost simultaneously, just beyond the far side of the trees I heard a whack of a golf ball accompanied by a dismayed, "Aagh!" And realised my error.

So much for telling my better half not to put off the golfers!

We proceeded along the muddy path and could see another dog approaching from the opposite direction. Lady was quite happy to say hello but Emma, who had once been badly attacked, developed what looked like a baby shark fin as the hair down the middle of her back bristled up in a threatening gesture. It didn't go any further than a visual warning, but from then on, we always kept an eye on proceedings when meeting other dogs, judging her fear by the size of her heckles, ready to step in at any trouble, but nothing ever happened.

Our trek continued and, in the distance, I spotted a gate where the path led onto open ground, so this was the spot where leads had to be attached to pass the duck pond. The dogs obediently ran back to us while the leads were clipped on, then we all stepped across the bridge and onto the common. I had to keep looking down to see if I actually had a dog still attached to my lead, because she was so well behaved it was impossible to tell. My partner seemed to be undergoing the same experience, and we agreed it was a far cry from our usual dog walking tales.

They were let off again once away from the pond, and I threw the ball I had hidden in my pocket as far as I could up ahead. Both dogs charged after it, and the youngest, Lady, came back triumphant to return it so I could give it another throw. They jumped backwards not caring where they were going, legs poised, eyes fixed as I picked up the ball, then turned to run as I lifted my arm to throw. By the time the ball had left my hand they were already half way to where it was going to land, and again Lady had that extra youthful speed to be the victor in the chase.

This wasn't fair, I thought, so as they charged off for the next throw, I changed direction at the last minute, ensuring Emma was the closest to the ball and could grab it first. She made the most of it, prancing back with head held high, teasing Lady with it, and after having to almost twist her neck round the opposite way to prevent it from being stolen, proudly dropped it at my feet.

After a few more throws the dogs were panting and would definitely need to be on leads before we were anywhere near the bridge, because I was sure a tasty drink of dirty duck-pond water was going to be a great attraction.

Making our way back, the path seemed much longer than we remembered, and the going was made even more difficult as our feet kept getting stuck in the thick sludge, each time an extra helping of accumulating mud clinging to our Wellies feeling like extra lead weights. From the look on the other two faces in our pack, they were just as weary, even without the footwear, and we were all pleased to reach the gate.

Once inside, the dogs ran to greet the gardeners again, as if they hadn't already done it earlier, while we looked round at all the doors leading in to the house, not sure which we should use.

You could have had a sure-fire bet on it... out of about seven doors, we managed to pick the only one that wouldn't open, and of course, looking up I could see the cleaner watching us.

Assisted yet again with directions to a suitable entrance, we got out of our muddy attire, and took advantage of a rare invitation to delicious coffee by the cleaner. The dogs slurped their fresh water as we had a quick chat with the cleaner over a much- needed drink just before she left. It was only brief, as she was going on somewhere else, but it was perfect timing as we also had an item on the agenda and disappeared to smarten up to prepare for an interview with yet another client only a short distance away.

The dogs were happy enough to be left alone and could sleep off their walk, so this was the best time to set off.

We were following map directions from the internet, and everything was going according to plan, until we got to the last two instructions, one that said turn left at a particular junction, and the other (that we only read at last minute), stating that if you reached another point, you had missed the turning. We had already been concerned that we had gone too far, but reading the last line only confirmed it, especially as I had seen the 'gone too far' point a hundred yards previous.

I quickly turned off so we could double back, and as time was getting short, I sped along the route, searching for our missed road, while my partner put the address in the satnav, so we could confirm directions.

As our position was pinpointed by satellite, the voice from the satnav took over that of my other half, and instantly sent us off in a direction that seemed to contradict our other instructions, but blindly following orders, we were taken back in the other direction again, the traffic now five times worse.

Somehow, yet again, we made our destination by the skin of our teeth, found a lucky parking space and rushed to the gate to announce our arrival. Via the intercom, the gate swung open and three dogs, a mother, son and daughter all in matching white fluff, much like little clouds on legs, ran around our feet as we tried to step over them and introduce ourselves to the owner. He obviously rated their opinions very highly and had already made it quite clear on the phone that it was the pets that would be interviewing us, but I wasn't worried. Even as we were invited indoors, it looked as though all the dogs were quite comfortable with my partner, following her like as if she were a dog magnet and bustling to get prime position on the sofa as she sat down next to the owner. I could tell we were being watched closely by all, analysed even, and I almost started to feel a little uncomfortable but fortunately, he went to make coffee and his wife went in search of the cat, whose opinion was also no doubt taken in high regard. I sat awkwardly as the feline sauntered in and walked toward the settee, whereupon the decision was rapidly made that I looked suitable enough, so she jumped up and manoeuvred herself round until the most comfortable spot on my knee was found. Once in position nothing was going to make her move, even as I struggled to reach coffee, or grab our usual question sheet, but really, I was quietly flattered.

Her story was quite unbelievable, a beautiful Persian who had been passed along to several owners, none of whom wanted her, and she had ended up here, a cat amongst dogs. It soon became apparent that she was the boss out of this pack, so things hadn't turned out too bad, and she was loved more than ever.

We continued through details of dog food, electricity points, telephone etcetera when one of the dogs decided the file my partner was writing in looked far more suitable as a bed in which to catch forty winks. He walked over her knee, past her arm, hand, and just flopped onto the pages, and he definitely wasn't moving either. That must have assured the owners that our interview with their pets was going well, but now both of us had one arm or the other pinned down and didn't like to push these doted on animals out of the way, so coffees went cold, notes were abandoned, and we just stroked. After a while, a tour of the house was suggested, so they were finally lifted off by their owners, but they still insisted on following everywhere right up until the moment we said our goodbyes.

We got back in the car, and once we were back on the main road through the village, our journey back was straightforward. The dogs looked pleased to see us back, even if they had only just met us, and we let them out for some fresh air. My other half found a ball, and to the delight of Lady started throwing it, but Emma wasn't really bothered, she was more interested in getting some fuss.

We stayed outside for a while longer, but it was already close to dinner time, and my stomach was in no mood for waiting.

The rest of the evening was gone in a flash, the early morning and long day taking its toll, so by ten-thirty we were in bed, ready for a good night's sleep.

For some reason, another prospective client decided six a.m. on a Saturday morning was a good time to send a text asking if we could reschedule a meeting, and as if that wasn't bad enough, all I could now hear from just outside the bedroom window, was the piercing sound of one tiny blue tit, seemingly with aspirations equal to those of a burly farmyard cockerel intent on waking the whole neighbourhood. Once focused in on the sound, it became more aggravating every minute, so still flinching at every nagging chirp I thought I might as well get up.

Just as I was moving back the duvet, another text arrived, this time waking my other half, who, even half asleep immediately wanted to know, firstly the time, and secondly, the identity of the person who had dared to wake us. I explained against a backdrop of exasperated 'sighs' and disgruntled 'tuts', pointing out the decibel shattering tiny blue cockerel as well, so it wasn't long before my other half was also too agitated to go back to sleep, and instead lay on the pillow with eyes wide open, inwardly grumbling.

We both lay there for a minute, but by the lazy hour of seven a.m. decided to get up to let the dogs out, then blearily had breakfast and prepared for our walk. Yet again, I forgot the gate key, but my now clued-up other half took delight in reminding me to take it, and we set off to the golf course path again. Thinking it had been a one-off yesterday, we let the dogs go leadless, and what did they do? Went straight through the fence again, and wandered around in full view of yet another two golfers, who fortunately, were just as engrossed as the two yesterday, so for the moment went unnoticed. Somehow, we had now mastered the art of shouting authoritatively in a hoarse whisper, and after yet another heart flutter, persuaded our two obedient companions to exit through the next gap, and join us back on to the muddy path.

Later that day we were repeating the episode, (minus the golfers) and as we reached the open space, I could see a boisterous golden retriever heading our way.

Addressing the two dogs I said, "Look! Here comes one of your curly haired cousins."

Before I had chance to complete the proclamation, they were running over to greet whoever it might be, and then all spent a few seconds intertwining like some canine dosey-do, all looking extremely pleased with themselves. Picking up speed to catch up, we found out we had bumped into the brother of our client, so they really had met their cousin.

At four p.m. on the Monday, we received a call saying they would be back by five p.m. so we did our last check in every room, and then waited, the dogs looking on quietly, knowing something was imminent.

My other half, on seeing the car pull into the drive, quickly fluffed up the cushion where she had been sitting, and opened the front door, while I stood in the kitchen with the dogs, who were craning their necks as if would help look round the corner of the door frame.

Their owners appeared and they bounded to greet them with true Labrador enthusiasm, not just tails wagging, but the whole of their bottoms, right down to their back feet which were twisting with all the gyrating.

With rather more reserve, we also said our, "hellos" and after giving a run-down of the weekend, made our exit.

Chapter 11 — Dolly and Pepper

The sit in this short tale, was relatively normal, except for our actual arrival and first day, so worthy of a mention, as once more we were faced with yet another panic.

It began one Monday, and as cats are renowned for being self-sufficient, there was no panic to get to the sit. Their owner worked full-time, so they were used to being alone all day and the venue was only a couple of miles from our home, so we could set off late morning and arrive about ten minutes later.

It all sounded easy enough… famous last words!

There were a few things, however, that we should have taken into consideration.

Our usual pre-visit had happened a couple of months previously, the owner had already left in the early hours, so as far as the two cats were concerned, we could just be two burglars or two squatters raiding their property.

Things started well as we luckily found a rare space to park just outside the terraced house, but as we piled our bags into their territory, one of the cats watched suspiciously, ready to make a dash for it if necessary, and the other just made a dash for it anyway, rapidly disappearing with her belly practically slithering along the floor as if she was running through an extremely low tunnel. Feeling somewhat guilty about the unexpected intrusion, freezer items were quickly dealt with, then we went to formally introduce ourselves as friends. The cats, however, had absolutely no desire to be introduced, and it was plainly obvious that our presence was not wanted… and I mean *really not wanted!*

The one and only cat we could find kept hiding in the furthest corner of any room we entered, peering nervously with eyes like saucers, legs poised to make another emergency escape if we got too close, so it was probably best to leave them alone and let them come to us when they felt ready.

Perhaps ignoring them would be a better strategy!

I hoped!

We returned downstairs to unpack other kitchen items that probably weren't necessary, had lunch, then decided to go in the sitting room to watch television.

Sure enough, as we sat quietly (neither of us hardly daring to speak), the youngest cat, Pepper, at ten years, seemed to come round slightly as his hunger took more of a priority, and he dared come downstairs and venture into the kitchen. I had to follow to get his food, tiptoeing as delicately as possible on the wooden floorboards, then I averted my gaze as he hid behind a table leg to watch. He observed from a safe distance while I filled his bowl with biscuits, then only when he was certain I was leaving the room again did he approach his food.

A few minutes passed and he meowed at the front door needing to go out after his meal, so I edged down the passage, pressed against one wall as if I was in danger of being hit by a sniper, and stretched over to the handle. He shot out of the door like an arrow as the door swung open, so I closed it behind him, and, according to our notes, he would knock on the door when he wanted to come back in.

I couldn't wait to hear that I thought, hoping he would actually want to come back in, now his house had been seconded.

His older companion Dolly still hadn't been seen since our arrival, but we would have to find her soon, as she needed regular thyroid medication, so I optimistically got pate out of the fridge to hide the pill, then cajoled my partner into joining me on a cat-hunt, starting with her last known position, so it could be administered.

That was the plan! After finding her … but a fruitless search of every room meant more worry. She was twenty years old… her medicine was essential… we were the first sitters to be trusted with this task… and at the moment we were absolutely failing!

We checked every open room again, then returned downstairs, an aura of agitation now replacing the previous serene atmosphere. While my partner went back in the sitting room, looking under chairs, behind cupboards, I put the pill-laced pate back in the fridge and tried to remember if either of us had gone outside since our first encounter. I didn't think so, but I was getting that definitely sure, but not absolutely sure conflict. My other half walked into the kitchen to report on her fruitless search and for a while we debated the point, until a sudden movement got my attention.

My hopes of it being our cat were quashed as I turned to see a tiny black face staring at us through the glass patio doors, but it looked so desperate that I couldn't help wrestling with the lock to open the awkward entrance. She scrambled under the metal frame as soon as a gap seeming much too small appeared, one second outside, next second in, almost embodying the eye-deceiving slight of the magician's hand. If only our two cats had been that eager to see us!

The big attraction wasn't us of course, and she made a beeline for the cat bowls to check for any leftovers before anyone could put a stop to it. Having been disappointed at the lack of snacks to plunder, the neighbouring feline knew just how to play on her pretty face accompanied with a pitiful meow, the tried and trusted technique with which she was not unfamiliar, and having recognised two gullible targets, was soon enjoying a couple of cat treats.

Getting her to go out again was another story!

She was like lightening, so by the time you put her outside, got to the door handle to try and get the heavy patio doors closed, she was already back inside, giving you her best pose.

At each attempt, I was getting quicker at the doors, and eventually in a joint effort we managed to beat her determined scramble, only to be left with such a feeling of guilt at the lonely, dejected face staring back, one paw tapping the glass from the other side, that I immediately let her back in.

After that little bit of excitement, my partner decided to water the plants in the front garden, and enticed the visitor into following her out, so Pepper seized the opportunity to slope back in without knocking, while I constructed one of my cappuccinos, two of my cappuccinos actually, to savour in the back garden as it was a sunny day. For a while we both tried to relax, but always lurking in the background was the reminder of the pill, so downing the final swig of coffee, I went to comb the house again, our timeline for administering the medicine now running short. With another thorough but unproductive search undertaken, I returned downstairs stating with a fair amount of panic that my other half should help me find the absent patient. We looked under beds, in beds, behind cupboards, above cupboards, any and everywhere we hadn't investigated before! She was nowhere to be seen!

Having experienced the disappearing cat phenomenon before, we wanted to remain confident, but as time crept by and our search became more and more thorough, we reached the only possible remaining conclusion, that we must have missed her going out of one of the doors.

Could there have been a flaw in our vigilant security precautions?

Could she have sneaked out while we were searching another room? Or when we let Pepper out... or was it when the front door was open... or was it when we were drinking our coffee?

It didn't matter how many times we tried to work out how it happened, when it happened, where it happened... it had happened!

When it got to ten p.m. we were more than really concerned, we were both desperate after yet another exhaustive but fruitless search of the house, so went outside, not for the first time, to look for her.

As I opened the front door, the little black cat from next door shot through, making us both jump backwards in shock, and made another dash to the cat bowls. We were too flustered to be sociable at the moment, so after a chase round the furniture a few times, she was yet again put out, and the door pushed to, while I went to the front gate.

I couldn't believe my eyes!

Underneath our car I could see Pepper, and what's more, he was staring at another cat...

Could it be?

Is it?

They seemed to know each other, and I was sure he must be trying to reassure Dolly it was okay to come back indoors.

What good fortune!

I calmly (sort of calmly), walked back down the path to coax him back in, then perhaps she would follow. I called his name, then took up my sniper avoiding position flat against the wall to allow the widest gap at the entrance, and after a few nerve-racking seconds he started to walk up the path.

Please follow him! I was thinking!

Invitingly, I held the door wide open, but it wasn't going to be that easy. Instead of walking in, he stalled a couple of feet away (after all, he still didn't know who we were, or why we were there), so decided to play it safe and jumped up onto the front wall, with no intention of crossing the threshold. My heart sank, and I was just in the process of closing the door, when I saw his car companion walking cautiously up the path. Not daring to move, holding my breath for the umpteenth time, I tried to surreptitiously push the door wide open again, and fade into the wallpaper backdrop so as not to put her off.

Guess what! Yep... the wall was more inviting. She jumped up next to Pepper, and they both lay there, paws tucked underneath their chests, eyes watching every move, and resolve not waning in the least!

If he wasn't coming in... and he definitely wasn't... neither was she!

Against the advice of you-know-who from behind the door in the living room, I tried my best cat coaxing noises to get them to come in, but taking a discreet peep, I could see it was doing little to help the situation. Being telepathic, they were already staring at the spot where my eyes materialised, and the more I tried to invite Dolly back in, the more she looked ready to bolt. I hastily backed further away from the door, but it was already too late... she was gone! Unsuccessfully trying to close the door silently, my own telepathic powers were telling me I was in for another 'I told you so'! ... and the only way to avoid it was to quickly get out of the way, so I decided it was a good time for me to do more unpacking. I tiptoed upstairs, every creaking step guaranteeing failure in my quest to be silent, and walked to the front bedroom to shuffle clothes round in our suitcase for a couple of minutes. As I took a step through the doorway, I took a double take and stood like a statue, not daring to make a sound, not daring to move a muscle, gaping at our missing cat stretched out on the bed, incidentally looking nothing like the cat that I was, just a few moments ago, trying to persuade to come in. No wonder she had a questioning look in her eyes—a bit like... "What? Me? You want me to come in? Why?"

I knew Dolly had seen me and was primed for another bolt, so I tried to blend into the wallpaper once more, then stepped backwards out of the bedroom to relay the good news to my partner.

I blurted some sort of garbled explanation, trying to get the words out of my mouth too quickly, then wanting confirmation I said, "Come and look!"

There had been little point disturbing my better half, because by the time we got upstairs, she was nowhere to be seen again, which then activated yet another fruitless search.

Did this house have secret passages, I mused?

For a while, I started to doubt my sanity, wondered if I was seeing things, speculated if I had imagined seeing our missing cat!

As I contemplated the onset of madness, my perplexed other half returned downstairs.

Not one to ever give up, I remained resolute in my purpose, I could not give up until the reputation of my sanity was restored, so I set about the most thorough search yet undertaken, no stone would remain unturned.

Methodically, I began in the office at the far end of the house, looking under and behind every piece of furniture but to no avail. Next to the office was a small single bedroom. I looked under the wardrobe, behind the wardrobe, then did the same with the chest of drawers and a cupboard, deciding they were definitely free of hostages. That only left the litter bin and the bed. I checked the bin just to be sure then peered under the bed.

No sign!

As I pulled back the cover to continue my investigation, it occurred to me that it was extremely long, draping on the floor on both sides with plenty to spare, and could conceal cat paws between the bed and the wall easily. I knelt on the bed and tried to peek over the side, but the duvet and cover were so thick that they touched the wall and there was no space between. No cat was visible, and I nearly walked away, but something was still niggling at the back of my mind… I had to pull the bed away from the wall before I was happy.

As I did a long tail came into view, followed by the rest of an extremely worried looking cat, and although I was ready to shout, 'hallelujah' at the top of my voice, I decided on a more discreet method of jubilation, so parading a wide grin from ear to ear, I went to find my better half.

Chapter 12 — Ollie, Marley, Tom, and Rosy

We had never looked after a puppy so were relishing the thought of a few days with a five-month-old dachshund. Suddenly, we had big ideas about training him... we had seen many a programme on the dos and don'ts of dog obedience... we could be influential in his upbringing... we could help him grow up to be a well-balanced, confident, friendly adult.

However, that was before we met the idolised little baby with the adoring owners. One look from his big brown eyes and he could do whatever he wanted he could have anything his little canine heart desired.

We had to get there first, and the journey to meet everyone for the familiar pre-visit was not one of a tranquil nature. I had scribbled down the instructions given to me over the phone on the only paper I could find at the time, which turned out to be a couple of bits of ripped scrap paper, then trying to use one leg as a desk, whilst balancing on the other, propped up against a door frame with phone wedged between my shoulder and my chin, all meant my writing was never going to be easy to follow. As they dictated, I had tried to write down as many details as I could, positive that the owners must know the best way to their own house, and so confident was I in the fact, that I had neglected to check the directions on the internet, even bothered to bring the satnav, or try reading my own scrawl before we left.

Had I gone mad?

For a while, things were going to plan, as I had actually remembered to bring the instructions, but now I couldn't understand my own hieroglyphics, I seemed to be without page two, and let me tell you… it wasn't going down well!

Getting to the M20, leaving the M20 was easy, but arriving in the town centre, nothing looked anything like the instructions and a wild goose chase round a one-way system only intensified the situation further. I was sat next to an unamused, irritated and uncooperative 'not going to touch the map' partner, who continued for several miles of praying it was the right direction, until fortunately, I saw a name on a signpost that rang a faint bell in my memory from the telephone call. Then as luck would have it, by also picking out a well-informed local to ask directions, it turned out that we were on the right route after all, and it was just the third road along to our destination.

I could breathe again!

Deciding to park on the road rather than in their drive, we both jumped out and hurried to the front door, where a ginger cat scuttled away as we took him by surprise. After watching from a distance, he must have concluded that it was safe enough to come back to get acquainted until the door opened, so he sauntered over, meowing loudly, to enjoy a stroke, and shed a multitude of ginger hairs on our trousers at the same time.

The door suddenly swung wide open, and as we introduced ourselves, the cat hurried between everyone's legs, just as an almost identical cat circled around our legs to avoid him, ran out and disappeared in the garden.

"They're brothers," we were told, "but they don't really like each other."

In their youth, apparently, plenty of cat hair had been lost between them, but now a little older and wiser, the two rivals could just about pass on the doorstep without starting a skirmish.

I followed my better half, following the owners through the hallway, until we all came to an abrupt halt at the next door. I could hear some sort of scratching noise coming from the opposite side, and as the door was gently pushed open, through a slight gap I could make out one cute dachshund, and judging from the angle he was lying, he must have been doing an extremely convincing imitation of a draught excluder. Stretched across the width of the entrance, all four paws were pressed against the door to prevent anyone entering.

His Greta Garbo moment of 'vanting to be alone' was short-lived, as bit by bit he was edged backwards, until the gap was big enough for one person to squash through and move him. A few more shoves and he surrendered, jumping out of the way as if door barricading was from that moment, no longer a priority. Welcoming his owners, along with the strangers that accompanied them was much more important, and he ran between the four of us, eagerly greeting everyone.

I stared down at him, quite surprised. He was so long, altogether so much bigger than I had expected, he was long haired, and he didn't look like a puppy one bit.

In my head I had pictured a short haired, miniature dachshund, a completely different kettle of fish, and this character was a giant in comparison... but extremely handsome with it. With every step, his long wavy coat swished to and fro like a shampoo commercial, and he looked every inch a pedigree... from the tip of his extra-long nose, right through his extra-long body, to the end of his extra-long tail.

We learnt that ever since he had joined the household, the feuding cats had removed themselves out to the front of the house in disgust, and he lived in the back, the two factions hardly ever meeting, but it seemed a shame to me that it should be so divided.

The rest of our meeting went well, and we arranged to be back a few weeks later to do the sit.

Arriving on schedule, I just expected a quick recap on our instructions before they left, so was quite surprised to walk in to bags, cameras, boots, coats spaced across the hall carpet, the lady of the house finishing a few emails before even starting her packing, and the man of the house perusing E-bay before packing anything into one of their cars parked in the driveway. I had mulled over which car to park in front of, not to be in the way, so I hoped I had made the right choice.

We, or rather my partner, decided that we should take Tom the dachshund out for a walk rather than stand around not knowing what to do, so we grabbed a lead by the back door and off we went. Keeping to the roads for once, as our trusty Wellies hadn't been unpacked yet, our walk was quite enjoyable, and Tom seemed very well behaved... that is up until the moment a squirrel rushed in front of us and ran up a tree in one of the nearby gardens. My other half and I visibly jumped with shock as Tom let out a piercing, shrieking noise, something like a cross between a yelp, a screech and a baying wolf, and my other half jolted forward, as he, Tom tried to make a dash after it. That iron grip holding the lead soon brought him to an abrupt halt, so he tried again but made no headway, and it took a few minutes of calming down before we could resume our relaxed, steady pace. We had, however, discovered a very satisfactory 'walk around the block'.

If I was surprised that his owners weren't packed when we arrived, I was even more taken aback when they were ready to go in the short time we were out on our stroll. Everything had disappeared from the hall carpet, the car was packed, so after a final cuddle with their baby, they were off.

Back in the kitchen, a massive drawer had been emptied, and one of their two fridges had been designated for our use only, so unpacking our food was a doddle compared to normal.

So it was agreed, it must be time for coffee.

We took our mugs into a large conservatory, dominated by a full-size pool table taking centre stage, and sunk in to the two soft armchairs facing the television at the opposite side. Tom sat down in front of my chair, shuffling nearer as if preparing for a jump, so before anything could get spilt, I put my coffee on a handy small table, then tapped my knees as an invitation.

He made a tentative leap.

His front half was on my knee, but the back half was still on the ground. What a long dog!

I tried lifting my legs as a half way step, squashing to one side of the seat, and seeing if I could pull the back half up, but the chair swivelled round, and my elbow swished dangerously close to the coffee mug. The serious look I was getting from my better half did nothing to stop my suppressed amusement, as we spun back the opposite way, and I started to giggle, made worse by the sight of Tom supporting his weight on one back paw resting on my foot, while the other searched in mid-air for another step.

My sniggering seemed to be sucking away any strength I had… my arm muscles and my leg muscles felt about as strong as a wet lettuce. We had to give up!

I lowered him back to safe ground and took a deep breath. Tom watched, looking disappointed and totally left out, so I decided to move over to the settee where there was plenty of space, expecting him to follow. Instead he walked off towards the door into the kitchen. For a second, I thought he must be leaving, insulted to be the cause of amusement… but at the last minute he turned, and made one almighty charge at the settee. The additional velocity just gave him enough height to land on the cushion next to mine, and before I knew it, he had shuffled himself on to a comfy spot, and there he stayed until coffee time was over.

By late afternoon, it was time for a proper walk, fully attired in Wellies and all.

We had already decided to try and get cats and dog more acquainted during our stay, so as soon as the harness was firmly attached, I went ahead and opened the door firstly into the passage, then to the undisputed domain of the cats, the hallway to the front door. By the time my partner arrived at the doorway, Tom was already trying to fling himself at the cat food bowl, which shocked the cats so much they just made a dash for the door, and stood flat against it like pressed flowers, backs arched to the highest position. I could hear Ollie giving an eerie cat growl somewhere in the depths of his throat, while Marley opted for a much more audible hiss, but this just shifted the attention of our trusty canine from the unreachable food to themselves, and he started shrieking in excitement as he tried his utmost to get to them. With my partner hanging onto the lead, Marley was running on the spot, grappling to get a foothold on the long straw mat that stretched from one end of the hall to the other, each step dragging it further backwards until it was completely rolled up by our feet. Through the deafening racket I quickly unlocked the heavy door, deciding that perhaps an introduction wasn't on the cards today, and both cats shot out so fast, a 'catapult' wouldn't have made it any quicker.

My trusty partner was still straining to hold back our excited pal as we went out of the driveway, his eyes and nose searching every nook and cranny in the front garden as he veered from left to right, but gradually there were other things to divert his attention, and we could continue our walk, in peace. We followed a path at the bottom of the road, which in turn took us into a secluded valley with lots of blackberry bushes, plum trees, wild garlic, and numerous wild flowers… the only trouble was the steep wood-come-mud steps you had to negotiate to get there. Was I glad it wasn't me holding back the enthusiastic Tom on his extending lead as he ran ahead with excitement?

The following day was beautiful.

The cats had been fed, we had been for our walk, we had sunbathed in the garden over coffee, brushed all pets, and had now left Tom outside while we got our lunch ready. I heard him start barking for some reason, so abandoning kitchen duties for a minute, went to investigate, and walked round the garden, round the back of the garage, round the two sheds shouting his name, but he was nowhere to be seen. The barking sounded fairly close, which was a slight reassurance, but I was starting to worry, and the constant yapping was surely going to annoy the neighbours by now, so I ran back indoors to relate the situation, then ran back out, closely followed by my partner.

"He must have found a gap in one of the hedges," I said, when all hiding places in the garden had been exhausted.

That thought really got the heart racing!

He might be able to get through to the front and on to the road if the other garden isn't secure!

The barks weren't so continuous now, but following the sound to the loudest spot, I peered through the bottom of the hedge and could just about make out a furry shape, snuffling in the neighbour's garden. My better half kept calling his name, which I hoped wasn't also irritating the neighbours, while I tried to push some branches out of the way to get his attention. Surprisingly, he did come over and make the effort to get back through, but the foliage was much too thick. I could see him pacing up and down the hedge trying to find a gap for a while, but failing miserably went back to his spot, and started biting one of the bright red apples scattered under a tree.

I could see what the big attraction was now!

At least he was occupied there, and not trying to escape.

I left my partner calling to him, while I dashed through the house and ran next door to ring the doorbell, managing to startle the one cat relaxing on the doorstep, then the other under a car as I went. I peered round the side of the neighbour's house, checking for any escape routes, while I waited for someone to answer the door, and as soon as it opened I started garbling some high-speed explanation whilst almost edging myself through the door past him. The elderly gentleman shuffled down the hall and began unbolting several locks, then fumbled for a key to let the two of us out, while I pondered on the notion of everything except myself just having converted to half-speed. He was still pushing the door open as I scuttled past, eyes searching for the heavily laden tree as I rushed to where I thought Tom should be. There he was, still engrossed in apple eating, turning a totally deaf ear to the shouts from the other side of the hedge.

A miraculous cure occurred almost instantaneously, because he sure heard my feet stomping rapidly in his direction, and hastily spat out what was left of the fruit before turning, head held down low, desperately sad eyes staring pitifully up, and walking his slowest walk in my direction.

I made a dramatic grab as if he might try and run off, but he didn't, and he was safe!

I was so relieved that I couldn't be mad, and at a much more acceptable tempo, expressed my thanks to our neighbour before carrying the runaway back home.

On our return, there was no sign of any cat, and Tom, feet firmly planted back on home territory looked so pleased with himself, and ran through to the garden where my other half was still calling his name. He jumped up and stretched his body to its longest, just reaching her hand for a welcome home stroke, which took her completely by surprise, with no time to realise she could have stopped calling his name some time ago.

The next thing to do was barricade any gaps in the fence... we didn't want a repeat performance.

Funny I should say that, because the very next day we were sitting outside in the sun having morning coffee after our walk down into the valley, Tom keeping cool under the table after a massive drink of water. I was engrossed in a puzzle in the newspaper, while my better half perused the news, and neither of us noticed Tom wander to the hedge and start biting at a piece of the wire fence.

Another few minutes and the barking started!

We both looked up, looked at each other, looked under the table, then ran to the hedge. The hole from yesterday was still secure, so he had found another way through.

There was no point wasting time trying to get him to come back through the hedge, I might as well just go next door and apologise to the neighbour yet again.

Both cats were outside in the front garden, soaking up the sun as far away from each other as possible, and glanced up in turn as I passed their spot, but weren't really that interested. Hurriedly, I pressed the bell, shuffling from foot to foot as I gave him plenty of time to get to the door, but all seemed quiet. I stared through the glass quickly, trying not to look too nosy, but couldn't see any movement.

This plan was not going well.

I had waited more than long enough, and as intermittently turning to stare at the door while I walked back down the driveway didn't make him magically appear, we would need to enforce 'Plan B'.

I was trying to decide what that might be as I returned, and hurried over to my partner who was on hands and knees, peering through the hedge, trying unsuccessfully to persuade Tom to stop barking.

I clambered between two spiky shrubs, and stretched out my hand as if it had a goodie in it, but he wasn't interested, so I crawled a bit further. My partner held back the wire where it had been well and truly chewed, and I scrambled underneath, twigs and thorns pulling my hair, and grabbing on to my tee-shirt as if they were trying to prevent me ever leaving, but I made it to the other side only slightly scarred. Tom hardly noticed; he was too busy staring at himself in a large mirror leant up against a tree, and barked incessantly to warn the identical imposter not to come any closer. I crawled over, hoping our neighbour hadn't made an untimely return and was now watching the tale unfold from his kitchen window, ready to recount a full and true report of the whole episode.

I kept low to the ground just in case.

Tom jumped as I grabbed him and ushered him back towards the gap, and he was desperate to get back to the intruder but was rapidly steered in to the waiting grasp of my better half.

He was back, now it was my turn.

The shrubs were just as persistent at keeping me out as they had been letting me go in the first place, and I emerged looking more like the 'Man from Atlantis', bits of plants threaded through my dishevelled hair, and clothes adorned with long strands of green foliage. While I was brushed down, it was Tom's opportunity to get away without a telling-off, and by the time we had rechecked the boundary, and blocked every slight gap, any weak looking bit of fence with a heavy plant pot, surrounded with boulders or piles of rocks he was snoring away in his favourite position… upside down in his bed.

Our barricading was quite successful and there was no further occurrence over our stay, but I would be informing his owners on their return.

Permission had been given to let Tom off the lead in the valley, but we hadn't attempted it yet, especially after hearing tales of him chasing rabbits and disappearing for ages, but it seemed a shame that he couldn't charge around in such a big open space, and tire himself out in the process, so the following day we decided it was time to give it a try. At first, we must have looked like an army patrol guarding a prisoner, I marched at the front, Tom in the middle, my partner watching from the back, and it was working quite well. He didn't like wandering in the thicket too much, because he usually ended up with briars and twigs stuck in the long hair on his legs, or somewhere even more delicate, and wouldn't budge till they had been removed, a process which could take almost delicate surgery at times. There we were in our smart formation, just going back up the seventy odd steps to the top path when he spotted a squirrel, and gave chase in the woods. He was oblivious to any shouts from behind, so while my partner went back to the bottom, doing that familiar call, I followed his route through the trees, struggling to balance on the steep bank littered with a number of branches and vines to either duck under, or not fall over. I was just about able to keep him in view, while I tottered unsteadily from the back, but the squirrel wasn't hanging about, jumping from tree to tree into the distance until it disappeared. Tom slowed down with nothing to chase, and it looked as though his ability to hear was making a comeback again, because he was peering in the right direction, but making absolutely no attempt to return to my better half. He just plonked himself down where he was, and stared at her through a slight gap in the trees. I could see his neck twisting to keep her in view as she worriedly paced across the field below, but he still didn't make a move.

While his attention had been diverted, I had almost caught up, and only a few snapping twigs alerted him to my approach, but by then it was too late to make a getaway, and he walked towards me, head bowed, waiting for a telling-off (which he got). I shouted down to my better half that he was found, then back on the lead once more, I escorted Tom back to the steps and we all went home.

He was ready for a drink by the time we got back, and hardly noticed the cats, one observing from the safety of a car roof, the other lounging smack in the middle of a flowering plant, a flat flowering plant that is, watching us walk to the gates, and as soon as we were through he was head down, in the bowl of water for an age.

While he slept off his hike, we went to the front and brushed the cats, which they both absolutely loved. It was essential to make sure there was always a fair space between them, because one or the other would frequently flop on the floor in ecstasy during the pampering, and if a loose paw or tail hit the other it was practically the equivalent of a slap in the face with a gauntlet. The relaxing mood would be firmly shattered in an instant, as paws and claws were put on high alert, ears pulled back flat, all accompanied by a mean scowl.

At night they managed to be civil, and while Tom was safely tucked up in bed in the kitchen, they would come upstairs with us, and enjoy a bit more pampering. If I tried to do a puzzle, Ollie would keep tapping the end of the pencil, so anything I wrote was unreadable, while Marley would keep nuzzling his head into the back of the book my better half was trying to read. Instead of reading a few pages, she would end up reading one page over and over after losing her place,

Eventually we would both give up… two smug cats getting the attention they rightly deserved.

One night Ollie was in a particularly lively mood, and as I was getting comfortable in the bed, moving both cats out of the way to get enough space, he leapt on my foot, pinned it down with his front paws and started biting through the duvet. Marley jumped down and took refuge under the dressing table, as I yelped and pulled it out of the way, but that was it!

He was in a right hunting mood.

Every time I tried to move, he made a lunge, and from the shuffling and sighing from the other side of the bed, I sensed my better half was on the verge of suggesting all cats be removed. I quickly pushed him out of the way, but he spotted my hand sneaking back under the covers, and made another dive, claws stabbing repeatedly, as the music from 'Psycho' played in my mind. I stifled a few more whimpers before lying totally motionless as if the music had just stopped in a game of musical statues, and eventually I must have fallen asleep.

The rest of our time was fairly uneventful, the daily routine running smoothly, apart from a couple of the Greta Garbo moments, which I soon found a way to deal with. If I couldn't get in, I would wait quietly for a few seconds, then suddenly bang on the door and it would make him jump out of the way in shock. It worked every time, so I think he must have just got bored, and gave up.

On the day we were leaving, the house was spic-and-span, the cats and Tom were smartly brushed, and our car seemed to be crammed with just as much as when we arrived, which was strange because we'd used up most of our provisions, so we were all ready. Somehow the pet owners managed to get in without any of us hearing them, and as they peeped round the door Tom looked up sleepily from his cosy position between the two of us on the settee. In the brief second before he realised who had walked in, they could see he was quite content, but then it was complete mayhem, as he squealed, jumped, ran, flopped over to have his tummy tickled, jumped up to race round again, and eventually brought to a standstill by a big hug.

I had written down everything they needed to know, especially the fence situation, so we said our goodbyes, stroked all pets, and were soon heading home.

2nd visit

After a New Year break, we were off to stay with Tom the dachshund again. He looked pleased enough to see us but was definitely subdued compared to last time... Was he going to be the first dog sensitive to his owner's departure?

We kept an eye on him during a quiet uneventful evening, all three of us succumbing to absolute lethargy until the only course of action was to get an early night for once, so my half-asleep partner went out of the back door with Tom, while I opened the front door to get Marley and Ollie, the ginger cats in from their last outing of the day. The hinges creaked loudly as I swung open the door, and the two of them appeared from opposite sides of the garden, their casual saunter changing to a trot in a subtle race to be first indoors, and more importantly, the first one to the food. Not breaking with tradition, a last-minute snack was always needed to sustain them through the dark hours, and it was the only time they would share a bowl, although they never looked each other in the eye, particularly from such close proximity, as it would surely be seen as a sign of a challenge. While they munched away, I wandered back in to the kitchen.

No one was there!

Strange that they weren't back yet, I thought, poking my head round the frame of the back door, and instantly getting a full-frontal view of my better half marching back from the garden, stern face moulded into a now wideawake deep frown. I ducked back quickly, just in case I was the cause, and moved to a safe distance before she stomped in.

"What's wrong?" I gently enquired, "Where's Tom?"

"He won't come in," came the exasperated reply… "and he keeps running off when I get anywhere near him… so I can't put him on the lead."

I suggested a double attack… between us we could corner the absconder and have him in his bed before you know it.

My simple strategy was far too naive.

This was turning into a fantastic game through the eyes of a playful dachshund, and he thwarted all attempts of capture, so confident in his talent that he would come teasingly close, leaving it to the very last second before making a dash. By now I could practically see a red-hot aura glowing around the head of my partner in the dark, as her patience was running so thin it was practically transparent, and within seconds a curt voice informed me I could do it on my own.

I tried the friendly voice, the angry voice, the calm assertive voice. I went through a whole repertoire of voices, but I might as well have saved my breath.

Feeling fairly agitated, I was sure my expression now resembled that of my partner a few minutes ago, and I utilised a similar stomp towards the back door, closing it behind me while I reassessed options. Slightly unnerved to find my other half stood in the dark kitchen like some ghostly apparition resigned to unrest, unable to move on while some business remained unfinished, I walked past to get to the 'goodie cupboard'.

Any discussion would be pointless at the moment, so still in silence, I opened the back door again, peered into the darkness and rustled a bag of dog treats, optimistically expecting Tom to run to my side... but nothing happened.

I took a step nearer to the garden and did the same... I called his name... I rustled the bag... I called his name.

It usually worked!

Didn't he know this game of hide-n-seek had been over ages ago?

I turned back towards the kitchen, to see if my ghostly partner had any other suggestions (knowing none of them would be repeatable), and would you believe it, there between the flowers was Tom, the dog. He had been observing all my efforts sitting just behind me, barely a yard away.

He was soon in that bed let me tell you!

The following morning, as usual, I was the first to get up, so having showered and dressed, I went to get the morning order of one dog and two cat breakfasts underway.

I served the cats their dried food and a bowl of wet food which they always tucked into eagerly, then immediately lost interest once the gravy had been consumed, then I could let Tom out of the conservatory, and get his breakfast while he went out. Opening the door, I knelt on the floor for our usual greeting of head nuzzling, tummy tickling, and a few kisses and I felt relieved to see him looking more like his normal self.

He wasn't out long, then I tidied the kitchen while he did his usual examination of the contents in his bowl, picking out bits of chicken whilst avoiding any dog food.

Walking past the glass doors of the conservatory again, I spotted something in the middle of the floor... now I understand... it was the result of an upset tummy... no wonder he looked subdued yesterday (I could see why my other half always let me check everything out before emerging from the bedroom).

My clean up didn't take too long, and I went to give Tom a sympathetic stroke, so he knew he wasn't in any trouble. I stared down at his apologetic brown eyes, put out a consoling hand, then luckily, just before stroking him I spotted the fur on his neck all stuck together with the same substance I had just cleared up.

Thank goodness I had spotted it first!

But then I remembered earlier... I squirmed at the thought of our first greeting of the day... but surely, I would have noticed if I had touched that coagulated fur, stroked it, even kissed it... wouldn't I?

The first thing on the agenda after our walk today would definitely be a dog bath.

A few days later, and this was one of those occasions, of which there are not many of, that I was grateful my trusty other half was still enjoying the warmth of a cosy duvet with no intention of giving it up until necessary.

I, on the other hand, had done all the morning chores and thought I would make preparations for our next call of duty. We were going straight to the next sit from here, and taking our own bedding, which as yet, needed the clean covers putting back on, so now would be an ideal time to do it.

I went to our car, got the pillows from the boot, then the king-size duvet from the back seat where it had been nestling under the seat cover, and quickly transported it through the front door before any could drop on the floor. The only place I could deal with it would be in the living room.

Sure enough... as soon as I put the duvet down, an inquisitive little dog firstly stood all over it while he sniffed and examined it thoroughly, then having noticed how comfortable it was, stretched his extra-long dachshund body straight across the middle and lay down.

I let him enjoy the moment while I squashed the pillows in to the pillow cases, then with one final almost envious look I set about removing him and wrestling the duvet cover in position. It is usually the latter that I have trouble with, but in this case, I seemed to have discovered a talent of Tom dog that was previously hidden... he could defy gravity. Even with the duvet held almost vertical he would not give up his spot, and stayed anchored until he was practically upside-down like the man in the advert for superglue. We were locked in a silent duel for a moment but gradually his antigravity super powers wore off, and he ungracefully rolled off the edge on to the carpet.

In the corner of my eye I could already see Tom making another approach, thinking this was another fun game so I quickly slung the cover across the floor and grabbed two corners of the duvet to push them in... but too slow!

Tom was now trying to nuzzle his way on to the duvet again and in doing so was getting himself all tangled up in the cover... the beautifully ironed cover that is... the beautifully ironed cover that my partner had spent quite some time doing, particularly hampered by her broken wrist (That's another story, but I'll save that for another time)!

I pulled it away, shuffled him back onto the carpet bit by bit, then listened to make sure there was no movement from upstairs. This time he couldn't be bothered to come back, that game was getting boring, so I grappled with the gigantic duvet until the cover was in place, and was so glad when (amazingly still looking freshly ironed) it was safely back in the car.

The rest of the day was quite ordinary, the weather not brilliant, so I had been playing pool against myself, while my other half soaked up plenty of television viewing. It was not until I went to top up the cat food bowl at teatime that it occurred to me that I had only seen one cat all day.

That in itself, was not so shocking as they avoided each other as much as possible, but when it came to food, Ollie was never one to be at the back of the queue. I opened the front door to see if he was waiting to be let in, but no sign. I walked into the bedrooms to see if he had got shut in by accident, and still no sign.

It was too early at the moment to put out a missing person's alert, so I left Marley enjoying a stress-free meal alone for once, and went back to join in the television viewing, but every now and then, one of us would check the front door. When it got to nine o'clock, this was definitely out of the ordinary, so after opening the front door for the umpteenth time, yet another cat search was set in motion. My better half checked the rooms that I had already checked downstairs, looking under tables, chairs, in cupboards, under settees, so off we went upstairs to do the same. Just as I walked past our bed to look underneath the wardrobe at the far corner, a paw shot out from under the valance, and tried to grab my foot.

I jumped a mile, accompanied by a loud, "Agh!"

This brought my other half running, and the paw shot out again as she passed.

Panic over!

Yet again things went well, and the only other mild anxiety was caused by the owners themselves.

We were expecting them about eight in the morning, but because the car was safely off the road, the packing of the boot had been done the previous evening, still leaving plenty of bags and trolleys to get into the back, and we still had to wash the bedding, and pack fridge and freezer things up.

I awoke slightly dazed, because I'd already been awake a few times, 'things to remember before leaving' running through my mind, and other such questions. It was still dark, so I wasn't sure what the time was, but I gradually started thinking I had heard a phone somewhere in the distance... was it a dream?

Now I was wide awake, so quickly got dressed and ran downstairs to dial 1471 to see if I had been correct, and sure enough, there had been a call at five-forty and I could see the answerphone flashing rapidly with a message. I pressed play.

"Just to let you know that our plane arrived early, and we should be back in about fifteen minutes."

What time was it now? How long ago had the message been received?

I charged back up the stairs, cats meowing through one door, Tom whining through the other, and gently woke my better half with a shout of, "Are you awake? I'm putting the lights on. They'll be here in quarter of an hour."

Even before her eyes had got accustomed to the sudden blast of light, my partner was already heading to the en suite, then was back in a flash to help unmake the bed. I scooped up the sheet, duvet cover and pillowcases, and ran off to the laundry, while she got dressed, and by the time I had fed the cats and Tom, she was downstairs, our bedroom things standing in the hallway. Very impressive!

It was now my turn to amaze, by actually squashing everything in to the car, including the fridge and freezer bags, which had now joined the end of the queue, and it felt almost a military style operation, the way things were falling into place so quickly and efficiently.

We were just trying to shut the back doors of our car, without anything falling out, as their car pulled in to the driveway… although I don't know how… I was still half asleep.

Later that Year

This was it!

A first email had asked if we would be happy to do it.

The second had suggested it might be happening.

A phone call confirmed it was really going ahead.

Yes... we were going to take charge of our first puppy... eleven weeks old.

Were we excited?

You bet!

Rosy was to be the new friend for Tom the dachshund, and even though he had been less than a year old when we first met, this was our first real puppy.

We knew the owners would have already left when we arrived at the house, but we were met at the door by their cleaner, who invited us in, then smiling broadly, beckoned us to follow her into the kitchen. We trailed behind quickly, then stood motionless, watching intently as she leant over a baby-gate and lifted a dark little bundle in to her arms.

The second she turned back to present our latest companion we were both immediately besotted, captivated by the two sleepy eyes staring back at us, and the temptation was just too much for my other half to resist.

Accompanied by a loud "Ahh!" She scooped the warm little body into her own arms, and after allowing me a couple of strokes, disappeared into the conservatory to sit and cuddle Rosy in comfort.

I looked round for Tom, expecting him to be wanting his fair share of attention, but he was nowhere to be seen, so asked if he was outside.

"No...he's gone with them on their canal boating trip," came the reply. "He's got his own life jacket specially."

I smiled at the thought of his long body enclosed in the jacket, long-haired tail swishing out at the back, his four short legs proudly bouncing along the deck, and no doubt he would think he was Captain.

My other half had returned by now, and placed Rosy back in her bed the other side of the baby gate, but she didn't want to sleep. Instead, Rosy took a few steps on to the kitchen floor, crouched, and suddenly a puddle started to form between her back legs. There was a sudden commotion as the two of us and the cleaner made a useless attempt to open the kitchen door and get her outside, but we were all too late. She was put out anyway, but obviously nothing would happen now.

The cleaner mopped the floor as two sad eyes stared at her through the cat flap, and just the sight of that little face looking up as I peered out of the window made me open the door immediately.

She got straight back in the bed and settled down to more resting.

The cleaner clattered the bucket outside to wash, then carried on with the chores until lunchtime, while we went to and fro, putting our bags in various rooms, so by the time we had finished, it was time for her to leave… not before giving Rosy another little hug first.

"Have a good weekend," she called, looking back and waving at the two of us stroking Ollie and Marley in the doorway, then just before getting in her car, added, "and see you Tuesday."

Ollie waited for the car to disappear, then wandered out in to the front garden, while Marley decided it was time for a quick snack, and walked over to the food bowl.

It was almost a race back to the kitchen, to see who could get to Rosy first and pick her up for a cuddle. *She must wonder what's happening,* I thought!

Separated from her litter mates and brought to a new house only a couple of weeks ago, just getting used to living with new people and another dog, and now left alone with another two total strangers.

That little puppy was about to be smothered in affection.

(I wonder if I'd have thought that after waking every morning to cleaning up puddles and packages on the kitchen floor, but that was par for the course I suppose).

The rest of the day was easy, no dog walking because Rosy couldn't go out until her injections had taken effect, and the cats weren't hard work, so I spent quite a while on the pool table. It's a good job that my better half was engrossed in snuggling the cute Rosy, otherwise the clanging of the balls as they catapulted round the table missing the pockets would have soon worn thin. Any time either of us saw the tiny puppy slightly awake, she was rapidly whisked outside before any accidents could happen, and so far, so good.

When it came to her dinnertime, neither of us wanted to miss it, and Rosy definitely looked eager.

I measured out the dried food, then starting as we meant to go on, I held up the bowl and gave the instruction to "Sit!" in a commanding voice.

She was far too busy staring at the bowl as if I wasn't attached to it, so I tried again.

My partner gently pushed her bottom to the floor, but she hardly noticed, fixated on the out-of-reach food, and wondering how to get at it. She immediately stood up and tried balancing on her two stubby hind legs but that definitely wasn't going to work.

A few attempts later, we were becoming somewhat of an annoyance to the hungry Rosy, but eventually she sat and waited for the bowl to be placed on the floor, then once the signal was given, she could tuck in.

And boy did she tuck in!

She ate like ten starving lions… and there was hardly time to blink before she was licking round an empty bowl, sliding it around the kitchen floor, to get any last bit of flavour from the glaze round the edge. I fully expected the food to make a sudden reappearance, but it was staying put, so that was a relief.

Not long after, we all went for a wander round the garden, until Rosy had done anything that needed to be done, which was scooped into the special bin, and we could all go back and relax for a while... as if we needed to... we had hardly done anything all day!

When it came to bedtime, that was a different story.

It had already occurred to me that this was going to be her first night totally alone.

Previously she had been with her brothers and sisters, then she had Tom for company (even though there was a gate between them at night apparently), and now there was no one.

Her little face looked as sad as a little face could get, as we gave her a last goodie before saying goodnight, then turned off the lights and disappeared upstairs.

It wasn't long before a little whinge started building up in to a louder whimper.

My partner shouted her name, and it went silent for a few seconds, but soon I could hear the moans starting up again, so I took my turn. We must be resolute!

"Rosy! Shh!"

It went quiet again.

I kept listening, expecting more of a battle, but we were lucky because it didn't happen again, and before I knew it, I was waking up to a new day.

As soon as I walked into the kitchen, before even speaking to Rosy, I grabbed the keys, unlocked the door and walked outside, just in case any excitement would cause a little accident, not that I thought my arrival was that exciting, but who knows. I stroked the squiggling little bundle, who had run outside behind me, then waited while she sniffed round the lawn for the perfect spot, and I knew it was safe to go back in. I had already spotted on my speedy dash through the kitchen, that a little cleaning up would be required on my return, but it didn't take long... and she was only a baby after all. Rosy had curled up in her bed, and was almost asleep by the time I had finished, but the second I opened the cat food tin, she was running between my legs like a wild thing... sniffing the air, using the cupboard doors to lean on, while she stood on her back legs and stretched to her longest. I gave her a few stern words, but she was soon pacing the floor again, taking in the delicious aroma with a somewhat glazed expression.

After ordering her back into bed yet again, so I could negotiate the journey to the door without tripping over and getting cat food all over the carpet, the smart Rosy watched until I left the room, then even before the door had time to shut properly, I could hear her claws tapping on the cupboard doors again, and I was praying the empty tin wasn't too near the edge. The cats hardly had time to get out of bed, as I slung their bowls on the floor and shot back out of the door again, saying I'd be back to see them soon.

For once, everything was okay. The tin was still safely out of reach, Rosy had given up and was back in bed chewing on one of her toys by the time I got back.

Another nice easy day ensued. The cats and Rosy had grooming and pampering sessions, although Rosy was trying to get the brush in her mouth at every opportunity, I kept practising and not improving on the pool table, while my other half caught up on the television viewing, and reading.

What a day!

Bedtime came round again, and we had not been upstairs long before the woeful cries of a lonely puppy started building up in volume. She sounded so sad... I could feel myself weakening... but we must be firm I told myself, unwavering in our protocol... but she was only a few weeks old.

One shout of her name, and silence prevailed once again, but it was only brief!

It eventually took a visit downstairs to order Rosy back to bed before we could all get some sleep, but considering this was only her second night alone, she was doing really well.

The following day began for me with another kitchen floor cleaning episode after letting Rosy out in to the garden, but there would be no extra snoozing for my other half. Once the cats had been fed and Rosy had demolished her breakfast in record time, I went back upstairs to rouse my partner, because after breakfast we had to go to the vet. It was the day for her last vaccination.

We made sure Rosy had another walk around the garden before leaving, then my better half got in the passenger seat, placed a blanket on her knee, and I lifted Rosy in. Rosy nestled herself in to a cozy ball, not one bit interested in what was happening, and looked as though she would be asleep in another couple of minutes, so I shut the door and got in the other side.

It was easy getting to the next village, just one right turn about ten minutes down the road, then as no one was behind, I could drive along slowly until we spotted our port of call, and I pulled into the car park.

Our entrance into the vet's surgery started a chorus of 'Ahh' from the receptionist, a nurse and the only other client in the waiting room, as they noticed the adorable little face peeping out from the warm blanket, and none of them could resist stroking her, which she absolutely lapped up.

We sat down as the vet appeared and disappeared back into his room just as quick, with barely enough time to call out the name of the other customer, but she jumped up and pulled the lead of her less than eager dog to follow. He obviously knew this place!

I could hear mutterings through the closed door, and it was starting to make me feel nervous, so I was quite relieved when they reappeared looking fairly happy, and it meant we could get our turn over with. After another couple of minutes, the vet made his entrance again, called the name 'Rosy', and even he couldn't resist a smile before turning back. We followed briskly, then my partner untangled the blanket so Rosy could stand on the big white table in the middle of the room, while I confirmed her name and address, then we all circled round while the vet examined ears, eyes, and paws… *little did she know what was coming next,* I thought, looking at the little trusting face.

After a few more questions, the vet turned his back and grabbed a small bottle and a syringe… *here we go* …then asked us to stroke Rosy as he grabbed the scruff of her neck. While I tensed at the thought, the needle was in and out, and she didn't even notice.

"All done," he said. "She can go out in two weeks' time."

After a quick, "thank you," Rosy was rewrapped in her blanket and whisked outside, while I went back to reception to explain that the bill was on the owners' account, then we were back home.

On our last day, the three of us were in the kitchen when we heard the front door open, and a call of, "We're back," from one of the owners. A split second later, startling the three of us, the door to the dining room blasted open as Tom headbutted it on his way through, then stampeded into Rosy knocking her flying, before charging straight out of the kitchen door, which fortunately was open, and into the garden.

Poor little Rosy! She got up and followed, and was promptly barged into at full thrust again, as Tom ran back in. I wanted to tell him off for being so rough with our little baby, but thought better of it as I was stood next to her rightful owners. My eyes kept wandering to the rough and tumble occurring outside as I gave them a quick rundown of our week, and at one point Rosy had Tom's long ear in her mouth, so at least she was standing up for herself. She would be okay!

Our work here was done, it was time to leave... but we would only be home for a few days before returning for a six-week stint.

Our brief visit home was soon over, and we were back. It was a beautiful sunny day, the front door was already wide open, and cases were being hoisted out to the car, so we waved at one of the owners as he manoeuvred bags round into the boot to make enough space, and he signalled us to go inside, after we stroked Marley of course, who had bothered to run over and say hello (and transfer a few cat hairs), before we vanished into the dog zone.

I called a friendly, "hello" as we walked through to the dining room, which was like a starting pistol for the two dachshunds to go mad, racing between us, hardly allowing their other owner a chance to speak over their barks of excitement. Eventually, once things had calmed down, we had a final check of everything we might need, and before you know it, the owners had made their quickest ever exit.

It was far too boring watching us unpack, and the two dogs ran off into the garden... it looked as though

Rosy was giving as good as she got, so we left them to it.

When it was done, it was time for another excursion to the valley, and although Rosy still couldn't go out walking, she had her own puppy carrier, much like a baby, and could come along with us to get to know the area. I volunteered for carrying duties, thinking it would be the easy job, while my other half put Tom on the lead, but we had barely got to the end of the road and that small puppy was already feeling like a ton weight. She was having a great time, head twisting and turning at every noise or movement, watching everything that was going on from her vantage point, and boy, did she get some adoring fans as we came across other dog walkers.

As far as I was concerned... the sooner we got home, the better, and every muscle in my back was in agreement!

Fortunately, there were only another couple of baby carrying days left, because by the Wednesday, the vaccination had taken full effect, and it was time to go for a real walk, on a lead.

Rosy was not particularly impressed at being tethered to someone who dictated where she should go, and didn't take an immediate liking to the idea, but as Tom was out in front, she eventually decided to follow, slowly and cautiously, but we were on the move. We didn't go too far on our first outing... it would have taken all day for a start, but it was an introduction to the outside world.

The following Monday, dinner for us was earlier than usual, because we had an appointment at the vet's surgery, where they were holding the first session of a puppy class... and we were signed up!

Tom could not come along, he had already seen it, done it and won it, and watched us from the other side of the kitchen's baby gate, like an incarcerated offender as we gathered everything required. It was recommended that Rosy hadn't eaten before the class, so we needed treats to reward good behaviour, her favourite toy, a tug of war toy for socialising with other puppies... it was like going to school.

We had allowed plenty of time for Rosy to have a walk round before going in... in fact we had allowed so much time that we were the only car in the car park, and the surgery was in darkness, but we didn't want to give a bad impression by being late. My partner walked round the corner to a grassy patch under some trees and waited, but Rosy wasn't getting the idea, and just sat down.

They walked a bit further and stopped, and she sat down again.

They were still going up and down the same patch as the lights suddenly came on in the surgery, and although it was another few minutes before anything happened, we still got there before anyone else. Once we had registered with the instructor, the only thing to do was sit making polite conversation, hoping someone would join us soon, so just as another gaping silence filled the room, I was quite relieved to see car lights turn into the car park, and soon a young cocker spaniel plus the owner walked in. The friendly little puppy came straight over to Rosy, and unlike the amicable exchange I expected, was greeted with a snappy growl, and sent on her way.

I was quite shocked... I pictured this being like a puppy party, playing games with new friends, and having a great time. Surely living with Tom, had provided some socialising techniques, but they weren't surfacing at the moment.

In fact, every time an excited puppy came through the door, I could hear Rosy growling quietly as she tried to keep out of their way, and I too hoped they didn't venture in our direction... this wasn't going well! All the other owners were comparing stories, all the other puppies were happily meeting each other, their tails wagging furiously, and we were sitting alone, hanging onto Rosy who was just furious all over, full stop.

When everyone had arrived the class began, and we all had to introduce ourselves and our puppies, which were all very close in age, but varied immensely in behaviour. A young Labrador accompanied by elderly owners just fidgeted on the end of a lead, no number of commands making her sit still, while a tiny chihuahua, dressed in a very trendy jumper was obedience itself. He was totally bald apart from a Mohican hairstyle, and according to his owner, had numerous outfits in his wardrobe to keep warm, which we would all doubtless be seeing over the weeks.

When it came to our turn to stand in front of the class, I already knew my partner would be volunteering myself to go through the 'sit' command with Rosy. We had already done this at home, along with 'stay', 'down', and 'roll over', so I shouldn't have been anxious, but I still hadn't got over her unfriendly, unpredictable behaviour yet, and it was making me uneasy. I needn't have worried... she did it straight away, particularly with the promise of a tasty reward at the end, and we returned to our seat, top of the class. Rosy would do anything for food, which was one predictable thing about her... the only trouble was that when the other puppies took their turn, she was straining at the leash trying to steal their treats as well, and insisted on barking at them incessantly. The instructor kept trying to make light of it, although her expression told a different story, but we couldn't keep her quiet, both my partner and I trying to tell her off discreetly, and completely disrupting everyone else's concentration in the process.

We were really going to enjoy six weeks of this!

It was probably just twelve hours later, when I let Tom and Rosy out in the garden the following morning, and as usual, they raced off to chase any squirrels, and if not chase each other instead. They were usually gone for a few minutes, so I had time to prepare and deliver two cat breakfasts and two dog breakfasts, but as I walked past the back door, a pitiful little face with those sad eyes was peering up. Rosy had come straight back and was standing on only three legs, the back one on the right-hand side dangling limply. I coaxed her to approach, but could see she was unhappy to put any weight on it, and preferred to do a little hop, so I lifted her up the two steps and plonked her on the kitchen floor to have a look.

I didn't want to be hasty!

This phenomenon had been witnessed before, and as I recall, the symptoms could disappear as quickly as they came on.

Before I could examine the wounded paw, she slowly limped and hopped her way to the bed at the far end of the kitchen, and curled up.

Now I was worried!

Rosy was constantly on the go, and this was definitely out of character.

What should I do?

My better half had passed her first aid course, and she would know at once if medical attention was required. I ran upstairs, blurting out my story as I swished the curtains wide open, knowing retribution for the deed was unlikely under these circumstances, and within a few minutes, back in the kitchen, my partner called Rosy over. Her forlorn little face looked up sorrowfully, then she stumbled out of her bed trying to balance on three legs rather than four, and slowly hopped towards the two of us. My better half could watch not a second longer, and scooped her up, offering copious amounts of sympathy, so I examined the underside of the foot for thorns or any wounds but couldn't see anything wrong. I was soon on the phone, and fortunately we were near enough to the surgery to make the nine o'clock appointment.

Rosy nestled on the comfy lap provided, and I pulled out of the driveway… just as every mother in the area was dropping their children off at the nearby school!

In both directions, cars were lining practically the whole road, others were causing delay as they tried reversing into barely adequate gaps, and the remainder were circling like hungry sharks, waiting to pounce on the first space that came available, and ready to fight for it. Weaving in and out of the congestion were parents who had abandoned their vehicles away from the skirmish, hanging tightly onto the hands of their uniformed offspring as they steered them to the school gates, probably hoping for a little respite before they returned to collect them again later. I joined the chaotic frenzy briefly, but instead of the direct route, took the first left turn, which initially would take us in the opposite direction, but would be quicker in the long run. The first few yards looked dicey, but once we were round the first corner it was plain sailing.

We arrived at the vet's surgery in plenty of time, and the puppy trainer, now in the guise of receptionist came over to offer more sympathy, and ask what had happened, but there was no time to reply. A woman struggling to carry a massive cat basket emerged and we were called straight in. My other half placed Rosy on the floor, and her discomfort was plainly obvious as she limped over to the scales, so the vet lifted her on to the table and started to feel every bone and joint individually, working his way down from the spine. As he pressed the offending foot, she let out a squeal, and further investigation meant a lot more squealing to follow, but he could feel no broken bones. An X-ray was going to be the only way to really confirm no underlying problems, and as breakfast had been neglected in the morning's proceedings, it meant Rosy could be left at the surgery now, and we could pick her up later in the afternoon.

Did we feel terrible walking out without her... the rest of the day we counted the hours until we could go and pick her up... and the next time we saw her, she was wearing a bright pink bandage wider than her other three legs put together, and a plastic cone round her neck to stop her chewing it. She looked up sleepily as she was handed back to my partner, the anaesthetic not having totally worn off, while the vet explained that he could find nothing serious, but a tiny bone in her toe may have a fine crack in it. After a week she would have to come back to have the bandage removed and see how she was walking.

Did such a tiny crack merit such a giant bandage?

I thanked the vet while my other half carried Rosy out to the car, and she looked much more awake once she realised she was coming home with us.

Back at the house I ran ahead to unlock all of the doors, then my partner walked in with the patient. Tom came over and sniffed at the strange pink leg Rosy had acquired, and the lampshade looking collar around her neck, then was ready for some more rough and tumble... but that wouldn't be happening!

She was put in her bed in the conservatory, surrounded with her with favourite toys, given several treats, cuddled, stroked, brushed, attention lavished on her... but the only thing Rosy could concentrate on, was that massive pink bandage... and how to get rid of it.

Her extra-long dachshund body was able to reach the top of the white dressing underneath the vivid covering, even with the cone round her neck, so any time she was left alone, it provided an opportunity to nibble at it. By the evening, long strands of chewed white cotton trailed behind her every step, as if she was the faithful companion of Jacob Marley, and twice we trimmed it, re-stuck it, pushed it back under the luminous bandage, but it was never going to last long!

It held on a few days but eventually we had to return to the vet early, the bandage completely in tatters, barely hanging onto her leg, but it had one bonus. Once the vet had checked her foot, he considered her okay to go without it, as long as she didn't run, or walk too far... taking it easy for another week (Does a dog ever do anything else).

The flip side of this, however, was that there would be no avoiding puppy class this week, as I had hoped.

So, on the Monday we all took our places again. The Labrador was stretching her lead to its longest to reach a pile of toys in the centre of the room, the stylish chihuahua was modelling his latest outfit, and the other puppies were all playing together nicely, all except ours again, but now at least we had a valid reason.

As the class began, owners had to sit in a circle in the centre of the room... I briefly considered the possibility that we may have stumbled on some black magic cult by accident, and if I had heard even one note of a chilling hypnotic chant, I would have been off. Volunteered yet again, I, the gullible one, joined the scramble to the lower circle watched by my better half, then the puppies had to sit on our laps. The idea was to pass them round the group, each person talking to and stroking every other puppy in the room to get them used to other people.

Passing the parcel is much easier than a wriggling puppy it took no time to discover!

After the puppies had completed their three-hundred-and-sixty-degree trip, we all returned to our seats, some easier than others, and were told that every student would have to do a party piece at the final class, and top of the class would be presented with a red rosette. I couldn't imagine anyone but the bald chihuahua, who was so well behaved getting that prize, and felt a little sorry for Rosy, as Tom had been the star in his class, and his red rosette was proudly hung on the notice board at home.

Six weeks passed by quicker than I expected... Rosy was walking normally, and now she had grown, Tom was not so rough with her. She was slightly friendlier at the puppy class now that she had got to know the other puppies a bit better, and the cats were happy keeping to their half of the house, with their night visits upstairs, so everything was in order for the return of their owners.

I had left lots of notes, because they would probably be jet-lagged, and the only thing left unfinished was the final week at puppy class.

We got an email the following week saying she had beaten everyone with her party piece, and her red winner's rosette was proudly exhibited on the notice board next to Tom's.

What a triumph!

Chapter 13 — Springer Surprise

Having met this family of three dogs, consisting of mother, father, and daughter, I can hereby declare that whosoever named this breed of spaniel the 'Springer Spaniel' to be an extremely astute individual. Petra could spring above the tallest grass obstructing her view, Brady could spring from the boot of the car like a fired cannonball, and Riley might not have had a cool motorbike, but he could spring over any fence (ninety-nine percent of the time) just as easy as Steve McQueen trying to escape.

At our pre-visit, their owners had seemed grateful that we would even take on this sit, but we couldn't detect any reason not to, and staying at an oast house for a week would be a first.

The actual morning of the sit was the foggiest I had seen for years. It reminded me of our holiday in San Francisco, driving back from Carmel, laughing as we compared the incoming fog to the horror film of the same name.

Not for long!

Within twenty minutes it had enveloped the whole area, until the car just ahead was barely visible, and driving at a snail's pace meant things only got worse as the daylight faded away, resulting in a painfully slow crawl back home in the dark, with a long queue of impatient drivers tailing behind.

Let's just say it wasn't two relaxed holidaymakers that returned to their hotel room that evening!

Anyway, that's another story! I'll return to here and now.

Having learnt from the experience, we had allowed ample time today for crawling through the mire, but had now arrived much too early, neither of us in the mood for waiting around in the bleak weather, so threw caution to the wind and decided to risk an impromptu early arrival.

Turning carefully into the awkwardly angled drive, I accelerated up the muddy track towards the gate with only a narrow space either side, crunched over the pebbles to the end of the drive then reversed into a space next to the garage, fully expecting the noise to have announced our arrival to both owners and dogs… but no one appeared.

We sat expectantly for a few minutes, but when there was still no movement my better half decided to get a couple of bags from the car to put by the front door, hoping we might get noticed. We must have been, because suddenly an upstairs window flew open, and a slightly embarrassed owner grasping a soggy towel leant out apologising for his appearance, then asked if we could wait outside for a few minutes as he wasn't quite ready (we had already noticed). His wife in the meantime was out, having gone to do a final check at work before jetting off.

We both nodded as he said he wouldn't be long, waited for the window to close again, and rapidly scuttled our bags back into the car.

Soon the back door opened, and surrounded by his three faithful companions, a fully dressed owner, wearing a broad grin strode over, apologised again and invited us into the kitchen to have coffee to pass the time until his wife got back, so we could all go over the instructions together. The three dogs circled us, tails wagging ferociously, then dashed indoors ahead of their owner, ready to greet us just as enthusiastically as we walked in, as if we hadn't just seen them outside. They were too full of energy to stay in one place for long, and rapidly disappeared together, maybe waiting for her to return too.

As soon as car tyres rattled across the pebbles outside, the three of them were jumping, or should I say springing at the back door, which immediately swung outwards and slammed into the outside wall the second the handle was turned. They charged at the car, racing and jostling for position as they went, then all three returned like a circle of bodyguards around their other owner, looking extremely pleased with themselves.

She walked into the kitchen holding out a hand for a formal shake, but she was much friendlier than the action suggested, and we all seemed to get on like a house on fire as she joined in for the coffee drinking.

Even after coffee and going through all the instructions for a second time, there was still plenty of time before they needed to leave for their flight, and we knew a practice visit to the park was on the cards if time allowed, especially as it was a drive away and we were going to be using their car, so that was the next thing on our schedule.

"Do you want to drive us there?" the husband enquired.

Well, it's one thing driving someone else's car, it's another thing driving it while they are sat next to you watching your every move, but it's another thing completely when you are totally disorientated with visibility that's about as far as you could throw a ball for three spaniels... I politely declined for the outward journey, knowing I would have to be the one driving back.

After a quick journey down one junction of the motorway, we arrived at a massive country park, and the two of us scrambled out, then stood amidst the damp fog while the owner opened the boot and grabbed three leads as the dogs leapt from the back of the car. They immediately scattered in different directions to do what a dog has to do, and he tried to keep watch whilst juggling the leads and several plastic bags at the same time, trying to get just one bag to open so he could do his collection and disposal as quickly as possible. Once he had, we set off around the park at a fine pace, various landmarks being pointed out en route, but all I could see in the poor visibility were vague shapes somewhere in the mist, and I wondered if my partner would remember his directions any better. I was sure she would!

By the time our brisk circuit of the park was complete, the six of us were completely sludge splattered, and I was surprised that the back of the car was even opened to allow the muddy trio in at all, but not an eyelid was batted. The owner then handed over the key, and I took my place in the driver's seat (which I could have done with being higher), as he jumped in the passenger seat, and my other half disappeared in the back.

In actual fact, you didn't need the key!

To start the car you just had to press a button, put it in to gear, and away you go.

So this is what taking my driving test felt like all those years ago, I pondered!

I slowly reversed, straining my neck left and right several times to check nothing was coming, and caught sight of my better half in the mirror, also looking both ways as backup, not exactly confidence boosting. At least the bad weather had ensured the car park was fairly quiet.

I drove to the exit and on to the main road, trying to find a balance somewhere halfway between being careful, but not looking too nervous, and in the end decided it was better to stop analysing, and just get on with it. That seemed to work, and the only tricky bit was turning the sharp corner into their drive again, as the estate car was quite a bit longer than I was used to, but thankfully all went well, and I pulled up next to the house, confidence still intact.

With hardly any time to breathe a sigh of relief we were immediately off again, on another short drive, because our return coincided with the time that the owners should leave, and as we had their car, we had been asked to drop them off at the nearby station (another first)!

It was good that the three dogs had used up plenty of energy and ought to need a nap, I thought, as they were shut in the kitchen.

We were back in ten minutes, and I imagined them to still be weary, but they were too interested in our bags to be tired, and followed with boundless excitement each and every time we walked out to the car. Their exuberance over nothing in particular was highly commendable if not somewhat misplaced, but I soon realised that through the eyes of a spaniel, absolutely everything merited the exact same treatment… with one hundred percent, full on, in-your-face unbounded enthusiasm at full pelt.

Our next visit to the country park later that day was slightly unnerving. We followed the exact same procedure as the morning run, and hoped the dogs would fall into the routine just as if we were their owners, but every time they charged off, I could feel my heart flutter a little. Of course we had permission to let them off the lead, and had been told that they were very well behaved and would always come back, but sometimes the response an owner and a sitter get, are two different things completely. The fog had cleared so our walk was a little more interesting, and we met plenty of other dogs as we trudged our way through the mud, so it was a relief to find that our three really were very obedient, and were usually too busy exploring to cause any trouble.

This seemed easy enough!

The following day, the car park was heaving as everyone took full advantage of the much brighter weather, and it was quite difficult to even find a space, so eventually we had to park much nearer the road than we would have liked, right round on the opposite side. We didn't want the dogs to charge off in the wrong direction, so it would be better to put them on leads, and get through the gates before we dare let them off.

Walking them on a lead, it seems, was a different story.

For a start, they expected to jump straight out as soon as the car stopped, and weren't happy to be cornered in the back before even attempting to get their leads on. Trying to clip them in place took several attempts as they jumped eagerly towards the door, all trying to push in front of each other. Eventually, my better half, two leads in hand and slightly agitated, stood by the car waiting for me, gripping the third lead for all I was worth, while I locked and checked the car doors before setting off.

It was like a chariot race... without the chariots!

From the back I could see my partner trying unsuccessfully to slow her two dogs down, arms stretched out wide as if she was holding the reins of a marauding bull at the country show, and in the meantime, I had discovered Petra was stronger than she looked, and skidded along behind in the mud as she tried to catch up with the others.

"That must have looked good," I said, hanging onto a fence, relieved that my partner had managed to stop just the other side of a gate, so we could all regain some composure.

At least we could let them off now.

As the leads were unclipped, the energetic trio bounded off, and Petra, began her search for a tennis ball that might have been lost somewhere in the vast space. She hardly ever came back empty mouthed, and had an endless ever-growing supply at home. The other two raced between the trees, reappearing at intervals to check the whereabouts of everyone else before vanishing again, and enjoying every minute until our circuit was almost complete.

It was all going so well, and we couldn't have been a hundred yards from the car park when Riley's nose began sniffing the air, his eyes gradually glazing over as if he was in a trance... and could, I'm sure, have easily eaten a raw onion, thinking it was an apple. My partner and I both called his name, the volume of panic in our voices building to a magnificent crescendo, but he couldn't hear a thing, he was mesmerised by some intriguing scent lingering on the other side of a menacing looking barbed wire fence, and he wanted to find it.

I cringed as he coiled back to judge the height before making a leap at it, and couldn't even look at the next bit... but when I actually dared open my eyes, I could detect no evidence of dog impaling...

In truth I could detect no evidence full stop, because he was nowhere to be seen.

My better half, followed by Petra and Brady, had already dashed over to the spiked barrier, and began shouting his name in a very authoritative tone.

I joined in, shouting in the gaps between her calls, as if we were the new Chas and Dave rehearsing the follow-up to *Rabbit, Rabbit,* at the same time scouring the long grass for signs of movement.

Fortunately, within seconds he was back, as if it was just a continuation of the chase with Brady... and whatever the big attraction had been, must not have been so attractive after all. He started to scramble under the barbed wire 'army style', but had to give up after discovering his tummy not to be as toned as it once was... so it looked like he was going to have to do the return jump.

This time I was more confident in his 'springing' ability, and watched as he measured up the distance... but something must have gone amiss with the calculations, because while his front paws just managed to stretch themselves safely back on solid ground, one of the back ones was hooked in the top of the fence, leaving his undercarriage pressing against the dangerous barbs.

He was well and truly snared.

My partner was close enough to grab him and try to stop him wriggling around, while I tackled the top of the wire to try and release his foot... he could already be facing a twisted or sprained ankle, perhaps broken bones in the toes or foot, so we didn't want a ripped abdomen to add to the list.

I hurriedly bent the wire round until the top loop came unhooked, then stretched it further apart while my better half manoeuvred his rear end back to safety. Happily, Riley looking none the worse for his entanglement, gave his whole body, a thorough shake, sniffed his back leg, then ran off with his packmates, who had been waiting patiently for far too long.

He was absolutely fine, apart from maybe a little embarrassed.

Out of the three of them, Riley was the stroppiest.

At night they all slept in the kitchen, but as soon as he came in from the garden, there would always be at least one attempt to dash up the stairs to get to the bedroom. He also wasn't shy of employing a threatening growl if he was in a bad mood.

One day he decided to take possession of the car when he had sneaked into the front seat, while the door had carelessly been left open. Calling him was useless, and shouting at him just made him growl again.

What could persuade him to come out?

We pretended the other two were getting the best tasting treats ever, then while he rushed to see what he was missing, I rushed round the back of the car and slammed the door.

Everything else went fine with our stay, for a change, and we were soon heading to the station to pick up the owners.

Christmas Sit

After a family discussion, we had decided to accept another sit beginning two days after Boxing Day, going over New Year and taking us up to January the fourth, once again with permission for my mum to accompany us as it was the Festive season. The owners of Riley, Petra and Brady were yet again amazed that we were even available, as normally we had an extremely busy schedule, never mind willing to work over Christmas, so were ecstatic when they found out we had agreed.

Everything had been arranged, so I was surprised only one week later to receive an email from them, asking if we were still prepared to go ahead with the sit, as unforeseen circumstances had occurred, and the resulting situation may have entailed extra work.

What could it be? I thought as I continued reading.

The next sentence stopped me in my tracks!

I grabbed hold of my laptop and immediately rushed off to read the email out loud to my other half. It went on to explain that they had discovered Brady was pregnant, and although they expected to be back by the time the birth occurred, those sorts of things didn't always stick to an exact schedule, and there was a possibility that it could happen while we were in charge.

Apparently the three of them had been kennel mates with the in-laws' dog at a wedding, but didn't realise they now had a new dog, fully intact.

My speechless other half stared, potato peeler static in one hand, half peeled potato in the other... and I stared back, already playing the scenario through in my mind, and discovering all manner of 'what if's' in the process. In fact my imagination could have run riot for the rest of the day with endless possibilities, but the silence was eventually broken by my no-nonsense other half declaring that as long as she had plenty of surgical gloves, she was willing to go ahead with the sit if I was. Rather less confident, I concluded that I would be okay as 'assistant to midwife' if necessary, so decision made, I left my better half peeling the rest of the potato, while I disappeared to send our reply.

It wasn't long before I got another email thanking us, and thanking us again, also saying we should expect a book on 'whelping' to arrive in the post, to prepare us for any emergencies.

The book arrived a couple of days later, and I started perusing the pages, sitting next to my better half engrossed in a newspaper.

I was looking at pictures of a 'whelping box', studying lists of things needed at the birth… then I got to the part entitled, 'What could go Wrong'!

I felt worse every second as it warned of breach births, legs getting stuck, the umbilical cord wrapping round the unborn puppy… and by the end I was in a cold sweat, suffering from severe palpitations, and felt as if the blood had completely drained from my head with the thought.

I read it again to my other half who also cringed at the possibilities, but we consoled ourselves with the thought that lots of puppies were born every day with no problems whatsoever.

I put the book with our packing, out of sight, and decided to forget it until after Christmas, when we began our sit.

The day after Boxing Day I drove back to London after spending Christmas at my mum's house, car laden with our luggage, my mum's luggage, Christmas presents, sale items we had acquired over our short stay up north, as well as our three overindulged bodies, no doubt all more than a few pounds heavier after the amount of food, chocolates and alcohol that disappeared into them over three gluttonous days.

The car had to be completely unpacked when we arrived home, as vehicles in this area were regularly relieved of their contents overnight, so the following morning I was attempting to cram our luggage back into the car, this time with food and drink to find space for as well. It was usually difficult enough when there was just two of us, but with an extra person travelling with extra bags, and a whole corner of space reserved to seat an aforementioned extra passenger, I worried that it would result in squashed knees, crushed shoulders and a whole load of grief for the luggage packer. My only defence would be to suggest leaving behind some of our not entirely 'essential items' and that was never going to happen.

Everyone squeezed into their place, and I manoeuvred into my seat, the steering wheel just leaving enough space for my legs to move between the pedals, but so close to my chest that my hands and shoulders were practically touching. No one was comfortable but the journey turned out to be easier than expected, hardly any traffic, route already known, and only squeaky windscreen wipers to cause any irritation on the way. That didn't stop my mum spending a fair amount of time with eyes closed, catching up on her beauty sleep, although according to her she was just resting her eyes.

Knowing we were too early, and not forgetting our last early arrival here, I drove straight to the local Sainsbury's, were we could all take a quick bathroom break, so it wasn't the first thing that everyone needed to do the moment we arrived at the house. The toilets were actually so far into the store that I managed to avoid buying coffee for everyone, because there was no time left when we had completed the trek.

Passengers wedged back into their spaces, I drove to the house, turned into their awkward entrance, where luckily the gate was open, then parked between the garage and the swimming pool as I had done before. Again no one appeared, so I went to the front door and knocked, waited a few seconds, then was taken completely by surprise as being greeted as if I was one of the family. In the meantime Petra and Riley had charged through the doorway, full of their Springer enthusiasm and run over to the car where my other half was helping my mum out of the car, and following slowly behind was an extremely uncomfortable looking Brady. Her stomach looked distended to its limit and beyond, and with only the momentary glance I dare take as she waddled and panted her way back, I was already getting sweaty palms. This brave attempt to act normal was fooling no one, and I hoped I was being more successful as we walked in talking to her owners, my underlying anxiety level edging up another notch as, in the corner of my eye, I caught sight of her flop down heavily on the floor to get a tummy tickle.

I was quite relieved when we had leave the room to go and see the utility room by the back door, now transformed into the whelping area. A massive cardboard box was padded out with cosy blankets on top of a heat pad, adding even more cosiness to the nest, with a baby gate to keep the area secure if the other two dogs got too interested. As it was open, Petra jumped in to give it one more test, and would have nestled in quite happily, but was promptly ordered to leave, so ran off back into the other room again, to see what she was missing. We were shown plastic gloves, towels, more blankets, a spare heating pad, another copy of the dreaded whelping book, all close at hand if the time should come, so the owners had provided everything we could possibly need. I felt slightly better to find out that a recent scan had revealed just four puppies, hoping that it should make things quicker if anything should happen, but anyway... why should it? They weren't due until after we had left.

There was not much more to say, but we were invited to finish any leftover food and wine, given all the phone numbers in case of emergencies, then that was it… a kiss and a cuddle for each dog, with an extra-long one for Brady, and off they went!

Well, over the next few days I spent many hours staring at Brady. She wasn't allowed to go out on the walks of course… fortunately for her, because the weather was terrible, and we were being blasted with freezing cold rain or sleet on every visit to the country park. There was no shelter in the wide, open space, and sometimes the wind was so strong it actually pushed you backwards, but the other two dogs couldn't have cared less. Petra was searching every nook and cranny for lost tennis balls, while Riley charged round the field looking for anything, and us getting soaked through was of no consequence. As soon as we got back, I would check on Brady, and usually she had spent the time lying next to my mum, getting plenty of tummy tickling, and nothing seemed to be happening, so all was well.

This time we were using our own car for ferrying to and fro, so my partner had covered the back seat in numerous layers of towels, to stop muddy paws soaking through to the upholstery. The only trouble was that the first time they got in, Petra jumped into the back seat, just using it as a springboard to catapult herself over to the front passenger seat before I could stop her, and my other half spent the journey sitting in a patch of soggy muddy paw prints. She was not happy!

In the end, we had to have a regimented order of entry into the car, starting with my better half, then the two dogs, who couldn't jump on the driving seat because of the steering wheel, then last of all, me, of course. Everyone was happier all round.

It was on New Year's Eve, when we got back cold and wet from our trek, this time in icy snow, that I noticed Brady panting more than usual. She looked anxious and kept pacing in and out, round the garden, back and forth. I was anxious myself, and kept trying to lead her to the whelping box... but she was having none of it, whereas the other two dogs were the exact opposite, trying to get in it at any opportunity, and had to be reprimanded more than once. My partner tried to persuade her to lie down amidst the warm blankets, but it was useless. Over the day, she kept wandering in and out, and every time I followed, waited, then followed her back in, watching for any signs, but still nothing happened. I vaguely remember toasting in the New Year, but really couldn't concentrate, my mind was on other things.

Before we went to bed, Brady was put in the whelping room, and Riley and Petra locked out, much to their disgust, and perhaps things might happen overnight.

On New Year's Day I went downstairs after an extremely restless night, walked quickly past Riley and Petra, and wouldn't have been surprised to see four puppies nestled in the box with Brady... but nothing!

Quite disappointed, I opened the back door to let the dogs out, and while the other two ran off, Brady went very slowly, and seemed wobbly on her legs. She crouched down awkwardly, then just walked back in and flopped back on the bed. I grabbed the dreaded book quickly, read through a few paragraphs, and reassured myself that the panting, the pacing, the agitation were all symptoms just before giving birth, but how could I be sure... I had never witnessed it before. It would be New Year's Day of course... nowhere open... no one to ask advice. I would just have to get my better half up to have a look at her.

I was already imagining long legs getting tangled up, especially as the father of these puppies was a red setter, and what if they were too big as there were only four of them! I was unable to keep my fears to myself, and had relayed them all the way down the stairs to my better half who also looked concerned, and turned to the exact same pages in the book, read aloud the exact same paragraphs, then we stared down at Brady together.

She looked glum.

With Riley and Petra locked out of the kitchen I opened the door again, and she wobbled outside, went to the nearest part of lawn, crouched then walked straight back inside as before, had a drink of water and lay down. No titbits could entice her to eat, and she was looking totally miserable. Was this normal? Was she okay?

We would have to leave her for a while, to chauffeur the other two off for their expedition round the country park, but after yet another battle against the elements, the four of us, looking rather bedraggled soon returned. My mum was in the kitchen making tea and toast as the back door burst open, and Brady made an effort to get up and greet the returning pack, which made us feel a little more at ease, but the effort of standing up with all that weight in her stomach soon became too much, and she made her way back to the bed.

By the afternoon, Brady was still looking extremely uncomfortable, there was still no sign of puppies, I was getting more and more worried that things might be going wrong, and made the decision that even if it was a bank holiday, I would have to call the vet.

It was going to be an expensive undertaking, so I phoned the son of the owners first, explained the situation and asked if I should go ahead… but anyone who has a pet would already know the answer.

I was soon describing the symptoms to the emergency vet, who said we should take her into the surgery as soon as possible, so after arranging a time to meet, I rang the son back to let him know, and he and his partner immediately said they would come over to take her.

By the time they arrived, Brady didn't want to move at all... she was too heavy to be carried, so my better half suggested we slide a duvet under her, and we grabbed a corner each. With a heave-ho she was lifted out of the door, across the garden and into their car, we asked them to keep us posted as the door was slammed shut, then they left. Nobody said a word for a few minutes, all lost in our own thoughts, but there was nothing more we could do but wait, and inwardly I was concerned that the news may not be good.

What seemed like hours later, the phone rang and it was the son. I hardly dare ask what had happened, but he explained that the vet was quite concerned Brady would not be able to have the puppies naturally, so she would have to undergo a caesarean overnight, and he would give us a call in the morning to let us know how it went.

I knew I had made the right decision now, and thanked him for the call, before dashing to tell the others... and I could see another sleepless night ahead!

What a New Year!

I was the only one up when the phone rang in the morning. Rather blearily I answered, but the news soon had me wide awake. The operation had gone well, Brady was extremely weak, but was now the proud mother of thirteen puppies, a fourteenth sadly hadn't made it.

Was I hearing things?

Thirteen!

No wonder she was uncomfortable. No wonder her stomach looked ready to explode.

Remind me never to trust a scan again!

She would have to stay in for a couple of days, and the puppies needed to be fed by hand as there were so many, which meant someone would have to stay with them in the surgery overnight (I could practically feel the bill going up with every word), but at least she was okay.

I couldn't wait to tell my fellow worriers, and I knew they wouldn't mind being woken up for the news. That's all we could talk about for the rest of the day!

The following morning, I phoned the son once again to check everything was still going well, and asked if we might visit the new mother and her brood, so arranged to meet them at the vet's surgery when it was convenient. We arrived first, even after driving past and missing it twice, so after explaining who we were to a receptionist, were allowed through to a very clinical smelling room in the back. Lying there surrounded by the thirteen totally black tiny puppies was a tired looking Brady, but as soon as she caught sight of us, she stood up, scattering the little black bodies in several directions, and I was worried she might stand on one of them, but they were all fine. We both gave her a cuddle and she nuzzled her head in to my partner for sympathy, then we both turned back to the cage and gaped in amazement at the actual space the thirteen babies took up. They had regrouped and were nestled together spread across a wide expanse of the warm blankets, and we were still marvelling at how they all ever managed to fit inside Brady, when the son and his partner arrived. After a quick hello, they immediately scooped up a tiny puppy each, which caused simultaneous squeaks of displeasure at being pulled from the warm bundle, because they were about to have a lesson in puppy feeding, so we didn't want to get in the way, and felt happy to leave now we had seen that Brady seemed okay. I quickly tried to take a couple of photographs, which turned out to be just one big blur of black on a blanket, then had a brief conversation with the son before we said our goodbyes.

What a New Year this was turning out to be!

It was a couple of days later, around six o'clock, when we received a phone call from the son again saying Brady and her puppies were well enough to come home, and they would all be arriving in a couple of hours. Before I had chance to panic, he went on to explain that they would be staying over to look after the puppies, so it looked like we were in for a full house.

As soon as the phone call ended, as usual, I rushed to relate the news, and everyone started scurrying round from room to room, tidying our things out of the way, so it would be nice and neat for their arrival… the whelping book was put well out of the way!

It was all done by the time lights appeared at the end of the drive, and as soon as the car was parked, my partner and I opened the back door to welcome them all back home.

Brady jumped out looking more her normal self, as Petra and Riley ran out to meet her, all looking excited to be a family again, then they all charged back indoors and ran between us to get stroked, as if all three of them had just arrived, but it meant they were occupied while the thirteen newcomers were smuggled in.

It didn't take long however, for the new scent to be detected.

Although Brady wasn't interested (I suppose she was savouring a bit of alone space), and had disappeared to get a stroke from my mum, Petra and Riley, noses twitching high in the air, followed the trail to the room cordoned off next to the kitchen, and came across a chorus of high-pitched squeaks coming from the puppies. They were blindly scrabbling around their new unfamiliar bed, not finding the warm body of their mother to nestle into, and made a din with it… so Riley took one look, and shot off up the stairs to get to the bedroom and out of the way.

Petra stood staring for a minute, head tilting first to the left, then to the right as if she was trying to understand the new language, but she seemed to be quite happy in their company. Before the puppies got too distressed in their new surroundings, Brady was ushered in with them, and it was as if she was magnetic… within a few seconds they were all snuggled together, ready for another nap, and I think Petra, watching everything closely, wished she could have been in there with them. She was their grandmother after all!

Meanwhile, at the other end of the kitchen, there was no time for napping. Bottles were lined up across the counter, a milky powder being measured in to each, and all waiting for the kettle to fill them up. Once they had been cooled to the perfect temperature, two puppies were removed from the litter, and their disgruntled squeaks were soon silenced as the bottle was popped in their tiny mouths.

They lay contentedly, each wrapped in a blanket, tiny paws flexing in mid-air, enjoying their first meal at home… *only eleven more to go after this,* I thought. My mum and other half couldn't resist having a turn at feeding the puppies, while more bottles were being prepped up, but I was too worried about doing it wrong, and went back to the kitchen to see if there was anything I could do.

It was in the middle of this massive task that the son suddenly mentioned that he had spoken with his holidaying family, and had agreed to take over all duties at the house, meaning we could go home early.

Why didn't he mention it earlier?

What a relief for us!

I didn't envy the sleepless nights ahead, feeding the puppies every few hours to make sure no one went hungry, and by the time it was done, it would surely be about time to start the cycle again.

While they continued the conveyor belt in the kitchen, I waited for my co-sitters to complete their task, then for us it was one mad panic to get everything packed up, and crushed back in the car, ready to leave. Needless to say, it wasn't done as neatly for our return journey... things were practically thrown in bags, thrown in the car, and I could see leg space was at a definite minimum from the lack of care. By now it was getting on for ten o'clock, and with an hour and a quarter drive ahead, then unpacking at home, we didn't want to stay longer than necessary, although I felt bad at leaving a job unfinished. We all said goodbye, stroked the dogs, and wished them well, then my mum and better half went to crush in their minimal spaces while I had a final check around the house to make sure we hadn't left anything. You can imagine the look I got from my partner, already flattened up against the side window of the car when I appeared with a rogue bag that had somehow been left halfway up the stairs. My mum was already nursing a large bag totally obscuring her view at the front, so the only place it could go was in the back, on her lap.

It just squashed in, right in front of her face, practically touching her nose... and it was not a happy face that the bag was hiding. I quickly gave the door a final push with my bottom to close it, then ran round to the driver's door.

I hoped the couple were too busy feeding the puppies to be watching our departure, as I shoved myself into the driver's seat, pushed as far forward as possible, leaving barely enough room for my knees to squeeze under the steering wheel, but I started the engine, took off the handbrake by contorting my wrist round something protruding from the back, and we were on our way.

It was a slow process for everyone, trying to prise themselves from the car by the time we arrived back in London. I scrambled out first, my back doing most of the complaining about the uncomfortable journey, as I went to get the bag that held my partner captive. The expression that greeted me from behind it was still not a happy one, and she couldn't move at all, so I dragged the bag, she pushed it and it suddenly shot out. Muttering a few choice words under her breath, but loud enough for me to hear, my better half grabbed the car door and hoisted herself half way up, then I took her hand and pulled her the rest of the way, hoping a mound of bags wouldn't fall out behind. I left her to get the blood circulating, and went to relieve my mum of the other bag, which I carried to the front door, while they both stretched themselves back into shape. I unlocked the front door, and turned off the alarm.

My mum went straight to the kitchen to make tea (after all it can cure almost anything), and as soon as the car was empty, we all flopped together in our television room, a place we don't get to see very often, to look back on the whole incident.

Our New Year may have started in panic, but had ended perfectly, with new lives beginning their journey in the world... just one of the things that definitely made pet-sitting an absolute pleasure.

FINDI
WORCEST~~ER~~SHIRE
MILESTONES

The Worcestershire Group
of
The Milestone Society

CONTENTS

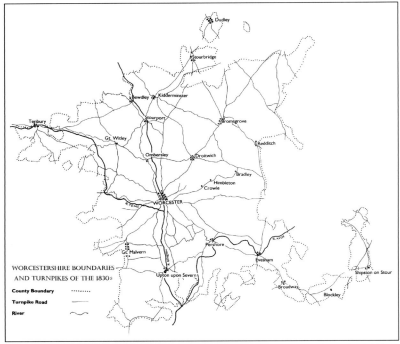

Map showing the Worcestershire boundaries and turnpike roads in the 1830s

Published in 2007 by The Milestone Society
ISBN 978-0-9557538-0-0

Copyright © 2007 Worcestershire Group of the Milestone Society

Introduction

Today one is confronted by a bewildering array of road signs of varying colours and sizes. However, as little as a hundred years ago there were only milestones, a few direction finger posts at cross roads and an occasional town name board.

Milestones were introduced by the Romans as an integral part of their road system which was vital for control of the country. Placed every thousand double steps – a roman *mille passuum* or 1618 yards – they were usually cylindrical in shape with laudatory inscriptions about the Emperor and often without mileage and destination information. In Worcestershire, even though several Roman roads crossed the county, only one of their stones is believed to have survived and is now in the Commandery Museum in Worcester. Discovered in Kempsey in 1818 it is a flat freestone slab 33 inches high by 20 inches wide and the inscription has been translated as *"Emperor Valerius Constantinus, pious, fortunate, unconquerable, Augustus."*

The milestones along our present roads are a legacy of the turnpike era or subsequent County Council and Rural District Council activities. Initially milestones were put up voluntarily by turnpike trusts; however, from about 1744 most turnpike acts had clauses requiring trustees to set up stones or posts stating the distances from nearby towns. In 1766 this requirement was made statutory by the General Turnpike Act and it was periodically renewed in succeeding statutes.

The 1752 Turnpike Act for the Roads around Upton upon Severn required the trustees *"to cause the said Roads to be measured and Stones or Posts to be thereon, and in or near the Sides of the said Roads, erected; each Stone or Post at the Distance of one Mile from*

another." Whether they complied is not known, but an entry in the Order Book of the Trust at the beginning of 1828, required the Surveyor to *"immediately cause Stones to be set up near the sides of every turnpike within the District at the distance of one mile from each other denoting the distance of every such Stone from the town of Upton upon Severn measured from the extremity of the Town upon each road and that he do also cause to be painted in legible characters on a board at the Entrance of every Town and Village within this district the name of such Town or Village."* That Order perhaps provides a firm date for some of the attractive milestones with their plates that are seen around Upton today.

In the middle of the nineteenth century there were between four and five hundred miles of roads in the county under the control of various turnpike trusts with presumably a similar number of milestones. The intervening years have not been kind and several hundred have been lost, damaged or removed, although initiatives in the late 1890s and again in the 1930s added new markers or replaced missing ones. During the Second World War all road signs and many milestones were removed or defaced on government orders for security reasons.

Fewer than 200 survive in Worcestershire today and this account records all those known to exist and their present condition in the summer of 2007. Unfortunately they continue to be damaged, most commonly by verge cutting machinery. Milestones are no longer used practically other than by walkers or cyclists but they are attractive in their own right and provide a link with an earlier time when the advent of the turnpike system revolutionised transport throughout the country

Turnpike Roads

In Elizabethan times the provisions of the 1555 Highways Act governed the way roads were maintained and repaired with the responsibility resting on individual parishes. Each householder was obliged to work (or pay someone to work on his behalf) for four and later six consecutive days a year under the supervision of usually two annually appointed, unpaid, parish Surveyors of Highways. Those who owned a team of horses or oxen had to make them available with two labourers and a cart and any necessary tools when required. Parishes failing to keep their roads in a suitable condition ran the risk of being indicted and fined by the justices until improvements were made. This arrangement was just about adequate for quiet rural backwaters but failed completely where the roads were subject to heavy use especially in winter when travel often became dangerous and frequently impossible. The radical solution that those using the roads should pay for their upkeep through the payment of tolls was first tried in 1663 on a stretch of the Great North Road passing through Hertfordshire, Cambridgeshire and Huntingdonshire. Initiated and overseen by the local Justices of the Peace, it was not long before control of subsequent toll road schemes became vested in independent trustees or commissioners drawn from the local land-owning classes.

After a comparatively slow take up, it was not until the following century that the toll road approach gathered pace. Turnpike acts were obtained through the initiative of local people who foresaw the potential advantages arising from improved roads and communication.

In Worcestershire the earliest turnpike act appeared in 1714 for the road from Worcester to Droitwich. Twelve years later the first act dealing with all the principal roads into the City of Worcester was passed. In subsequent acts these roads were extended further and further into the surrounding countryside. The peak period for new turnpike acts in the country (known as "Turnpike Mania") occurred between 1751 and 1772 when 389 individual acts went through parliament. Those for Worcestershire included the roads around Droitwich, Bewdley, Kidderminster, Evesham, Tenbury, Stourbridge, Upton upon Severn and Great Witley. They provided a network that linked the county with the important towns in the adjoining counties and especially the rapidly developing industrial areas of Birmingham and the Black Country.

All turnpike acts follow a fairly standard pattern in that they identify the roads to be improved, list the names of prominent local individuals who, if they took the necessary oath, could as trustees direct the business of the trust including authorising the erection of tollgates, toll houses and milestones. The acts specify the maximum tolls that might be charged and the roles of the individuals who when appointed by the trustees would carry out the day to day tasks of the trust. These included the Clerk who was usually a local solicitor able to give legal advice, organise the record keeping, call meetings and so on, a Treasurer to hold and dispense funds and a Surveyor who supervised the road building, repair and maintenance.

There were no charges for those on foot but for others the tolls depended on the number of animals either alone or pulling carts or carriages and in the early acts the wheel widths.. The royal family, the mails, carts carrying military equipment, individuals going to church on Sundays, funerals or parliamentary elections and those engaged in transporting a variety of agricultural implements and materials all escaped tolls.

The acts also set out penalties for toll evasion and other offences, describe arrangements for road improvement, the procedures for raising money to carry them out along with a host of technical detail covering financial matters and the corporate status of the trust. The raised money was in effect a loan or mortgage and seen by some as an investment opportunity with the interest coming from the tolls paid by those using the road. Other calls on the toll revenue were to pay employees, meet the expenses of the officials and the ongoing costs of road maintenance and improvements. Another significant expense was for the periodic renewal of a trust's governing act as the lifetime was usually limited to around 21 years. Thus for each trust there are likely to be several acts. On each renewal the opportunity was usually taken to increase the toll charges and include additional roads. In the second half of the nineteenth century many trusts experienced financial difficulties due to competition from the growing railway network and pressure grew to finance the road system in other ways. This resulted in the majority of the turnpike trusts being wound up between 1860 and 1880. The last activity of the turnpike trustees was to sell all the trust assets and with the money realised pay off the outstanding mortgagees in full or as a percentage depending on the amount raised. Usually any surplus funds went to the parishes through which the road passed. The care of the roads then transferred initially to local Highways Boards and after 1888 to the newly formed County Councils.

Toll houses are the other legacy of the turnpike era and whilst most have been dismantled or substantially changed over the intervening years a few remain adjacent to the highway with their characteristic frontages.

Single storey brick toll house at Fairfield

Double storey Cotswold stone toll house at Overbury

Worcestershire

Worcestershire is one of England's smaller counties ranking 33rd in size among the counties in existence prior to the 1974 reorganisation. It is an eighth the size of Yorkshire and not quite as large as any of its neighbours, Herefordshire to the west, Gloucestershire to the south, Warwickshire to the east, Staffordshire to the north and Shropshire to the north-west. During the turnpike era the boundary of the county was rather different from today with several detached parishes in adjoining counties and various projecting spurs and indents. These detached parishes have since been assigned to the counties in which they were located, and those parishes on spurs or next to indents swapped with or gained from adjacent counties. Some of the greatest changes have occurred in the north east corner of the county where large areas have been reassigned firstly to Birmingham and more recently to the new West Midlands County. The net result of these changes is that several sections of turnpike roads formerly in Worcestershire are now in adjacent counties with the consequent loss of several milestones. In this account only those milestones within the current county boundaries are described.

Milestones and Markers

It is believed that some early mileage markers were made of wood but none have survived and they were replaced by the more durable stone pillars that we know today on which the distances to nearby towns were engraved. However, the readily available local stone weathers badly and it was periodically necessary to re-engrave them. This ever-present problem was overcome towards the end of the eighteenth century by putting the distance information onto cast iron plates fixed to the stones and in the county this became the method of choice until the end of the turnpike era. Thereafter the stones continued in use but at the end of the nineteenth century the county council and one of the rural district councils introduced additional triangular cast iron structures. A further change occurred following the recommendations of a government committee to standardise the size of letters on road signs so that they could be read by passing motorists and to make the public aware of road numbers

when the county authorities designed a wholly new milestone. Made of concrete these T shaped pillars have fixed to them two cast iron plates, the smaller one showing the road number and a larger one beneath displaying the mileages to the nearest town either side of the milestone. These particular mile markers introduced in the early 1930s are unique to Worcestershire and over 50 remain of about the 100 originally installed. They were conceived by Harold Brooke-Bradley the deputy county road surveyor and in more recent times have been described as Bradley stones in his memory.

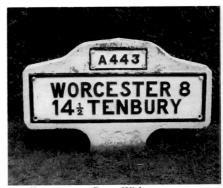

Bradley stone at Great Witley

Milestones are the property of the local Highways Authority and it is an offence under section 13(2) of the Highways Act 1980 for anyone to pull down or obliterate any inscription with those convicted liable to a fine. Those milestones deemed to be of "special architectural or historic interest" are included on a statutory list compiled by the Secretary of State under the Planning (Listed Buildings and Conservation Areas) Act 1990. Listing provides a degree of legal protection but currently only about 30 of the milestones in the county are listed and it is hoped that more will be included in the near future.

Engraved or First Generation Milestones

These milestones from the early turnpike period are comparatively rare in the county as the local sandstone is subject to serious erosion. A fine one at Knightwick bears the legend "To WORCESTER / 8 Miles / LONDON 120". Another at Stanford Bridge has been moved from the roadside to a garden nearby and is engraved on one side and has a metal plate on the other. The engraved legend facing the road is To / LONDON / 125 miles / To / WORCESTER / 13 / To / TENBURY / 9 whereas the later metal plate with pointing direction fingers records Bromyard / 8½ miles / Worcester / 13. A taller engraved milestone, around five feet tall has been moved from its original position north of Evesham to outside the town's museum. It records the distances to Alcester, Birmingham, Worcester, London and Stratford using the Roman numbering system which was generally replaced around the 1750s. Adjacent to it is another, smaller, moved stone that is badly eroded but the legend Evesham 3 is clear.

Two other engraved stones where the legend fronts the road are known. One on the bridge over Bow Brook at Feckenham records "To / Alcester / 6 / To / London / 108 / Miles". The other is in Broadway, which was the main road from London through Worcester and onward to Aberystwyth before the bypass was built. It states "To / LONDON / 90 Miles / Morton 8 / Stowe 10 / WORCESTER / 21 /". The lower section of the stone is indistinct although the word Evesham is discernable. At the bottom is a small metal plate recording the stone's restoration in 1953 following the "world war defacement".

With the change to plated milestones the old stones were generally reused and there are examples of the plates fixed on top of the engraving. Another approach was to turn the stone and three are known with engraved legends now on the side away from the road. The one in Cookhill gives the mileages to Redditch and Evesham while the one south of Ombersley and the one in Hillhampton only have the words "To LONDON" visible.

Re-positioned engraved milestone outside Evesham Museum

Close up showing the Roman numerals on the Evesham Milestone

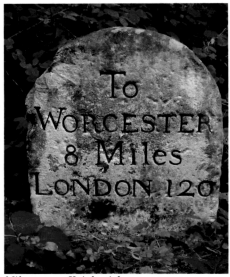

Milestone at Knightwick

Repositioned milestone at Stanford Bridge

Milestone on Bow Brook Bridge at Feckenham

Upper part of the Broadway milestone

Lower plate on the Broadway stone recording the restoration and Second World War defacement

Plated or Second Generation Milestones

There are approaching a hundred second generation milestones remaining in the county and the majority lost their plates during the war although a few survived and others have since been replaced with replicas. The late Mr Alfred Wilkes who worked for the county Highways Department from 1918 to 1969 remembered the central government instruction in 1940 to destroy the milestones. Each Highway unit went about the task in a different way. In some, milestones were buried or the legends chipped off or filled with concrete. In Worcestershire where most of the stones had cast iron plates, many of these were levered off and the pieces thrown in the scrap to help the war effort. A few of the stones in the Malvern area had their plates obscured by a layer of putty and a coat of white paint applied. In at least two cases the metal posts on the Leigh to Alfrick road were dug up and hidden in the back of the hedge. It is believed that all the Bradley stones were taken back to the Highways depots.

One of the tallest at over four feet is the one mentioned above south of Ombersley. In addition to the "To London" engraving on the back there are indentations on both the back and the front where plates were formerly fixed. The one at the back is rectangular with a curved lug top and bottom for the fixing bolts whereas the one at the front is the twelve-sided plate which appears to be another Worcestershire peculiarity. This pattern although of different overall dimensions also occurs on several of the stones on the Worcester to Bradley Green road and on all of those between Ham Bridge and Stanford Bridge. The latter road has the distinction of being one of the last county roads to be made a turnpike in 1845 and at a little over four miles is one of the shortest. Undoubtedly some of the most impressive engraved plate milestones in the county are those around Upton with pride of place going to the three big ones that measure approximately 18 by 28 inches where the distances to Upton and Ledbury are surmounted by the village name of either Upton or Welland. They are unique in that the lettering is incised rather than in relief. Village names also appear on some other milestones of the Upton trust in Hanley and Eldersfield although the plates are smaller. Two without village names unusually have pointing finger direction markers.

The plates for these second generation stones were cast in local foundries often 200 or more years ago and one of the attractions of this type is to observe the variety of plates, the use of abbreviations to fit the available space, the variability in letter alignment and the different fonts chosen. The Redditch 3 Evesham 13 plate has perfect lettering and is unusual in having a curved top to mirror the stone and integral raised bolt holes. The Pershore plate has a mix of upper and lower case lettering including the old form of "s" with some very unusual forms for the numbers. It also gives the distance to London which is not common but was of relevance to mail charges before the advent of the penny post. The Blakedown stone recording the distance only to Birmingham abbreviates the city name to four letters and only has room for a small "s" on the word miles but the stone in Clent goes even further with two abbreviations, economy over the use of miles and a variety of font sizes. Plates of the Worcester turnpike trust which was the largest in the county and at its peak responsible for over 156 miles of road and subdivided into 8 separate districts, used the simple one destination legend "To Worcester Cross x miles".

Milestone on Eldersfield Common

Milestone at Shelsley Walsh replated with the characteristic Worcestershire 12 sided plate

Milestone south of Ombersley showing the remains of the bolts set in lead and the often present OS benchmark

Massive Plate of the Upton Trust at Welland

The Blakedown Milestone on the Kidderminster to Birmingham road

Evesham Trust Milestone in Pershore

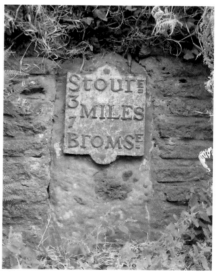

An early second generation Milestone at Clent

- 11 -

Milestone at Astwood Bank on the Evesham to Redditch Road

Plated Milestone at Hanley Swan

Worcester Trust Milestone on Malvern Wells Common

Another of the Upton Trust indented plates on the outskirts of the town

Third and Fourth Generation County and District Council Mile Markers

There are two types of these replacement markers, the third generation triangular cast iron ones and the fourth generation concrete T shaped Bradley stones. Eight of the former survive in the area around Suckley, Knightwick and Alfrick with two others in the south of the county near Sedgeberrow and Wickhamford and one at Rochford in the north-west. There are more in adjoining counties. They were made in the foundry of M & W Grazebrook at Dudley and are dated 1898. The top triangular panel has the parish name and on the vertical faces beneath the pointing finger marker are the names of nearby villages or towns and the distances. One is unusual in having a distance in a fraction of a mile and yards. At the bottom of the right hand side as you face the marker is the detail of the foundry and at the bottom of the other is either the legend Martley Rural District Council or County of Worcester and the date.

Mile marker of 1898 at Knightwick

The 50 or so remaining Bradley stones were designed for the motoring age and introduced in the 1930s to replace existing milestones. They are made of a concrete/stone aggregate with steel reinforcing rods. Cast at Dawley in Shropshire, they are about 5½ inches from front to back and 40 inches wide. The total height is four feet and usually a little over two feet is exposed above ground. That below ground tapers outwards to 20 inches at the base. There are two recesses into which cast iron plates are bolted. The upper one has the road number although subsequent changes in Ministry of Transport road numbering means that several are now incorrect. The larger lower plate has mileages to the stated places with the distance either before or after the town name to indicate the direction. Below the lower plate are the indented letters CCW apparently to distinguish Worcestershire County Council from the

Mile marker at Suckley

adjoining Warwickshire County Council. It is believed, although not confirmed, that the plates were cast in the Bromsgrove Guild workshops and as such the font is simple and elegant without unnecessary serifs. All except one show two place names one above the other. That with a single name is on a dual carriageway and it is believed originally there was a stone opposite showing the place in the other direction.. In the case of the one showing the village name Cleobury Mortimer it was necessary to adopt a smaller font to get the place information onto one line.

Unidirectional Bradley stone on the dual carriageway at Ombersley

Bradley stone at Far Forest

Mr Brooke Bradley who is believed to have designed these milestones lived for a number of years in Little Witley and is buried in the churchyard. A plaque has been erected on the bus shelter overlooking one of the stones to commemorate his association with the village.

Obelisk Milestones

Two of these survive in the south of the county near the Gloucestershire boundary. The one in Bredon, not far from the church and the historic manorial barn, is a tapering pillar to which is fixed a similarly tapered cast iron plate bearing the date 1808 and the village name below which are the distances to six nearby towns.

The Bredon Obelisk dated 1808

The obelisk in Beckford, erected to commemorate Queen Victoria's Golden Jubilee in 1887, gives the mileages to 27 nearby towns and villages. In 1953 an addition was made to mark the coronation of Elizabeth II and 50 years on, the monument was recently cleaned and refurbished.

Queen Victoria Golden Jubilee Obelisk at Beckford with distances engraved on three of the lower panels

East side panel

ASHTON	2
ELMLEY CASTLE	5
PERSHORE	8
DUMBLETON	3
BROADWAY	6
EVESHAM	7
ALDERTON	2
WINCHCOMBE	6
TEDDINGTON	5
STANWAY	6

South side panel

TEDDINGTON CROSS	1½
CLEEVE	6
CHELTENHAM	9
ASHCHURCH	4
TEWKESBURY	6
GLOUCESTER	16
UPTON ON SEVERN	12
MALVERN	19

West side panel

OVERBURY	1½
KEMERTON	2
BREDON	4
TEWKESBURY	7
ECKINGTON	6
PERSHORE	10
UPTON ON SEVERN	10
MALVERN	17
WORCESTER	18

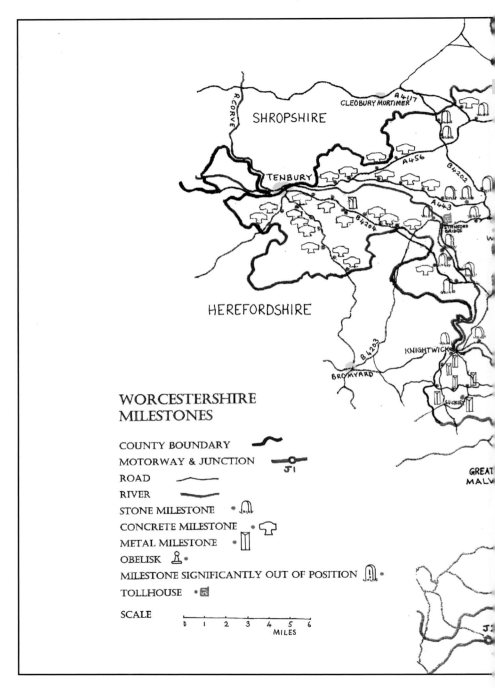

SHROPSHIRE

CLEOBURY MORTIMER

TENBURY

HEREFORDSHIRE

KNIGHTWICK

BROMYARD

SUCKLEY

GREAT MALV

WORCESTERSHIRE MILESTONES

COUNTY BOUNDARY

MOTORWAY & JUNCTION

ROAD

RIVER

STONE MILESTONE

CONCRETE MILESTONE

METAL MILESTONE

OBELISK

MILESTONE SIGNIFICANTLY OUT OF POSITION

TOLLHOUSE

SCALE

0 1 2 3 4 5 6
MILES

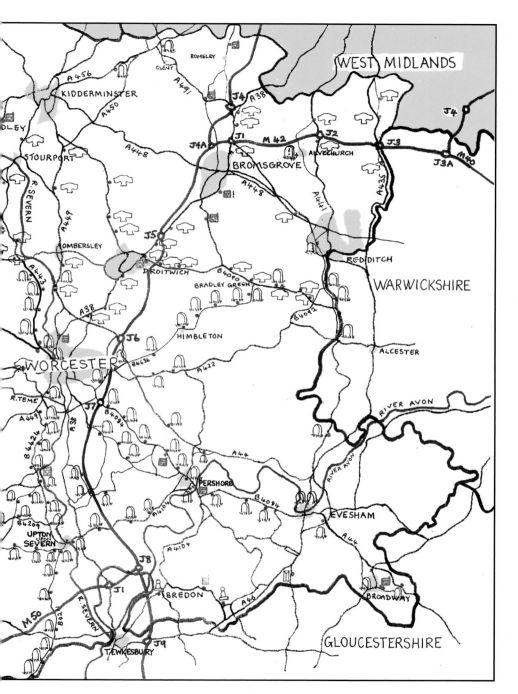

Milestone Society

The Milestone Society was formed in 2001 with the aim of identifying, recording, researching and conserving for the public benefit the milestones and other way markers of the British Isles. The Society is organised on a county basis and the Worcestershire group meet regularly and has recorded and photographed all the milestones that are believed to remain in the county as well as carrying out research into Worcestershire's turnpike trusts. Details of the milestones have been placed on a national database with those from other counties and the information is available for use in a variety of ways by official and other bodies.

Over the years milestones have suffered through neglect and both accidental and malicious damage. Undoubtedly the most significant harm occurred in 1940 following the government decree to remove all signposts and milestones when the country faced the possibility of an enemy invasion.

Today many milestones are often hidden or buried in wayside hedges and one of the group aims is to make them visible by cutting back vegetation and repainting so that not only can a wider public appreciate them but equally importantly further damage by verge cutting contractors is prevented. The following series of photographs illustrate the typical problems and work needed to restore many of the existing milestones.

The Worcestershire Group is involved with the County and local parish councils and others to reinstate damaged stones, re-erect fallen ones and to initiate and actively support programmes to replate second generation stones at particular sites and on specific routes.

Plate-less milestone near Powick Bridge sinking into the ground

Milestone at Hanley Castle tipping over sideways

Milestone at Callow End showing a damaged plate and also separation of the top of the stone from the base due to a serious impact

Another badly damaged plate at Hanley Swan

Badly eroded stone at Pensax showing five bolt holes and OS bench mark

The milestone at Clows Top on the Cleobury to Abberley turnpike was the first to be raised to its original height and replated and after that the group began the project to replate the existing stones on the Worcester to Great Witley road and to replace and plate a missing stone in Hallow. That project was completed in April 2005 when the local MP Sir Michael Spicer unveiled the final link in the chain of eleven milestones. More recently all four milestones on the Shelsley turnpike from Ham Bridge to Stanford Bridge have been replated and work is in hand, again with the support of local people, to do the same on the road from Worcester to Bradley Green. A more challenging task was to prepare a mould and cast a new reinforced concrete Bradley stone to replace one damaged outside the electricity sub station at Feckenham and produce new cast iron plates for it, a project generously supported by National Grid Transco PLC.

Newly cast Bradley stone and plates at Feckenham

First milestone to be re-erected to its original height and replated by the Society with the help of others at Clows Top

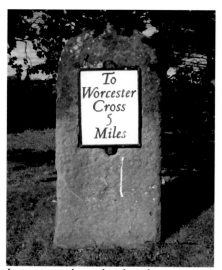

An original Bradley stone at Feckenham

The Group would welcome any information about past or present Worcestershire milestones and this should be sent to Worcestershire Coordinator and Milestone Society Secretary Terry Keegan, The Oxleys, Tenbury Road, Clows Top, Kidderminster, Worcs, DY14 9HE from whom details of the Society can also be obtained.

Last stone to be replated on the Worcester to Great Witley road project

Gazetteer of Worcestershire Milestones and their Inscriptions

The following gazetteer records all the milestones and markers identified to mid 2007 within the present Worcestershire county boundaries. They are listed by road number and each entry gives the grid reference, the side of the road, the material it is made of, the parish in which it is located together with any inscriptions if present. In some parts of Worcestershire (eg most of Redditch District) there are not parish councils and in those instances the name in the parish column is that of the District Council. The abbreviation S, M, C in the material column indicates whether the stone or marker is made of stone, metal or concrete The OS criteria or convention consistently record first and second generation milestones as MS and the third generation metal markers as MP. Confusingly Bradley stones can be recorded as either MS or MP. Not all the milestones in the gazetteer are marked on the Ordnance Survey maps and some the OS show are no longer in position.

A 38 Birmingham to Tewksbury (including part of the old A 38 north of Bromsgrove which is now unclassified) and various side roads

Grid Ref.	Side of Road	Material	Parish	Milestone Legend
SO 974757	E	C	Catshill	A 38 / WORCESTER 16 / 10 BIRMINGHAM
SO 969744	E	C	Lickey	A 38 / WORCESTER 15 / 11 BIRMINGHAM
SO 968727	E	C	Lickey	A 38 / WORCESTER 14 / 12 BIRMINGHAM
SO 924663	E	C	Dodderhill	A 38 / WORCESTER 9 / 17 BIRMINGHAM
SO 915650	E	C	Dodderhill	A 38 / WORCESTER 8 / 18 BIRMINGHAM
SO 905638	E	C	Droitwich Spa	A 38 / WORCESTER 7 / 19 BIRMINGHAM
SO 895623	E	C	Droitwich Spa	A 38 / WORCESTER 6 / 20 BIRMINGHAM
SO 879597	E	C	Martin Hussingtree	A 38 / WORCESTER 4 / 22 BIRMINGHAM
SO 866588	E	C	North Claines	A 38 / WORCESTER 3 / 23 BIRMINGHAM
SO 852475	W	S	Kempsey	Plate missing
SO 864418	W	S	Ripple	Plate missing
SO 878500	W	S	Norton by Kempsey	Plate missing
SO 889491	E	S	Norton by Kempsey	Plate missing
SO 897479	S	S	Drakes Broughton & Wadborough	Plate missing
SO 862467	E	S	Kempsey	TO / WORCESTER / CROSS / 6 MILES
SO 869453	E	S	Croome d'Abitot	Plate missing
SO 881454	S	S	Croome d'Abitot	Plate missing

A 44 Broadway to Leominster (including a section of the old A 44 which is now an unclassified road)

SP 114373	N	S	Broadway	Plate missing
SP 105375	N	S	Broadway	TO / LONDON / 90 MILES / MORTON 8 / STOW 10 / WORCESTER 21 / EVESHAM 6
SP 073408	N	M	Wickhamford	Top; Wickhamford Parish Left face: Evesham 3 / Pershore 9 Right face Broadway 2¾ / Morton 11:
SP 053428	S	S	Evesham	Plate missing
SO 932498	S	S	Stoulton	Plate missing
SO 822546	S	C	Rushwick	A 44 / 2 WORCESTER / BROMYARD 12
SO 791551	S	C	Cotheridge	A 44 / 4 WORCESTER / BROMYARD 10
SO 777552	S	S	Cotheridge	Plate missing
SO 764553	N	S	Broadwas	Plate missing
SO 742562	S	S	Doddenham	Plate missing
SO 729557	S	S	Knightwick	TO / WORCESTER / 8 miles / LONDON 120

A 422 Worcester to Alcester

SO 936544	N	S	Upton Snodsbury	Plate missing
SO 951548	N	S	Grafton Flyford	Plate missing

Unpainted Milestone on A 441

Nearby milestone on the A 441 replated with marble

A 435 Birmingham to Evesham (including the old A 435)

SP 079766	E	C	Wythall	A 435 / ALCESTER 13 / 7 BIRMINGHAM

| SP 078751 | E | C | Wythall | A 435 / ALCESTER 12 / 8 BIRMINGHAM |
| SP 084719 | W | C | Beoley | A 435 / ALCESTER 10 / 10 B BIRMINGHAM |

A 441 Birmingham to Evesham (including the old A441)

SP 038657	E	S	Redditch	REDDITCH 1 / EVESHAM 15
S9 044626	E	S	Redditch	REDDITCH 3 / EVESHAM 13
SP 046610	E	S	Redditch	REDDITCH 4 / EVESHAM / 12
SP 057580	E	S	Inkberrow	Plate missing On back: TO / REDDITCH / 6 / MILES / EVESHAM / 10

A 442 Droitwich to Kidderminster

SO 884661	E	C	Hampton Lovett	B 4192 / 8 KIDDERMINSTER / DROITWICH 2
SO 881675	E	C	Elmbridge	B 4192 / 7 KIDDERMINSTER / DROITWICH 3
SO 879705	E	C	Rushock	B 4192 / 5 KIDDERMINSTER / DROITWICH 5

A 443 Worcester to Newnham Bridge via Great Witley

SO 840554	E	S	Worcester City	To / Worcester Cross / 1 / Miles
SO 832569	E	S	Worcester City	To / Worcester Cross / 2 / Miles
SO 826563	E	S	Hallow	To / Worcester Cross / 3/ Miles
SO 828598	E	S	Grimley	To / Worcester Cross / 4 / Miles
SO 827614	E	S	Holt	To / Worcester Cross / 5 /Miles
SO 818626	W	S	Holt	To / Worcester Cross / 6 / Miles
SO 805632	N	C	Holt	A443 / WORCESTER 7 / 15 ½ TENBURY
SO 791637	N	C	Little Witley	A443 / WORCESTER 8 / 14 ½ TENBURY
SO 792636	S	S	Little Witley	Plate missing
SO 778646	N	S	Little Witley	To / Worcester Cross / 9 /Miles
SO 766656	N	S	Hillhampton	To / Worcester Cross / 10 / Miles
SO 752662	N	S	Great Witley	To / Worcester Cross / 11 / Miles
SO 715675	N	S	Stockton-on-Teme	Plate missing
SO 703680	N	C	Lindridge	A 443 / 7¼ TENBURY / WORCESTER 15
SO 685686	N	C	Lindridge	A 443 / 6¼ TENBURY / WORCESTER 16
SO 672690	S	C	Lindridge	A 443 / 5¼ TENBURY / WORCESTER 17
SO 655692	N	C	Knighton-on-Teme	A 443 / 4¼ TENBURY / WORCESTER 18

A 449 Kidderminster to Little Malvern

| SO 846720 | E | C | Hartlebury | A 449 / WORCESTER 11 / 3¼ KIDDERMINSTER |
| SO 840688 | E | C | Hartlebury | A 449 / WORCESTER 9 / 5¼ KIDDERMINSTER |

SO 845628	W	C	Ombersley	A449 / STOURPORT 7
SO 844612	W	S	Ombersley	Plate missing
SO 844612	W	C	Ombersley	A 449 / STOURPORT 8 / 4 WORCESTER
SO 836526	W	S	Worcester City	Plate missing
SO 784476	S	S	Malvern Town	TO / WORCESTER / CROSS / 7 / MILES
SO 775466	S	S	Malvern Town	TO / WORCESTER / CROSS / 8 / MILES
SO 775447	W	S	Malvern Wells	TO / WORCESTER / CROSS / 9 / MILES
SO 773433	E	S	Malvern Wells	Plate missing
SO 773417	E	S	Malvern Wells	TO / WORCESTER / CROSS / 11 / MILES
SO 768404	N	S	Little Malvern	MALVERN 3 ½ MILES / UPTON 6 / LEDBURY 4 ½

A 451 Kidderminster to Great Witley

SO 819738	W	C	Kidderminster	A 451 / KIDDERMINSTER 2 / 1¾ STOURPORT
SO 767666	E	S	Great Witley	Plate missing

A 456 Birmingham to Leominster through Kidderminster and Bewdley

SO 874779	S	S	Churchill & Blakedown	To / BIRM / 14 / Miles
SO 772748	N	C	Bewdley	A456 / BEWDLEY 1 / 13 TENBURY
SO 772748	N	S	Bewdley	Plate missing
SO 757743	N	S	Bewdley	Plate missing
SO 742739	N	S	Rock	Bewdley 3 Miles Cleobury 5 Miles
SO 669699	E	C	Lindridge	A456 / 5¼ TENBURY / BEWDLEY 9
SO 655695	W	C	Lindridge	A456 / 4¼ TENBURY / BEWDLEY 10
SO 640693	N	C	Knighton-on-Teme	A 456 / 3¼ TENBURY / WORCESTER 19
SO 627687	N	C	Knighton-on-Teme	A 456 / 2¼ TENBURY / WORCESTER 20

A 4104 Pershore to Little Malvern

SO 949456	E	S	Pershore	UPTON / 8 miles/ Evesham / 6 / LONDON / 102
SO 918428	N	S	Defford	Plate missing
SO 904425	S	S	Defford	Plate missing
SO 878419	S	S	Hill Croome	Plate missing
SO 856409	S	S	Ripple	Plate missing
SO 839399	S	S	Upton-upon-Severn	Upton / To Ledbury 9½ Miles / to Upton 1 Mile
SO 824398	N	S	Upton-upon-Severn	Upton / To Ledbury 8½ Miles / to Upton 2 Miles
SO 810401	N	S	Welland	Plate missing

SO 795401	S	S	Welland	Welland / To Ledbury 6½ Miles / to Upton 4 Miles
SO 779404	N	S	Little Malvern	Plate missing

A 4112 Tenbury to Leominster

SO 593668	E	C	Tenbury	B 4553 / LEOMINSTER 8 / 1 TENBURY
SO 582656	E	C	Tenbury	B 4553 / LEOMINSTER 7 / 2 TENBURY

A 4117 Bewdley (Callow Hill) to Ludlow

SO728746	N	C	Rock	A 4117 / BEWDLEY 4 / 4 CLEOBURY MORTIMER

Partially buried stone on the A 449 at Little Malvern

Bronze plate on milestone on the A 456 at Rock

B 4078 Sedgeberrow to Winchcombe

SP 025382	E	M	Sedgeberrow	Top: Sedgeberrow / Village / Left face: Winchcomb / 6 ¼ Miles / Right face: Evesham / 4 Miles

B 4083 Pinvin to Pershore (the old B 4084)

SO 958480	N	S	Pinvin	Plate missing

B 4084 Worcester to Evesham (the old A 44)

SO 882519	N	S	Whittington	TO / WORCESTER / CROSS / 3 / MILES
SO 894512	N	S	Norton-juxta-Kempsey	TO / WORCESTER / CROSS / 4 / MILES

SO 915490	N	S	Drakes Broughton	Plate missing
SO 928482	N	S	Drakes Broughton	Plate missing
SO 933467	S	S	Pershore	Plate missing
SO 961451	S	S	Wick	Plate missing
SO 991445	S	S	Cropthorne	Plate missing
SP 006439	S	S	Cropthorne	Plate missing

Milestone at Drakes Broughton on the B 4084. When plated, the legend was To Worcester Cross 7 miles.

Milestone at Norton on the B 4084 with the surviving To Worcester Cross 4 mile plate.

B 4088 Evesham to Alcester

SP 055498	W	S	Harvington	Plate missing

B 4090 Droitwich to Alcester

SO 913631	N	C	Hanbury	B 4090 / ALCESTER 12¾ / 1 DROITWICH
SO 930628	N	C	Hanbury	B 4090 / ALCESTER 11¾ / 2 DROITWICH
SO 974627	N	C	Hanbury	B 4090 / ALCESTER 8¾ / 5 DROITWICH
SO 987619	N	C	Stock & Bradley	B 4090 / ALCESTER 7¾ / 6 DROITWICH
SP 003614	N	C	Feckenham	B 4090 / ALCESTER 6¾ / 7 DROITWICH

SP 005613	N	S	Feckenham	To Alcester 6 / To London 108 Miles
SP 018612	N	C	Feckenham	B 4090 / ALCESTER 5¾ / 8 DROITWICH
SP 031605	N	C	Redditch	B 4090 / ALCESTER 4¾ / 9 DROITWICH

B 4096 Lickey to Redditch

SP 010683	W	C	Tutnall & Cobley	A 448 / 2 REDDITCH / BROMSGROVE 4

B 4120 Alvechurch to Hopwood

SP 028744	N	C	Alvechurch	A 441 / BIRMINGHAM 9 / 4½ REDDITCH

B 4194 Astley to Bewdley

SP 802691	E	S	Astley	Plate missing

B 4196 Holt Heath to Stourport

SP 804652	E	C	Shrawley	B 4196 / WORCESTER 8 / 4 STOURPORT

B 4202 Cleobury Mortimer (Mawley) to Abberley

SO 708736	E	S	Bayton	CLEOBURY 3 / WORCESTER 17
SO 712721	E	S	Bayton	CLEOBURY 4 / WORCESTER 16
SO 738684	E	S	Abberley	Plate missing

B 4203 Great Witley to Bromyard

SO 737661	S	S	Shelsley Kings	Plate missing
SO 713658	N	S	Stanford with Orleton	To / LONDON / 125 Miles / To / WORCESTER / 13 / To / TENBURY 9. Reverse side: BROMYARD / 8½ MILES / WORCESTER / 13

B 4204 Worcester to Tenbury

SO 826564	W	C	Lower Broadheath	B 4204 / 2 WORCESTER TENBURY 18½
SO 786585	S	S	Kenswick	Plate missing
SO 735610	S	S	Clifton-upon-Teme	Plate missing
SO 705632	S	C	Clifton-upon-Teme	B 4204 / 12 WORCESTER TENBURY 8½
SO 677654	N	C	Hanley	B 4204 / WORCESTER 14½ / 6 TENBURY WELLS
SO 663655	S	C	Hanley	B 4204 / TENBURY WELLS 5 / 15 ½ WORCESTER
SO 651666	N	C	Eastham	B 4204 / WORCESTER 16½ / 4 TENBURY WELLS
SO 638671	W	C	Rochford	B 4204 / 17½ WORCESTER / TENBURY WELLS 3

SO 638671	W	M	Rochford	Top: ROCHFORD Left face: TENBURY WELLS / 3 MILES Right face: WORCESTER / 17½ MILES
SO 625675	N	C	Rochford	B 4204 / WORCESTER 18½ / 2 TENBURY WELLS
SO 611679	N	C	Tenbury	B 4204 / WORCESTER 19½ / 1 TENBURY WELLS

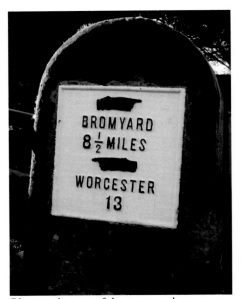

Plate on the rear of the stone on the B 4203 at Stanford Bridge

Milestone on the B 4211 one mile from Upton upon Severn

B 4209 Malvern Wells to Hanley Castle

SO 783424	S	S	Malvern Wells	Plate missing
SO 799426	S	S	Hanley Castle	HANLEY / UPTON / 4 / MALVERN / 4 MILES
SO 814429	N	S	Hanley Castle	HANLEY / UPTON / 3 / MALVERN / 5 /MILES

B 4211 Great Malvern to Gloucester

SO 839441	E	S	Hanley Castle	Plate missing
SO 838426	E	S	Hanley Castle	UPTON / 1½ MILES / MALVERN / 5½ / WORCESTER/9
SO 844395	E	S	Upton-upon-Severn	UPTON / UPTON / 1 / GLOSTER / 15 / MILES
SO 841379	E	S	Holdfast	Plate missing
SO 836365	E	S	Longdon	Plate missing

SO 848336	E	S	Longdon	Plate missing
SO 842325	E	S	Eldersfield	FORTHAMPTN / UPTON / 6 / GLOSTER / 10 / MILES
SO 833311	E	S	Eldersfield	ELDERSFIELD / UPTON / 7 / GLOSTER / 9 / MILES
SO 822299	E	S	Eldersfield	ELDERSFIELD / UPTON / 8 / GLOSTER / 8 / MILES

B 4214 Tenbury to Bromyard

SO 603673	W	C	Tenbury	B 4214 / TENBURY 1 / 10 BROMYARD
SO 612662	W	C	Tenbury	B 4214 / TENBURY 2 / 9 BROMYARD
SO 623653	W	C	Kyre	B 4214 / TENBURY 3 / 8 BROMYARD
SO 627639	W	C	Kyre	B 4214 / TENBURY 4 / 7 BROMYARD
SO 633627	E	S	Stoke Bliss	B 4214 / BROMYARD 6 / 5 TENBURY
SO 644616	E	S	Stoke Bliss	B 4214 / BROMYARD 5 / 6 TENBURY

B 4424 Powick to The Rhydd

SO 833512	E	S	Powick	Plate missing
SO 837498	E	S	Powick	TO / WORCESTER / CROSS / 4 / MILES
SO 829484	E	S	Powick	Plate missing
SO 826469	W	S	Powick	Plate missing
SO 833456	E	S	Guarlford	TO / WORCESTER / CROSS / 7 / MILES

B 4636 Worcester to Crowle and the unclassified road on to Bradley Green

SO 864552	N	S	Worcester City	Plate missing
SO 892556	N	S	Tibberton	Plate missing
SO 921565	S	S	Crowle	5 / MILES / TO / WORCESTER / CROSS
SO 943586	N	S	Himbleton	Plate missing
SO 949596	N	S	Himbleton	
SO 964599	N	S	Hanbury	Plate missing
SO 978601	N	S	Stock and Bradley	Plate missing
SO 988602	N	S	Stock and Bradley	Plate missing

Unclassified roads in Beckford and Bredon

SO 919368	N	S	Bredon	1808 / BREDON / UPTON / 6 Miles / PERSHORE / 7 Miles / EVESHAM / 12 Miles / TEWKESBURY / 3 Miles / WINCHCOMB / 10 Miles / CHELTENHAM / 11 Miles

SO 974357	S	S	Beckford	North side: ELIZABETH II / CORONATION 2 JUNE 1953 / VR JUBILEE 1887 / BECKFORD East side: ASHTON 2 / ELMLEY CASTLE 5½ / PERSHORE 8¾ / DUMBLETON 3 / BROADWAY 9 / EVESHAM 7¼ / ALDERTON 2½ / WINCHCOMBE 6 / TODDINGTON 5¼ / STANWAY 6¾ South side: TEDDINGTON CROSS 1½ / CLEEVE 6 / CHELTENHAM 9¼ / ASHCHURCH 4 / TEWKSBURY 6 / GLOUCESTER 16½ / UPTON ON SEVERN 12 ¾ / MALVERN 19¾ West side: OVERBURY 1¾ / KEMERTON 2½ /BREDON 4 / TEWKSBURY 7 / ECKINGTON 6 / PERSHORE 10 / UPTON ON SEVERN 10 / MALVERN 17 / WORCESTER 18

Milestone in Hanbury Parish on the unclassified road from Worcester to Bradley Green

Milestone at Bradley Green on the unclassified road from Worcester

Unclassified road in Clent

SO 916801	E	S	Clent	Stoure / 3 / Miles / 7 / Brome

Unclassified road from Hanley Swan to The Rhydd

SO 824446	S	S	Hanley Castle	Plate missing
SO 813439	E	S	Hanley Castle	Plate missing

Unclassified Road from Ham Bridge to Stanford Bridge

SO 736612	W	S	Clifton-on-Teme	TO / WORCESTER / CROSS / 9 / MILES
SO 728624	E	S	Shelsley Walsh	TO / WORCESTER / CROSS /10 / MILES
SO 718636	W	S	Shelsley Walsh	TO / WORCESTER / CROSS /11 / MILES
SO 712648	W	S	Stanford with Oreleton	TO / WORCESTER / CROSS / 12 / MILES

Unclassified Roads to the west of Worcester and south of the A 44

SO 731557	W	M	Knightwick	Top: KNIGHTWICK Left face: TO WORCESTER / CROSS 9 MILES Right face: TO SUCKLEY / 3½ MILES / TO CRADLEY
SO 730505	N	M	Suckley	Top: SUCKLEY Left face: / TO WORCESTER / CROSS 9 MILES Right face: TO STOCKS / ½ MILE / 176 YARDS
SO 721545	W	M	Knightwick	Top: KNIGHTWICK / Left face: TO WORCESTER / CROSS / 10 MILES Right face TO SUCKLEY / 2½ MILES / TO CRADLEY
SO 716532	S	M	Suckley	Top SUCKLEY Left face: TO WORCESTER / 10 MILES Right face: TO BROMYARD / 4½ MILES
SO 728527	N	M	Suckley	Top: SUCKLEY Left face: TO WORCESTER / 9 MILES Right face: TO BROMYARD / 5½ MILES
SO 739529	N	M	Alfrick	Top: ALFRICK Left face: TO WORCESTER / 8 MILES Right face: TO BROMYARD / 6½ MILES
SO 763532	N	M	Leigh	Top: LEIGH Left face: TO WORCESTER / 6 MILES Right face: TO BROMYARD / 8½ MILES
SO 782534	N	M	Leigh	Top: BROCKAMIN Left face: TO WORCESTER / 5 MILES Right face: TO BROMYARD / 9½ MILES

Out of Position Stones (OOPSs)

Six further milestones not listed in the above gazetteer have survived but are now in new locations in the county and are know as OOPSs or Out of Position stones. The two outside the Almonry Museum in Evesham have already been mentioned. The larger of oolitic limestone is five feet high and two foot wide at the base and bears a small metal plate recording *"This stone believed to have been erected at the cross roads on the top of Green Hill in 1730 was restored and re-erected here in 1978."* It has the carved legend To / Alcester / X Miles / To Birmingham / XXIX Miles / To / Worcester XV Miles / London XCVI Miles / Stratford thro / Alcester XVIII Miles /. The adjacent badly eroded smaller stone has the legend Evesham 3 and it has not been established where it was originally sited.

A first generation engraved stone originally located on the road to Bromyard from Stanford Bridge is now in a driveway at Caunsell and matches the surviving Hundred House trust stone at SO 713658. On one side is the legend To / LONDON / 126 Miles / To / WORCESTER / 14 / To / TENBURY 8 and on the other there is a second generation metal plate BROMYARD / 7½ MILES / WORCESTER / 14.

Another plated milestone is outside the Alvechurch Local History museum and bears the legend To / BIRM / 10 / Miles. It was recovered from a nearby garden and the distance is about right although interestingly the letter format and plate size is the same as the one at Blakedown SO 874779.

A second generation stone from the A 38 that was replaced by the Bradley stone at SO 968727 is now in a nearby garden. It was salvaged in the 1930s but has since lost its original plate that bore the legend BIRMINGHAM / 12 / WORCESTER / 14. It is 40 inches high and 17 inches wide at the base and from the size of the indent the plate would have measured 18 inches by 12 inches.

The final known OOPS is one of the triangular 1898 County Council metal markers and is now outside a house on a narrow unclassified road between Eastham and Orleton. The nearby householder purchased it from an antique dealer in Ross on Wye and inserted the name of the hamlet Pipers Brook on both faces and altered the mileage to Tenbury to reflect the new location. It emerged that the marker originally stood one mile from Tenbury on the B 4204 at SO 611679 where there is now a Bradley stone. On the upper triangular panel are the words TENBURY / PARISH and on the left face WORCESTER / 19½ MILES / PIPERS / BROOK / and on the right face TENBURY / 4 MILES / PIPERS / BROOK / with both faces having the usual lower subsidiary details.

Further Reading

Haines, Carol *Marking the Miles*, Self Published, 2000 and available from the Milestone Society

Benford, Mervyn *Milestones*, Shire Publications Ltd, 2002, Princes Risborough

Printed by A&G Printing Co Ltd Stourport on Severn Worcestershire